VIETNAM
AND THE
SOVIET UNION

About the Book and Author

Examining the long and turbulent relationship between Vietnam and the Soviet Union, Douglas Pike traces its political, economic, and diplomatic history from the Bolshevik Revolution to today's deep and intricate alliance. He not only explores this extraordinary relationship but also outlines its great geopolitical significance for the entire region.

The current relationship is marked by greed, mistrust, and uncertainty, with both countries testing the utility of close military and economic ties. Convinced that the USSR was never adverse to sacrificing Vietnamese interests for marginal Soviet gains, Hanoi has little sense of obligation toward Moscow. By contrast, the Soviet Union sees its relationship with Vietnam as the promising and important exception to its efforts in Asia, most of which have resulted in only modest returns for considerable investment. The major determinant of the alliance continues to be the Sino-Soviet dispute.

Although Vietnam and the USSR are bound by mutual interests, they share neither common perceptions nor a common heritage. The forces uniting them seem as strong as the issues that would divide them. Professor Pike expects this balance to be maintained for the short term, but he argues that Vietnam's historical inability to sustain successful external relations may ultimately doom the alliance.

Douglas Pike is director of the Indochina Studies Project at the University of California, Berkeley. As a U.S. foreign service officer, he was posted in Saigon, Hong Kong, Tokyo, Taipei, and Washington. He is the author of five books on Vietnam, the latest of which is *PAVN: People's Army of Vietnam*.

VIETNAM
AND THE
SOVIET UNION

Anatomy of an Alliance

Douglas Pike

WESTVIEW PRESS
BOULDER AND LONDON

Copyright © 1987 by Westview Press, Inc.

Published in 1987 in the United States of America by Westview Press, Inc.; Frederick A. Praeger, Publisher; 5500 Central Avenue, Boulder, Colorado 80301

Library of Congress Cataloging-in-Publication Data
Pike, Douglas Eugene, 1924–
  Vietnam and the Soviet Union.
  Bibliography: p.
  Includes index.
  1. Vietnam—Relations—Soviet Union. 2. Soviet
Union—Relations—Vietnam. I. Title.
DS556.58.S65P54 1987   327.470597   86-29022
ISBN 0-8133-0470-9

Printed and bound in the United States of America

The paper used in this publication meets the requirements of the American National Standard for Permanence of Paper for Printed Library Materials Z39.48-1984.

10   9   8   7   6   5   4   3   2   1

CONTENTS

PREFACE

THIS BOOK IS a history of relations between Vietnam and the USSR, beginning in the earliest days when there was neither a Vietnam nor a USSR as such, and continuing to today's deep and intricate but uncertain alliance. It is written with primary emphasis on the Vietnam rather than the USSR perspective, since Vietnam is my professional field of interest and work; nevertheless, as evidenced below, my credentials as a Kremlinologist are at least respectable.

As Voltaire said, one turns over a library to write a book. In this endeavor I turned over an archive, the University of California's Indochina Archive at Berkeley, of whose vast holdings (3 million pages of documentation; 25,000 books and monographs; 35,000 maps, photographs, graphics) about 15 percent relate directly to the subject under scrutiny.

In the course of my research I traveled three times to the USSR, twice for conferences and once as a guest for two weeks of the USSR Academy of Science's Oriental Institute, during which time I talked with numerous Soviet specialists on Indochina and explored the Lenin library. I have also attended several U.S. conferences with Soviet scholars, and all of these occasions enabled me to develop a number of valuable professional relationships. Also I have systematically consulted Hanoi watchers and scholars working on Vietnam in the ASEAN states, Japan, and China. Finally, I spent a year and a half on sabbatical with the Congressional Research Service at the Library of Congress, where I walked the endless stacks examining relevant volumes.

My research uncovered less than one might imagine. I did not, for instance, find a single English-language full-length history of Soviet-Vietnamese relations. That fact was the primary reason I wrote this book. My research took on the character of a jigsaw puzzle, and the result is a multitude of fragments and piecemeal data assembled into an admittedly incomplete mosaic.

It is appropriate, and only fair to the reader, to set down my general view of that vast controversy we call the USSR, so that if there is bias or unintended prejudice present, it can thus be explained.

As an undergraduate at the University of California (Berkeley) in the early 1950s, I had the ambition to become a Moscow-based foreign correspondent, one who spoke the language, was well grounded in Russian history, and knew Soviet government, society, culture, and ideology. I took all the appropriate courses I could find. For one calendar year I studied the Russian language full time—five hours a day in class plus three in the language laboratory, hooked via earphones to a tape recorder—a time I recall chiefly as the most miserable year of my life. I remember saying to a fellow student over a beer that I now understood why the Russians were so hard to get along with; so would anyone who had to speak that wretched language.

Then, in an irony of wasted effort, I was off to Asia for twenty years of foreign service assignments, chiefly in Vietnam, during which I hardly once spoke Russian; by the time I finally made it to the USSR, two decades later, I had lost most of it.

Yet my education in Soviet studies stood me in good stead. When assigned to Saigon in 1960 I became at once interested in the newly formed National Liberation Front (NLF), or Viet Cong, and found that I could put to good use my knowledge of Marxism-Leninism, particularly in understanding the organizational structure and mobilizational strategy of the NLF, which had been heavily influenced by Leninism.

Years passed, the Vietnam War ended, and I was able for the first time to get to the USSR. It was a singular experience. I arrived with a great deal of intellectual baggage, but I soon discovered that much of my knowledge was out of date, that over the years I had assembled a clutch of stereotypes and misperceptions that were soon shattered. I found the Soviet Union to be both better and worse than I had imagined and was left with the conviction that every American, whatever his or her political outlook, should live for a few weeks in the USSR and bathe in the reality of the place. Over the years, with subsequent visits, my sense of the USSR evolved from sinister to sympathetic to respectful alienation.

Probably the most important fundamental question that can be asked about the era of history through which we are now passing is: Whither the USSR? It is for all of us literally a life or death question, but as difficult to answer as it is profound.

There are, I would argue, three general perceptions of the USSR held today by Americans, by West Europeans, and, to a lesser extent, by Asians—three perspectives that represent neither reality nor falsehood, since they exist in a dimension beyond factual truth. Actually they are philosophical categories manifested in the defining process that goes on in the head of each individual as a flood of information and opinion about the USSR is translated into a coherent abstraction. The three perceptions can be found everywhere: in the press, in academia, and in state policy-making councils.

First is what might be called the Armageddon crowd, who believe that the USSR's motto is We Will Bury You. Their perception of the USSR is that it regards itself as history's instrument, with messianic roots going far back into history, predating even the Czars. Ideologically driven, the Kremlin leaders view our times as a great global struggle in which there can ultimately be only one winner, and whatever is required they mean to be it. The enemy here is seen as the Soviet system, totalitarian at home and imperial abroad. It cannot be turned, it cannot be pacified, it can only be defeated.

Second are the Preservationists, who hold that there is but one immutable law of history—change—and whose slogan is Time Is on Our Side. They see the USSR as an expended revolutionary force, once dangerously aggressive, now essentially benign because it is so conservative in terms of taking risks, at best only an uncertain bully. The USSR as a system is weak, living permanently on the edge of crisis from which it can never escape because the system can never be made to work well. Its leaders are still traumatized by the destruction of World War II. They are proud of what they have achieved in a short time, fearful of losing it, and seek only to protect and build. If the cause is to be advanced through adventurism it will be by surrogates, the Cubans or the Vietnamese. So long as opposition, primarily the United States, remains tough and determined, the USSR will be no particular threat to world peace. It may be a challenged, but not a true, enemy, and eventually it will be outlasted.

Third are the Institutionalists, who see the essential world condition as a permanent struggle for power among nations and transnational institutions. By the very nature of this struggle, none can ever dominate; thus much of the struggle is self-cancelling. The USSR in fifty years has moved from a position of inferiority to one of parity, but it can never go beyond. All reality stems from this present and continuing nuclear balance of terror. It fixes the limits of all political action. However, this is a dynamic condition and within its boundaries lie great opportunities to influence the direction of history, not by war but by determination, skill, and perseverance. Eventually this struggle will be contained within some supranational institution.

The important point to be made about these competing perceptions is that they are genuine and valid. We must always bear in mind, therefore, that everyone does not see the USSR through the same prism.

Yet these three perceptions are also policy-oriented, what might be called tactical views. There is another perspective, a longer, non-deterministic one which holds that both the United States and USSR, indeed all of the world's systems, are confronted by a common challenge—of an uncontrolled and uncontrollable science and technology—and that the capacity to adjust to this challenge, not ideology or rhetoric, will determine not only power and influence in the future but survival itself.

I am grateful to Robert Scalapino and Allan Cameron for their valuable comments on this book in manuscript form. And, for her practical and intellectual assistance, I am indebted to my wife, Myrna.

Douglas Pike
Berkeley, California

ACRONYMS AND ABBREVIATIONS

ARVN	Army of the Republic of Vietnam
ASEAN	Association of Southeast Asian Nations
CMEA	Council for Mutual Economic Assistance
Cominform	Communist Information Bureau
Comintern	predecessor of Cominform
CPSU	Communist Party of the Soviet Union
DRV	Democratic Republic of Vietnam
FBIS	Foreign Broadcast Information Service
FCP	French Communist party
GRU	Intelligence Directorate of the Red Army
GVN	Government of Vietnam
ICC	International Control Commission
ICP	Indochina Communist party
kw	kilowatts
kwh	kilowatt hours
mt	metric tons
NLF	National Liberation Front
p/a	per annum
PAVN	People's Army of Vietnam
PLA	People's Liberation Army (China)
PLAF	People's Liberation Armed Forces
PRC	People's Republic of China
PRG	People's Revolutionary Government (South Vietnam)
PRK	People's Republic of Kampuchea
RAND	Research and Development (Corporation)
SAM	surface-to-air missile
SRV	Socialist Republic of Vietnam
TASS	Soviet news agency
VNA	Vietnamese News Agency
VNQDD	Vietnam Quoc Dan Dang

APOCRYPHAL STORY

A Vietnamese diplomat is lunching with a Swedish diplomat in Paris. In the course of the meal, the Swede asks his colleague from Hanoi whether he is worried about the dangers inherent in his country's intimate embrace of the USSR.

Replies the Vietnamese: We survived French conquest, we survived American hostility, and we can survive Russian friendship.

INTRODUCTION

Soviet Overview of Asia

ASIA DURING OUR lifetime has been the scene of nearly constant political turmoil, social upheaval, economic chaos, and war in several forms. The pilots of Moscow's ship of state have had to chart a course through perpetually uncertain waters. Their navigational record overall is not impressive. Time and again in the past seven decades the USSR has found itself running against the tide of events, marooned in some policy backwater or grounded on the shoals of miscalculation. It erred enormously in handling China and, for years, Vietnam. It failed in Indonesia under Sukarno and in Cambodia with the Khmer Rouge. It missed enormous opportunities in Japan and probably in Korea as well. Its efforts to control events and influence decisions in Asian countries and within local Communist parties have continually been thwarted or ruined by the native spirit of nationalism. It has been plagued by weak party-to-party relations, and its influence at the government-to-government level generally has been less than elsewhere in the world. Often it has been obliged to withhold support from a left-wing political movement, to the detriment of its image, because the movement's coming to power would serve China more than the USSR. There have been some successes, most notably in India. But in general the USSR's experience has been to find itself at something of a strategic and tactical disadvantage in Asia.

The standard Moscow foreign policy approach has been to search for soft-spot opportunities and, when found, to exploit them. The rule seems to be: Push where softness is found, and keep pushing until resistance hardens. It is a rule that has worked better elsewhere than in Asia. Further, the dominant characteristic of Soviet behavior in Asia during the past fifty years has been reaction, not action. The USSR appears not so much to be operating from some master plan as to be

1

moving opportunistically to meet unfolding events. The latter requires skill in dealing with the subtle Asian mind, but the USSR has seldom demonstrated much finesse. Its historical record in Asia thus is clear: Despite considerable input and energy over the years, it has surprisingly little to show for past efforts. Probably this is why its present efforts in Vietnam are so important to it.

To what extent is the USSR an Asian nation, as opposed to a European one? Kremlin leaders warming to the subject stake a claim to Asian primacy by pointing on a map to the vast expanse of territory between the Ural Mountains west to the Pacific and from the White Sea south to the Caspian, noting that two-thirds of the USSR lies in Asia. But Asian memories are long, and when most Asians think about the USSR it is imperial Russia that comes to mind. The USSR is seen as a continuation of empire that enjoyed the benefits of extraterritoriality, a customs regimen, and residential concessions in Asia. The Czar had a legation guard in Peking, received a share of the Boxer indemnity payments, and laid special claims to northern Manchuria and the Chinese Eastern Railway. The Russians played the Great Game with the British over control of India's Northwest Frontier Province and took special interest in Mongolia (having incited a Mongol revolt in 1911). Imperial Russia had a long history of aggrandizement, fought Asians on many fronts, seized and held vast territories. Thus many Asians, particularly the Chinese, see the USSR as the last of the European colonial powers. What the Kremlin considers an integral part of the Soviet Union Asians see as subjugated lands and tribes under western-oriented domination. The USSR's interest in Asia differs from that of other western nations, however, in that regional developments affect it more. Soviet moves tend to be more purposeful and clearly defined than those of, say, the United States, whose interests are more amorphous and actions more inconstant. In truth, it appears that the USSR is not simply a non-Asian nation in Asia—as was, say, Great Britain—but neither is it simply a fellow Asian nation. It is a hybrid, and it does have and will continue to have peculiar interests in Asia.

Future Soviet behavior in Asia, if we are to use history as our guide, will be driven by a mission of empire. Moscow's ambitions may or may not have pre-Communist roots, but the recent record indicates that what it wants in the region is ideological dominance, to be achieved without Soviet participation in war. This theme—dominance without war—explains much of what the USSR has done in Asia in recent times, that is, since Khrushchev.[1] USSR policy in Asia may now be entering a time of historic change. This possibility has been suggested by some Kremlinologists speculating on the "revolution" that is being introduced into the USSR by the new general secretary, Mikhail Gorbachev.[2] One of the changes to be effected, according to this speculation, will be the treatment of Asia less in terms of ideological competition, as in the past, and more as a matter of strategic concern, as the USSR has always treated Western Europe. In any event, the question facing the countries of the Pacific Basin—including Vietnam—is, What are the limits of Soviet ambition? Is the arrival of Soviet military presence in the region simply orthodox pursuit of national interest, or is something more sinister under way—that is, Soviet political maneuvers and cold war actions that seek to change the fundamental balance of power in Asia?

It is with these grand strategy considerations in mind that we begin to trace the many-colored threads woven into the fabric of the relationship between Vietnam and the USSR.

NOTES

1. Western Asia, which borders on the USSR, may be the exception, as developments in Afghanistan since 1980 certainly suggest.

2. See the important Gorbachev speech made at Vladivostok on July 28, 1986, carried by FBIS *Daily Report* for the USSR (July 29, 1986), and "News and Views from the USSR," USSR Embassy Press Release (July 29, 1986).

One

THE FORMATIVE YEARS

Pretense and Reality

THE HISTORY OF Vietnamese-USSR relations until well into the decisive 1960s was nominal and cursory. There was neither much intercourse nor emotional attachment for either party. The heritage of those years, which continues to be influential today, is best expressed thematically. The earliest years, the 1920s, were an amalgam of pretense and reality for both Ho Chi Minh's little band of revolutionaries and the ruling Comintern in Moscow. The Stalin years of the 1930s and 1940s were a time of cruel indifference for Vietnamese radicals seeking Moscow assistance in ridding their homeland of colonialism. The last years of this formative period, the time of Nikita Khrushchev, witnessed the advent of a deeper and more complex association that left scars of distrust in Hanoi—scars that still have not disappeared. It is these themes that we seek to trace in this chapter.

EARLIEST YEARS

The history begins with the initial contact between the fledgling Indochinese Marxist movement and Moscow after the 1917 Bolshevik Revolution and the start of the slow filtering of Marxist-Leninist thought into Indochina. Here there is no large body of early documentation to be examined, no lengthy histories to be consulted. Rather, the record is one of scattered references in memoirs and brief passages in historical accounts devoted to larger events.

Hanoi historians today trace Vietnamese communism's spiritual roots back to 1903 and the July 30 meeting of the Russian Social Democratic Workers Party. This, it is held, was "the key turning point in the history of the revolution of the working class and laboring people in Russia, and in the world as a whole, including Vietnam . . . that set

4

the principles of a new proletarian party which later Ho Chi Minh fostered in founding the Communist Party of Vietnam from which stemmed the victories of the Vietnamese revolution . . . (and) the lines and orientations for economic development."[1]

Actually, there is no evidence that Marxist thought was at all influential among Vietnamese revolutionaries prior to the Bolshevik Revolution. According to Truong Chinh, Ho Chi Minh first began reading Marx (and Lenin) in a systematic and meaningful way in late 1919, initially in preparation for the December 1920 French Socialist Party Congress at Tours (which resulted in a French left split and the formation of the French Communist Party, of which Ho was a charter member).[2] Vietnam's other early great revolutionary figure, Phan Boi Chau, likewise did not begin studying Marxism until after the Bolshevik Revolution.[3] Vietnamese with revolutionary stirrings in the early days found their lodestar in the east—in Japan because of its turn of the century victory over Russia, and in China with Sun Yat Sen's 1912 revolution. If there was identification with the west among these young proto-Marxists it was not with Bolshevism but with the radicals of France, in the spirit of the Paris commune.

Lenin and the other Bolsheviks, prior to their revolution, had been aware of developments in Indochina, although clearly these were marginal for them in the general scheme of things. The earliest specific reference to Indochina the author has been able to find is Lenin's August 1908 article on the "tinderboxes of the world," in which he wrote,

> A look at the attitude of the French in Indochina shows that this time some of those who have taken part in the plundering of the colony feel uneasy: they helped the "historical government" of China suppress revolutionaries! They are also fraught with worry over keeping "their" Asiatic colonies on the edge of China intact.[4]

Much of what Lenin wrote about colonialism—including his important *Imperialism, The Highest Stage of Capitalism* (1916)—was generally relevant and did make specific reference to Indochina. A third early Lenin reference was to "rebellious plots in French-controlled Annam" in a July 1916 newspaper article on self-determination.[5]

The first post-revolutionary official pronouncement out of Moscow that even remotely could be related to Vietnam came in December 1917, a month after the Bolsheviks had seized power. It was Lenin's message to the Moslims in and out of Russia, a general statement that, in effect, defined the Communist revolution in Asia as liberation from colonialism.[6]

Of course, the Bolshevik Revolution in itself was profoundly meaningful for the revolutionary movement in Indochina. Previously, the Vietnamese revolutionary impulse that had arisen with the arrival of the French as colonialists in the 1860s was narrowly structured though amorphous. The Bolshevik Revolution became a fork in the road for Indochinese revolutionaries, offering them (or forcing them into) a choice of revolutionary routes, Communist or non-Communist.

Serious attention by Moscow to issues primarily concerning colonized Indochina began in mid-1920, when Lenin sent a draft report to the Comintern Second Congress that then went to a special commission and finally emerged as a policy statement titled *First Outline of Theses on the National and Colonial Questions.*[7]

The document deals with two issues: nationalities or ethnic minorities in the USSR and colonialism. The portion dealing with the latter is largely an elementary set of instructions on the thinking to be followed and the pitfalls to be avoided by Communist cadres in their organizational and operational activities in what today would be called the Third World. Lenin was apparently primarily concerned with ensuring that native revolutionary movements were kept under firm party supervision and ideologically uncontaminated by "petty bourgeois nationalism and pacificism." Organizational efforts, of necessity, were to be centered in the peasantry but would include whatever local proletariat was available. The party should always be self-contained, Lenin said, and should eschew the false opportunism represented by broad political movements such as the Pan Asian and Pan Islamic movements. Organizers were warned to be particularly wary of bourgeois-democratic tendencies that could either subvert the revolutionaries' character or co-opt the revolution. However, temporary relations, even alliances, were sometimes necessary, and they were permissible as a tactic. The sense of *Theses on the National and Colonial Questions* seems to be that, as most peasants were tradition bound, parochial in outlook, and stubbornly apolitical, the peasantry was a very weak reed. Lenin's pessimistic conclusion seems to be that not much could be created from such unpropitious material.[8]

Even so, the advent of *Theses* was significant. It raised the status of Asia and moved it closer to the center of Communist strategic thinking. No longer was Asia a mere contributor to world revolution. Now it was a major actor assigned an essential role. Asia, which principally meant China, was seen as capitalism's vulnerability. If Asian peoples could be organized and motivated to revolt, an avalanche could be set in motion. The revolt could best be accomplished by harnessing the hostile forces latent in the institutions of feudalism, colonialism, imperialism, and racism. It became part of a vision of the world transformed:

Conflagration in the hinterland would cause first crisis and then revolution in the imperialist citadels—and this could not be done without the contribution of the peoples of Asia. It was all succinctly expressed in Grigory Zinoviev's aphorism coined at the 1925 Comintern Plenary meeting: "The road to World Revolution lies through the East rather than through the West."[9]

Much later, Ho Chi Minh said that Lenin's *Theses* is what drew him to Marxism—it hit him like a thunderbolt, he told an interviewer. Truong Chinh describes Ho's encounter with Lenin's *Theses on the National and Colonial Questions:* "Sitting alone in his small room at Number 9, Impasse Compoint (Paris) he was extremely moved. Tears flowed down his cheeks. He shouted aloud, as if addressing a large crowd: 'Dear martyrs! Compatriots! This is what we need! This is the path to our liberation.'"[10] Perhaps, as with Chapman looking into Homer, it was a profoundly moving experience. Or it may simply have been that Lenin had raised the subject of colonialism to a transcendental level, something Ho had been attempting to do among the French left, but without much success. Possibly the legend is simply Ho's gesture of deference to the fountainhead of communism.

Much later, Vietnamese Communists speaking privately would argue that Ho Chi Minh at the time was more advanced in his thinking on the liberation of Asia than was Lenin, that he certainly knew more about organizing a revolution around the peasantry, and that Lenin's formula—which called first for ousting the colonial/imperialist power and then for achieving revolution—was not necessarily correct. Ho argued the two could be combined[11] and that, in any event, they were intricately linked. This was the burden of Ho's contribution to the debate at the Comintern's Fifth Congress (Eighth Session, June 3, 1924) in Moscow:

> My purpose in speaking here is to direct the attention of the delegates to the colonies, which to a large degree will determine the destiny of the world proletariat. Colonies supply the food and soldiers for the large imperial countries; if we want to defeat these countries we must begin by taking away their colonies. . . .
>
> Apparently you have yet to accept fully the thinking that the destiny of the international proletariat, especially the proletariat in countries that send forces to invade and occupy colonies, is closely linked to the destiny of the oppressed classes of the colonies. . . .
>
> Why in these matters of revolution have you not reorganized your tactics and forces? Why do you give no attention to the forces and the propaganda from the opposition

you wish to struggle against and topple? Why do you ignore the
colonies when the capitalists use the colonies to defend
themselves and oppose you? . . . It is the colonies that are the
foundation of counter-revolution. Yet when you talk about
revolution you give only slight attention to the colonial
question. . . .

Comrades, forgive my boldness. But I must say as I listen
to the debate by those of you from mother countries, I have the
impression you are trying to kill the snake by hitting it on the
tail, not the head. The venom and vitality of imperialism are in
the colonies, not the mother countries.[12]

The Vietnamese colonial complaint, voiced here and elsewhere,
was that while the Bolshevik and Comintern leaders paid lip service
to the liberation of Vietnam and other colonies, their strategic planners
were not acting on the logic of the utility represented by colonies.

Indeed, there was justification for Ho's criticism. Lenin's *Imperialism,
The Highest Stage of Capitalism* must have greatly disappointed him, for
it made no reference to the idea of revolution in the mother country
via revolution in the colonies. This writing was the logical place for
Lenin to deal with the concept, had he been so inclined. The idea itself
was not new, nor was it unknown in Moscow. Marx, using Ireland as
a model of thought, had seen the vulnerability that colonialism represented to the colonizing power. He recognized that denying markets
and resources to a European power, by means of revolution in colonial
and semicolonial nations, might well trigger revolution at home. Although
the early Comintern leaders endorsed the idea, they did not share Ho's
preoccupation with it. Or perhaps their attention was elsewhere, focused
on what they perceived as a greater strategic opportunity. As a result,
they treated colonialism in an undifferentiated manner, lumping it under
the rubric of the National Question. They spoke of liberation of the
European colonies, but in the context of the right of self-determination
of the colonial peoples. Most contended that this right would be realized
only as a by-product of revolution in the mother country. Trotsky was
perhaps the most insistent on this point: "The workers and peasants
not only of Annam, Algeria, Bengal but also of Persia and Armenia
will obtain the possibility of independent existence only on the day
when the workers of England and France will have overthrown Lloyd
George and Clemenceau and taken the state power into their hands."[13]

The early Comintern statement that most closely approached Ho's
thinking on strategy for Asia is found in the report that emerged from
the Sixth Comintern Congress (1928). It called for the overthrow of
"imperialism, feudalism, and landlord bureaucracy; establishment of
democratic dictatorship of the proletariat and peasantry on the basis of

Soviets; expropriation [and] nationalization of all land; and establishment of revolutionary worker's and peasants army."

The position of Trotsky and of others such as Zinoviev was quite clear; Lenin's was somewhat less so. In any event Ho's suggested strategy was ignored. It would not be the last time in which he and his Vietnamese cadres would differ with Moscow on grand strategy, later to be proved possessed of greater clarity of vision.

If Ho was not persuaded by Lenin's geopolitical thinking, he was greatly impressed by the Leninist concept of the organizational weapon in making a revolution. Strategy in mobilization and emotionalism on the evils of colonialism seem to have been the two characteristics of Lenin's writings that made the greatest impact on Ho, as evidenced by the half-dozen or so articles he wrote about Lenin and Leninism. This is typical of Ho's early rhetoric:

> The peasants in Vietnam and the hunters in the forest of
> Dahomey have heard that the people in a remote corner of the
> world have succeeded in driving away their exploiters, and are
> managing their country by themselves without any need for
> masters or governors general. They have also learned that this
> country is called Russia, that its people are very brave and the
> bravest man among them is Lenin. Mankind shared this joy and
> felt still happier when learning that after liberating his own
> people, this great leader will help emancipate other nations as
> well.[14]

HO IN MOSCOW

What could be called the start of true Vietnamese-Soviet intercourse began with the arrival of Ho Chi Minh in Moscow in the early 1920s.[15] Indeed, it is not much of an exaggeration to say that in the early years Ho Chi Minh *was* the relationship, personified.

Ho's political thinking had been shaped by the left in France during the decisive years after 1917, but he appears to have become increasingly disillusioned with the French Communist movement; thus the journey to Moscow became an intellectual break, a moving on to a new association if not to a new alliance. It was a perceptive shift. The inescapable fact was that the interests of the French Communist party in France and the interests of the Communist movement in Indochina were not the same; sometimes, in fact, they were diametrically opposed, a condition that ended only when French colonialism in Indochina ended. With his departure in 1925 (possibly excepting a brief return in the late 1920s)

Ho did not see Paris again until his return as an official state visitor in 1946.

Until recently, Hanoi historians glossed over Ho's years in Moscow, virtually to the point of exclusion. For instance, the official book-length biography published in 1970 by *Nhan Dan* (Hanoi, May 1970) reduced his early association with the USSR to a single sentence: "Ho stayed in the Soviet Union for a while to study the Soviet system and the experience of developing a Party in accordance with Lenin's theories." Such brief treatment of this subject in the early years probably was due to tactical considerations. It was obviously also a means of coping with the Sino-Soviet dispute, in that it downplayed Ho's early acts of commitment to either camp.

In any event, it was long asserted by many outsiders that Ho never had much to do with the USSR or for that matter with Marxism-Leninism and that whatever association there was had been forced on him by the French and uncaring others. But this was disputed, and for years the argument raged among observers concerning Ho's connections with and loyalties to Moscow. For years scholars of Vietnamese studies suffered from a dearth of information about what many were sure was fact: that Ho in 1924 began a close association with Moscow and committed himself to the system it represented, not only as a true believer in Marxism-Leninism but also as a Comintern agent. But for decades these scholars had as proof only scraps of historical evidence, much of it from suspect sources.

This drought of information ended after the Vietnam War, when a flood of official material began to pour out of Hanoi and Moscow. Detailed accounts of Ho's early years in Moscow were published, and his relationship was assertively traced. Memoirs from early Vietnamese party figures, such as Bui Lam, whose candid references to cadres studying in Moscow and the presence of Comintern agents at all the early party congresses and meetings, came as a refreshing relief to the official silence on Soviet influence in Vietnam that prevailed for fifty years.[16]

Today the early connections between the Vietnamese Communists and Moscow are stated in unequivocal terms by Hanoi historians:

> The October Revolution awakened the Vietnamese patriots and brought Marxism-Leninism, the truth of our age, to the working class and people of Vietnam, thereby lighting the way to national liberation and social emancipation. During the long night of slavery, Nguyen Ai Quoc (Ho Chi Minh), the first communist of Vietnam, found in Leninism the way to save the people, save the country. . . . Possessing absolute confidence in the path of

Leninism, he overcame countless difficulties, traveled to the Soviet Union, homeland of Lenin, and with that, laid the foundation for Vietnam-Soviet friendship. . . . Vietnamese revolutionary militants found in the Soviet Union a tremendous source of hope, confidence in inevitable victory and strong inspiration. Considering the Soviet Union to be the home of socialism, to be the beautiful image of the Vietnam of tomorrow, Vietnamese communists have, from the beginning, always considered protecting the gains of the October Revolution and supporting the Soviet Union as its international obligation.[17]

Another article says that Ho visited the USSR "frequently" in the period between 1923 and 1941, and that at one point he was moved to write a poem that included the lines:

Russia has done the unusual,
Turned slaves into free men.[18]

And, the account continues, feelings were reciprocated:

As Uncle Ho discovered the citadel of revolution, the Soviet people quickly recognized him as a genuine, outstanding revolutionary; and, through him, they recognized the nation of Vietnam and its unique culture. In December 1923, in an article entitled: "Visit with a Communist International Soldier: Nguyen Ai Quoc," the Soviet poet and journalist O. Mandelstam wrote: "From Nguyen Ai Quoc emanates a culture, not European culture, but perhaps a culture of the future. . . . The Vietnamese people are a simple and civil people. In the noble mannerisms and quiet speech of Nguyen Ai Quoc, I saw tomorrow, saw the quiet prospect of world friendship as vast as the ocean." The Soviet people have always shared the joys and sorrows of our people. When hearing that Nguyen Ai Quoc had died in a Hong Kong prison on 26 June 1932, the Communist International and the Far Eastern Communist College in Moscow held a funeral ceremony, many letters, poems, commentaries and books were written and countless meetings were held in the Soviet Union to remember him. And, through Uncle Ho, Vietnam acquired an increasingly important position and was especially admired by the Soviet people. In recent years in the Soviet Union, no country has been introduced in such glowing terms and with such warm feelings as Vietnam. As a result, the peoples of the two countries gained a deeper understanding of each other and their friendship became increasingly warm. Nurturing these feelings for the Soviet Union, Uncle Ho always taught our people to display profound gratitude; this feeling, which is "close to

piety," is one of the basic virtues, is a tradition to the loyal
Vietnamese. When drinking water, remember its source; with
gratitude to the Soviet Union, our party and people have always
believed that they must "make every effort to fulfill their tasks
regarding the nation and fulfill their international obligation to
the peoples of other countries."[19]

As far as can be determined, Ho never met Lenin; but this is likely
in any case, given that Ho achieved the importance that would have
drawn Lenin's attention only after Lenin's death. Hanoi biographies refer
to Ho "meeting Leninism" but never Lenin. Apparently early Soviet
leaders, such as Stalin and others who succeeded Lenin, did not know
quite what to make of Ho Chi Minh, and thus their opinions on him
were divided. Janos Radvanyi, a long-time Hungarian diplomat who
defected to the West, wrote that in the 1950s he discussed Ho with
USSR Foreign Minister V. M. Molotov and that Molotov "has a poor
opinion of Ho Chi Minh because he, and Pham Van Dong, were both
stubborn men, interested only in Vietnam and not in the international
movement. . . . I also heard other opinions too (in Moscow), some that
Ho was close to Moscow, others that his most intimate ties were with
Peking."[20]

Today in the USSR Ho's name is widely venerated. A Soviet
transport vessel bearing his name, commissioned upon his death on
September 3, 1969, calls regularly at Haiphong. There is a Ho Chi Minh
Square in Moscow and a Ho Chi Minh Foreign Language College in
Irkutsk. In May 1980 a memorial tablet was dedicated in front of the
building at 1 Kalinin Boulevard, Moscow—the Comintern office where
Ho worked from 1923 to 1925.

Two themes dominate present-day Hanoi historical treatment of
Ho in connection with the USSR and early Soviet-Vietnamese relations.
The first concerns reciprocated attitudes. There was, it is asserted, an
early and deep attachment by Vietnamese revolutionaries to the USSR
and to Marxism-Leninism, a sentimental tie and a psychological connection, purportedly because of the similarities of history, background,
and experience of the early Bolsheviks and the early Vietnamese Communists, one that is returned by the people of the USSR. The second
theme concerns the early USSR as "peerless example" and "guiding
beacon" for the Vietnamese revolutionaries, but no more. The rhetoric
is lavish—as noted above, the USSR is portrayed as a "tremendous
source of hope, strong inspiration, beautiful image"—but always abstract.
There is little reference to specific political/diplomatic support, virtually
none to early Soviet military assistance. In short, the debt to the Rome
of communism is strictly a spiritual one. Hanoi historians jealously

guard their heritage of the Vietnamese revolution as self-contained, self-sufficient.

This is a useful approach for both the historians and the Hanoi officials dealing with the USSR today. Tribute can be paid to those early Moscow and Comintern days in a tactful way that acknowledges what every older party cadre knows, that much was unsatisfactory in the initial encounter of the two Communist movements.

Moscow historians for their part offer a more material view of the early official association with the Vietnamese:

> The Comintern paid a great deal of attention to the question of training cadres of communist revolutionaries for the countries of the East. . . . The Comintern carried on extensive training of cadres of Vietnamese revolutionaries and provided them with all-around assistance via China. . . . A distinguishing feature of the relations taking shape between the Comintern and the communist movement in Vietnam in the 1920s was that the Vietnamese Communists joined the Comintern as members of the French Communist Party and not as representatives of an independent Communist Party of Indochina for the simple reason that it did not exist at the time. In that period the Vietnamese revolutionaries trained at the Communist University of the Toilers of the East or at the Chinese revolutionary military academy at Whampoa, were preparing to work directly in the country and form a Marxist-Leninist party of the working class. The activity of Ho Chi Minh, Tran Phu, Le Hong Phong and other revolutionaries and their contacts with Communists in Russia, France and China in many ways contributed to the emergence of close links between the Vietnamese revolution and the world communist and working-class movement.[21]

Whereas earlier the Moscow connection with the revolutionaries of Indochina had been downplayed or denied outright, today the Soviet claim is vaunted:

> The relations between the revolutionaries and the working people of our countries (USSR) have existed since the 1920's. During this period Ho Chi Minh and many other patriots in Vietnam came to the Soviet Union to study communism. The victorious Soviet proletariat extended its support to the liberation movement in Vietnam. The Soviet Union became a guiding star and strategic ally of the Vietnamese revolution.[22]

THE COMINTERN RELATIONSHIP

The Communist International or Comintern (later, Cominform) was created in March 1919 with headquarters in Moscow as the institution by which, in theory, the worldwide Communist movement would govern itself and which, in actuality, the Kremlin rulers would use as a mechanism to control Communist movements everywhere. Initially the Comintern transcended the USSR and had an international character about it. Under Stalin it became purely a tool for Soviet enforcement and repression. In the years under consideration here, there was still a difference between the USSR and the Comintern.

The Second Comintern Congress (1920) placed Indochina administratively under the French Communist party (FCP) within which (beginning in March 1922) a Colonial Commission was charged with devising a strategy and setting down the party line for party members in Indochina and other French colonies. Much of the FCP's public activity was executed through international front organizations, such as Peasants International, the Red International of Labor Unions, the Communist Youth International, and the Anti-Imperialist League, which had branches in Indochina and other French colonies.

A second chain of command from the Comintern to Indochina, via China, was required because most Vietnamese revolutionaries were outside of Vietnam, in Paris or in Canton: "In the 1920's the Comintern had no direct contacts with the revolutionary movement in Vietnam. It cooperated and maintained contact with the Vietnamese revolutionaries through its sections, the Communist Parties of France and China."[23] The control mechanism for Asia was the Comintern's Far Eastern Bureau (*Dalburo* in Russian), which operated clandestinely out of Shanghai and, as the Southern Bureau, out of Hong Kong and Singapore.

The Comintern in the 1920s met periodically in congresses and discussed Indochina, at least briefly. Such discussions apparently were strategic in nature. Regarding the question, for instance, of whether Indochina could repeat the success of Mongolia where a people's republic had been established in 1924, the Comintern's conclusion (1924) was that circumstances were not the same.

Much Comintern activity with respect to Indochina was exhortatory. This rather passionate "appeal" to the Communists of Annam, sent February 27, 1924, was typical:

> O, My Brothers. O, My Brothers. Direct the destiny of your own land. Come to the desires of heaven and no one can conquer you. For five years an association has been functioning in Russia which plans to unite all the workers of the world. This

association carries the name of the Communist International. Without the courage of its promoters, it would not be in existence today. At the present time it is very powerful and aims to come to the support of the millions of workers scattered over the globe. It is especially interested in the fate of the unfortunate peoples living in colonies, such as you Annamites, whose lot has been frightful ever since the day the French barbarians came to loot and destroy. . . . Energy and courage are needed today. It is necessary not only to fire the rifle and wield the sword against these barbarians who have enslaved you, who oppress you, but it is also necessary to defy these hypocrites. Their words are lies. They appear to aid you and bring you to the path of progress but in reality they have poisoned you and are even attempting to exterminate the Annamite race. . . . In all the lands of the earth there are tremblings as the red flag of our Association flies. The hour of victory approaches. O my brothers! Workers of the world unite![24]

Hanoi historians, more than is justified, today place the Comintern at the center of early Vietnamese revolutionary planning and activity. Some typical examples follow:

- In 1918 the forerunner of the Comintern in Moscow began "propagating Marxism-Leninism in Indochina in preparation for the founding of a revolutinary organization and a Communist party." On April 25, 1920, the French Consul in Vladivostock informed his government that a Vladivostok-based group was planning to organize a propaganda operation in Saigon and elsewhere. On November 8, 1920, the French in Saigon expelled the Soviet official M. Antonikovski and an associate for communist organizational activities. "These efforts of the Comintern greatly contributed to the progress of the revolution in Indochina. . . ."
- The Comintern "won the full confidence of Ho Chi Minh in 1920."
- "The Comintern had a deep impact on the revolution in Indochina after Ho became a communist and joined the Comintern at the Tours Congress in 1920."
- "Through the Comintern Ho found the revolutionary path for the Indochinese people. . . . Ho became a faithful and imaginative follower of Lenin in world proletarian revolution."
- The Comintern "guided the early cause through its assessment of the situation in Indochina and concrete decisions."
- The victories of the Vietnamese revolution were "largely due to the care and guidance of the Comintern."

- "When the British imperialists arrested Nguyen Ai Quoc and planned to hand him over to the French imperialists who, by the agency of the Royal Court of Annam, had condemned him to death in 1929, the Comintern, through the Anti-Imperialist League, issued an appeal entitled 'Save the Annamese (Vietnamese) revolutionary Nguyen Ai Quoc!', calling on all anti-imperialist organizations the world over to oppose the handing over of Nguyen Ai Quoc to the French imperialists and to demand his release."

- "After the 1930–31 revolutionary high tide (in Vietnam) the French imperialists drowned the worker-peasant movement in Indochina in blood, and all Party and mass organizations were disrupted. On 27 February 1932 the Executive Committee of the Comintern instructed the French, Chinese and Indian Communist Parties to do their best to help the Indochinese Communist Party and the revolutionary movement in Indochina to recover rapidly."

- "Under the guidance of the Communist International, Indochinese communists who were studying in Moscow worked out a 'Programme of Action of the Indochinese Communist Party.' This programme was approved by the Comintern in June 1932, sent to Indochina, and published in newspapers and reviews of the Comintern. It aimed at pointing out the immediate tasks of the communists and revolutionary masses, helping them to overcome pessimism in the face of temporary difficulties and setbacks and to draw lessons from their experience with a view to restoring and promoting the revolutionary movement and bringing the revolution to complete victory."

- "The Comintern made a great contribution to the training and fostering of our Party's first theorists. The first theorist trained by the Comintern was Nguyen Ai Quoc. The first cadre admitted to the University of the Peoples of the Orient in 1925 was Nguyen The Ruc. From 1925 until 1932 when the school closed down more than 40 Vietnamese cadres studied here."

- "The Comintern (in all) published in its journals nearly 100 articles on the Indochinese Communist Party and the Indochinese revolution written by such Indochinese communists as Nguyen Ai Quoc (using the pen names of Wang, A.F., N., W.), Le Hong Phong (pen names: An, Cho Moi). . . . The articles on Indochina denounced the barbarous plunder, harsh rule, and terrorist acts by the French imperialists in Indochina. When Tran Phu, our Party's General Secretary, died a courageous death, the Editorial Board of the *Communist International* wrote an article entitled 'In Memory of Comrade Ly Quy' (Tran Phu's alias). When Pham

Hung (alias Pham Van Thien) and two other comrades were sentenced to death, the Editorial Board of the *International Correspondence* wrote an article."

- "Under the leadership of the Comintern, two Vietnamese fought courageously in the Comintern-led International Brigade beside the Spanish people against the Franco fascists who, with the assistance of the German and Italian fascists, were attacking the Spanish Popular Front."[25]

The Fifth Comintern Congress (July–August 1924) upgraded the mechanism to supervise activity in Indochina and the Asian region. It became the Comintern's Eastern Department and was put under the legendary Michael Borodin and headquartered in Canton. The Southern Section of the Eastern Department (i.e., the Southeast Asian Section) was under Ho Chi Minh, who supervised organizational and propaganda work in Indochina, Thailand, and countries to the southeast from the mid-1920s into the early 1930s. The purpose of the new *apparat* was to increase efforts to foment revolution, or at least disorder, in Indochina:

> The decisions of the Fifth Congress of the Comintern (July–
> August 1924) prompted the Communist parties to increase their
> assistance to the national liberation movement in the colonies. Ho
> Chi Minh, who presented an analysis of the situation in the
> colonies, noted that the European Communist parties had to
> establish effective contact with the masses in dependent and
> colonial countries because only such a policy was consistent with
> the requirements of Leninism. "We must adopt concrete
> measures," he said. "I propose the following points:
>
> 1. To publish in *L'Humanite* a new feature of at least two
> columns weekly devoted to regular coverage of colonial
> questions.
> 2. To increase propaganda and choose Party members
> among the natives of the colonial countries in which there are
> already branches of the Communist International.
> 3. To send comrades from the colonial countries to study at
> the Eastern Communist University in Moscow."[26]

The early relationship between the Comintern and the Vietnamese revolution was a mixture of pretense and reality. Its character was largely a product of Ho Chi Minh's personality, which is why it is difficult to describe in objective terms. It appears that at best it was an alliance of convenience. There is no evidence that Ho ever refused or even questioned a Comintern order, but neither is there any example of his having sacrificed his interests for it. Somehow he managed to arrange matters so that he never got an assignment or instruction contrary to his personal interest or to that of the Indochinese Communist movement. Ho apparently considered the Comintern to be of limited utility to him and his cause beyond its valuable know-how in organization building. Nor did Ho ever seem to have the feelings of warmth and empathy for the USSR that he had for the French and France.

On the other hand, it is clear that Comintern theoreticians and the academies of Moscow never made a concerted effort to translate Communist doctrine into terms that would be meaningful in the cultures of Indochina or even to adapt Communist revolutionary strategy to the special circumstances of Vietnamese colonialism. In truth, Lenin probably never thought much about Indochina at all, and later Stalin's continental mentality prevented him from developing more than *provocateur* interest. This indifference was apparent to the early Vietnamese faithful. "Indochina is a country which seems to be forgotten by the whole world," said a Vietnamese delegate to the Sixth Comintern Congress in Moscow in 1928, voicing a plaintive complaint heard early and repeated frequently during the next four decades.[27]

THE INDOCHINESE COMMUNIST PARTY (ICP)

Communism in Indochina in the 1920s was marked by factionalism, doctrinal wrangling, and competition among personalized entourages. At one point three separate Communist movements existed—the Stalinists, the Trotskyites, and an indigenous group called the Young Vietnamese Revolutionaries Association—in addition to several well-organized nationalist (non-Communist) revolutionary movements.

Debate on forming a Vietnamese Communist party began at the Sixth Comintern Congress in 1928. Three Vietnamese were in attendance (as members of the French delegation): Ho Chi Minh, Nguyen Van Tao, and Le Hong Phong, all important early revolutionary figures. Tao took the lead in urging the Comintern in an August 17 speech to authorize the formation of a single Communist party in Vietnam out of the three existing "Marxist tendencies." Ho apparently considered the move to be premature and the Comintern concurred. In any event it was not until October 1929 that the Comintern officially instructed Ho, then working out of Canton, to effect the merger: "On February 3, 1930, under the instructions from the Communist International, Nguyen Ai Quoc (that is, our Uncle Ho) convened the Merger Conference to bring together the various communist groups of Indochina and establish the Communist Party of Vietnam, which later changed its name to the Indochinese Communist Party."[28]

At this merger meeting Ho was armed with a stern message from the Comintern's Executive Council warning that failure to move on the formation of a single party was endangering the revolution and adding that "the indecision and indifference displayed by certain groups toward the immediate formation of a Communist Party [are] absolutely enormous."[29] The Comintern asserted that, once formed, the new party "would have to accept the program, rules and decisions of the Comintern . . . [and] set up a united committee of representatives of all communist organizations to be headed by a representative of the Comintern."[30]

The leaders of the three Communist movements accepted the advice and a single party was created, at least on paper.[31] The Comintern Executive Committee at its Eleventh Plenum (twenty-fifth session) on April 11, 1931, declared that "the Indochinese Communist Party, formerly a section of the French Communist Party, is henceforth recognized as an independent section of the Comintern."[32]

Feuding did not end, however, much to the irritation of the Comintern, which, at the Seventh Comintern Congress (1935), declared:

Serious errors were committed in the merger. The unity
commission which administered the merger of various communist
groups into the united Communist Party made a series of
mistakes of which the most important was that the merger was
effected without an adequate differentiation and selection of truly
revolutionary forces from the existing communist groups. During
the ebb of the revolutionary tide some fellow-travelers who
joined the Party without being screened carefully enough during
the period of upsurge, voiced their defeatist feelings.[33]

This continuing factionalism was a manifestation of Vietnam's sociopolitical heritage. Whereas the thrust of history in Europe in the past 200 years was toward centralized power and the unification of political elements, the trend in Southeast Asia and Vietnam was toward political atomization. Internecine political warfare continues to this day. There was a second heritage at work: clandestinism in politics. Indochina's history is filled with accounts of conspiratorial politics, secret sociopolitical organizations, plots and counterplots, and spasms of political struggle both violent and obscure.[34]

The result consistently has been fragmented social institutions operating as vaguely defined political systems, which, combined, became a Communist organizer's nightmare. This may have been one of the reasons why the Comintern backed away from a more structured approach.

During the 1930s Lenin's concept of the liberation of Asia was fleshed out and its precepts disseminated. The strategy was first to oust the occupying colonial/imperialist power, then to supplant it briefly with a bourgeois-nationalist regime that included Communist party participation, and, finally, to follow with seizure and monopolization of power by the party. The model was the Bolshevik Revolution. Vietnamese Communists sought as best they were able to implement this three-stage formula for revolution just as it had come off the Moscow drafting board. However, it did not prove a credible guide, and the Vietnamese Communists concluded early that the reliable route to power was seizure with direct military force. Perhaps even Moscow theoreticians, reflecting Lenin's pessimism about Asia, found it difficult to entertain the idea of a colony successfully ousting the metropolitan state. The colony was weak, and the decisive test of power already had taken place with the establishment of the colony in the first place. Also, most early Marxist theoreticians were Europe oriented and believed that the only sure revolutionary instrument was an aroused and organized proletariat. They maintained that revolutionaries such as Ho and the Vietnamese needed to elevate and transform their anticolonial and nationalist sentiments into the higher consciousness of class struggle. Left to themselves, they would produce only a bourgeois (i.e., nationalist, noncolonial) state. Thus the Soviet model was never actually of much practical use in dealing with the French *colon*.

In later years the Vietnamese Communists would heap praise on the USSR for its valuable contribution in the 1930s to the cause in Vietnam. Much the same tack would be taken as that used with respect to the 1920s—namely, the use by the Vietnamese of the USSR revolutionary experience as an inspiration and an ideal they could emulate.

Examples of this idealization of the USSR in Vietnamese history— this "same historical chain"—are expressed in two major speeches by Party Secretary Le Duan. The first is in his famous "Forward Under the Glorious Banner of the October Revolution" speech (1967), the second in his speech at the party conference in Ho Chi Minh City in July 1976:

> The Vietnamese revolution is a component of world revolution
> and its successes have never been separated from the latter's. For
> the Vietnamese people, the victory of the October Revolution . . .
> is a great event in one and the same historical chain. . . . The
> October Revolution was a vivid lesson in an ingenious and
> flexible application of the theory on revolutionary violence and
> on insurrection for the conquest of power.[35]

> In the nearly 60 years since the Russian October Revolution in
> 1917, the proletarian revolution has advanced to victory after

victory. In order to prevent their own collapse, the imperialists mounted very fierce counter-offensives. The first was the intervention by 14 imperialist countries against the newly established Soviet government.[36]

The international significance of the October Revolution, and its meaning to Vietnam, Le Duan said, was as "a remarkable model of strategic and tactical conduct" for other revolutionaries. He credited Lenin and the Russian Bolsheviks with a formula still valid for the seizure of power. They created a "monolithic" party, forged a "worker-peasant alliance," and combined "armed struggle and political struggle into powerful revolutionary violence." This and later victories of the Soviet Union, he continued, "not only safeguarded the first socialist state but also generated favorable conditions for the triumph of revolution in a series of countries in Europe and Asia."[37]

Following Lenin's teachings on revolution in the Orient, the Vietnamese revolutionaries applied Marxist-Leninist principles to the concrete and specific conditions of Vietnamese society. The first political program of the Indochinese Communist Party, now the Vietnam Workers Party, clearly stated that in the era of imperialism and proletarian revolution . . . the Vietnamese revolution has become a component of the world revolution.[38]

Even so, the tendency in Hanoi then and now is to depict the USSR as long on emulation model and short on practical assistance. And, in fact, what Ho got from the heartland of communism initially was mostly philosophic advice, material help for the early Vietnamese cause being, to say the least, modest.[39] To a large extent the quality of the relations that existed is acknowledged now by Moscow historians. For example:

Speaking specifically of relations between the USSR and the Vietnam Communist Party above all we must speak of the attention with which Ho Chi Minh, founder of the Party of Vietnamese communists, followed the CPSU's experience. He constantly emphasized its significance for the development of the world revolutionary process and urged that this experience be taken into account in Vietnam. . . . Our parties' reciprocal ties are extensive. Imbued with the spirit of proletarian internationalism they help us to understand each other more deeply and effectively promote the elaboration of a joint approach to a whole series of various problems and the unity and cohesiveness of the two parties and peoples and their active participation in the socialist community's multifaceted life.[40]

However limited the early Moscow assistance may have been for the Vietnamese revolutionaries, the fact is that the truly old guard— such as Ho, Le Hong Phong, Nguyen Van Tao, and Nguyen The Ruc— had more Soviet than Chinese connections, although it might be argued that for all of them the French connection was stronger than either. It was only later that the conflicting claims by Moscow and China came to be made on Vietnamese communism's loyalty.

What Ho and the other early figures got from Moscow was what might be called the organizational weapon technology, the Leninist devices for mobilization, motivation, and leadership. These could also be called ideological contributions. However, these techniques (and the ideology behind them) had to be recast if they were to grow in local soil. The important point to be made here (and discussed in detail below) is that there was a great sea change in communism's passage to Asia. Emptied of much of its intellectual content, communism became more an instrument and less a philosophy. Moreover, although many outsiders consider Vietnamese communism to be a pale carbon copy of Soviet communism, there are many dissimilarities.

Whatever the reason, the Bolshevik Revolution as a model today has virtually no intellectual appeal in Vietnam, especially among the young. As discussed later, Vietnamese Communist cadres of subsequent generations came to regard it as a distant event of history that had lost whatever awe or magnetism it once had. It is, as one young cadre put it to the author, the thunder of a storm that has long ago rumbled its way to oblivion.

NOTES

1. Vo Chi Cong, *Nhan Dan* (July 29, 1983); see also *Tap Chi Cong San*, No. 7 (July 1983).

2. *Tap Chi Cong San*, No. 11 (November 1981).

3. Joseph Buttinger, *Vietnam: A Dragon Embattled*, Vol. 1 (New York: Praeger Publishers, 1967), p. 155.

4. V. I. Lenin, *Collected Works*, 3rd ed., Vol. 17 (Leningrad, 1935–1937), p. 217; and Lenin, "The Tinderboxes on the World Political Scene," *The Proletarian*, No. 33 (August 5, 1908). See also Lenin's "Notes on Imperialism," in *Collected Works*, Vol. 22, p. 184, for his reference to French colonialism.

5. Lenin, *Collected Works*, Vol. 30, pp. 66–67.

6. See "Message from V. I. Lenin, Chairman of the Council of Peoples Commissars, and J. V. Stalin, People's Commissar for Nationalities Affairs, to

all the Working Moslems of Russia and the East," in *Milestones of Soviet Foreign Policy* (Moscow: Progress Publishers, 1967), pp. 33–35.

7. See *Theses and Statues of the 3rd Communist International; Adopted by the Second Party Congress July 17–August 7, 1920*, reprinted as an appendix in Robert Turner's *Vietnamese Communism: Its Origins and Developments* (Stanford, Calif.: Hoover Institution Press, 1975).

8. Lenin's thinking about Asia in general, as well as the Comintern's handling of the "eastern question," is treated extensively in Charles B. McLane's excellent work, *Soviet Strategies in Southeast Asia: An Exploration of Eastern Policy Under Lenin and Stalin* (Princeton, N.J.: Princeton University Press, 1966), which includes a detailed account of the debate and difference of opinion that influenced the final version of *Theses on the National and Colonial Questions*; see especially pp. 12–24. It is clear these early Comintern figures reflected sharply divergent views on the proper policies for Asia/Indochina.

9. Frequently misquoted as "through Peking, rather. . . ."

10. *Nghiem Cuu Lich Su* (Hanoi), No. 132 (May–June 1970).

11. Historians of this early era, particularly those in Hanoi, probably give Ho Chi Minh too much credit for pioneer doctrinal thinking on the matter of whether revolution in Asia was possible, given the absence of a significant urban proletariat. It seems clear that M. N. Roy, the famed early Indian Communist figure, argued the case for a Communist revolution in Asian colonies as early as did Ho, if not earlier. Roy was advancing his arguments at the same time Lenin was publishing his *Theses on the National and Colonial Questions*. As far as is known, Ho, in his writings, did not take note of Roy's ideas. Roy was expelled from the Comintern in 1929 for branding as "imperialism" the Comintern's decision to entrust the Communist revolution in India to the British Communist party. For a discussion of the influence of Soviet doctrinal thinking on Ho and other Asian revolutionaries, see Robert Scalapino's chapter, "Legitimacy and Institutionalization in Asian Socialist Societies," in Robert Scalapino et al., eds., *Asian Political Institutionalization* (Berkeley: University of California Institute of East Asian Studies, 1986), pp. 59–94.

12. *Tap Chi Cong San*, No. 6 (June 1984), citing Archives of the International Party History at the Institute of Marxism and Leninism, Moscow.

13. *Der I Kongress der Kommunistischen Internationale: Protokoll* (Hamburg, 1921), p. 5; cited in McLane, *Soviet Strategies*, p. 8.

14. "Lenin and the Colonial Peoples," quoted in "Lenin's Image in Ho Chi Minh's Writings," *Vietnam Courier* (April 1985). For other typical examples, see "Lenin and Colonial Nations," *Pravda* (January 27, 1924); "Lenin and the East," *Tieng Coi* (January 21, 1926); and "Leninism and the Liberation of Oppressed Peoples," *Pravda* (April 18, 1955). For a lengthy discussion of Ho's writings on Lenin, see *Hoc Tap* (April 1970).

15. As with so many other details regarding Ho, the exact date on which he first arrived in Moscow is in dispute. Some sources say as early as 1921; biographer Nguyen Khac Huyen says he attended the Fourth Comintern Congress in November 1922; *Nhan Dan* (May 18, 1985) quotes Novosti Press Agency as saying Ho first went to Moscow in 1923 and was interviewed by a Moscow

journal called *Ognonyok* (Little Flame) about his visit. Other Moscow accounts state that he attended the Fifth Comintern Congress in 1924. Many references are in the context of the death of Lenin (January 21, 1924). It seems certain that he arrived before that date.

16. A typical example of the sort of documentation now being supplied by Hanoi is the publication in the party journal *Tap Chi Cong San* of the texts of three documents dealing with Ho's acceptance as a delegate to the Comintern Fifth Congress in Moscow in 1924: (a) a letter from Ho to a Comrade Petrov of the Comintern's Far Eastern Bureau requesting delegate status; (b) a reply by Petrov saying he would pass the request to the French delegation; and (c) a letter from the French delegation to the Comintern Secretariat requesting consultive delegate status for Ho. See "Nguyen Ai Quoc's Participation in the Fifth Congress of the Communist International (1924)," *Tap Chi Cong San*, No. 6 (June 1984) (JPRS-SEA 84-113). And for a particularly candid account of Ho's early association with the USSR, see Bui Lam in *Tap Chi Cong San*, No. 9 (September 1982); JPRS-SEA 82-610 (January 10, 1983).

17. *Tap Chi Cong San*, No. 11 (November 1985); editorial.

18. *Tap Chi Cong San*, No. 11 (November 1981).

19. Ibid.

20. Janos Radvanyi, *Delusions and Reality* (South Bend, Ind.: Gateway Editions, 1978), p. 20.

21. R. A. Ulyanovsky, *The Comintern and the East: The Struggle for the Leninist Strategy and Tactics in National Liberation Movements* (Moscow: Progress Publishers, 1979), pp. 468–469. Ho was apparently one of the early cadres trained at the Toilers of the East University; he wrote an article about class work there in the March 1924 issue of *La Vie Ouvriere*.

22. Radio Moscow International Service, January 30, 1986.

23. See Ulyanovsky, *Comintern and the East, passim*. Soon after its formation in 1920, the French Communist party established a special committee to promote the organization of revolutionary movements in French colonies. By the mid-1920s it was circulating party newspapers and journals in Vietnam. In 1925 the Saigon publishing house Annam published the *Communist Manifesto* in Vietnamese—the first Marxist work to be printed in Vietnamese (Ulyanovsky, *Comintern and the East*, p. 467). *Le Matin* (August 19, 1927) accused Moscow of attempting to wreck the French empire through the activities of the Soviet military attaché at Paris (M. Wolkoff) and the Soviet ambassador in Berlin (J. Kretensky). See *New York Times* (August 20, 1927). At the Comintern's Eleventh Plenum (March-April 1931) the Indochinese Communist party was granted alternate status membership in the Communist International and thus separated, at least on paper, from the Communist party of France.

24. Quoted in full in *L'Asie Francaise* (February 1925), p. 122. This was the first Comintern document specifically directed at Indochina in Vietnamese. It was a tract dated February 27, 1924, probably written by Ho Chi Minh. See also Buttinger, *Vietnam: A Dragon Embattled*, p. 517.

25. All of these examples were drawn from Nguyen Thanh, "The Communist International and the Indochinese Revolution," *Vietnam Courier*, No. 2 (February 1984).

26. Nguyen Thanh, "The Communist International and the Indochinese Revolution," *Vietnam Courier,* No. 2 (February 1984). The same article states that in the 1920s and 1930s two Comintern journals, *Communist International* and *International Correspondence,* published nearly 100 articles on Indochina, including those by Ho Chi Minh (under the pen names Wang, A. F., N., and W.), Le Hong Phong, and Nguyen Van Tao.

27. McLane, *Soviet Strategies,* p. 103, quoting *Inprecor* (October 25, 1928).

28. "The Communist International and the Indochinese Communist Party," in *Tap Chi Cong San* (Hanoi), No. 2 (February 1986), p. 41.

29. Ulyanovsky, *Comintern and the East,* p. 475.

30. Ibid.

31. In October 1930, Tran Phu, who had returned that spring from Moscow (where he had been studying at the University of the Toilers of the East), became the new party's first Central Committee secretary-general.

32. See *Vietnam Courier* (February 1984).

33. Cited in Ulyanovsky, *Comintern and the East,* p. 382, quoted from *The Communist International Prior to the Seventh World Congress* (Moscow, 1935), p. 484.

34. For a discussion of the institutionalized politics of clandestinism in Vietnam, see Douglas Pike, *Viet Cong* (Cambridge, Mass.: MIT Press, 1966), Ch. 1.

35. Le Duan, "The Same Historical Chain: Forward Under the Glorious Banner of the October Revolution," *Nhan Dan* (November 4, 1967).

36. Duan, *Developing Upon Our Great Victory and Continuing to Advance the Revolution* (Hanoi: Su That Publishing House, 1980), p. 17.

37. Duan, "The Same Historical Chain," p. 27.

38. Duan, *Developing Upon Our Great Victory,* p. 38.

39. At the time, of course, the Comintern did not receive much return on its investment in Indochina either; what it got were merely some proforma gestures of proletarian solidarity. For instance, the October 1930 Indochina Communist Party Congress issued a ten-point program, in which point number ten was "to support Soviet Union solidarity with the world proletariat and the revolutionary movements of the colonized and dependent people" (Buttinger, *Vietnam: A Dragon Embattled,* p. 561).

40. *Pravda* (May 13, 1980).

Two

THE STALIN YEARS
Cruel World of Indifference

JOSEPH STALIN DID not have quite the messianic impulse of most other early Bolshevik figures, nor was he as deeply committed as was Lenin to anticolonialism as the engine of Communist revolution in Asia. The experience of the 1920s, particularly the debacle in China, appears to be the reason for this negative attitude. Stalin seemed to regard anticolonial activity as a sometimes useful but generally undependable weapon against the capitalist world. All too often in the progression of revolution, things would go awry. Stage one, ousting of the colonials, would be followed by stage two, temporary installation of the bourgeois-nationalist-Communist united front. Then the revolution would stall and stage three, communist takeover, would be sidetracked as the new noncolonial regime turned anti-Communist. Further, Stalin was continentally oriented, his strategic thinking dedicated to the USSR as heartland. Finally, Stalin was preoccupied, first with consolidation of internal power and social reconstruction in the USSR, then with the rise of Hitler, and finally with World War II.

Most scholars of this period—McLane, Cameron, Sacks, and Brimmell[1]—regard the Vietnamese Communist relationship with Stalin as being episodic and sporadic and characterized by marked disinterest on both sides. Vietnam, which was largely ignored by official communism in France and China as well, avoided public association with the Comintern because of its temporizing on colonialism. The 1930s fixed a lone-rider quality on Vietnamese communism that it retains to this day.

It is difficult to establish the exact degree of control that Stalin and the Comintern exerted over the Indochinese Communist party during this period. One limitation was the fact that the ICP was still so amorphous that it had trouble applying the discipline necessary to make it a mainline participant in international Communist affairs. Stalin was not greatly interested in encouraging greater activism in Indochina; hence there was no need for much control. The Comintern as an institution of influence and control had begun to decline, particularly in Asia. As Allan Cameron expressed it:

> The early Communist movement in Vietnam was only on the fringes of Soviet control, even at the height of the Comintern period. Although Ho Chi Minh was indeed a Comintern functionary and, apparently, held positions of considerable responsibility for the Communist movement in Southeast Asia, Moscow's attempts at control were only sporadically effective and often encountered serious obstacles in the fractiousness of both individuals and groups within the Indochinese Communist Party (ICP) prior to World War II.[2]

One of the few visible examples of whip-cracking was the Comintern's preemptive veto of the name *Vietnamese Communist party*, which Ho had chosen in the 1930 merger. Two months after the christening, he was obliged to announce a name change. The Plenary Meeting, he explained, had decided to change the party's name to the *Indochinese Communist party* because "the Vietnamese, Cambodian and Laotian proletariat have politically and economically to be closely related in spite of their difference in language, customs and race."[3]

THE POPULAR FRONT

The decade of the 1930s was a bad one for the party in Vietnam. The party faced the difficult task of reconstituting itself in the aftermath of a disastrous 1930-1931 experiment in open rebellion. It was seriously challenged by two nationalist movements, the Dai Viets and the Vietnam Quoc Dan Dang (VNQDD) on one side and the Trotskyites (who remained popular and powerful throughout the 1930s) on the other.

The party's most difficult period came in the mid-1930s, when the Comintern instructed it to support the united front movement, which sought to unite all countries and political organizations worldwide under a single stop-Hitler umbrella. In Indochina this meant abandoning the revolution and cooperating with the hated *colon*. The Comintern's rationale was that nothing should be done to weaken French opposition to fascist Germany. While that policy made sense in France, even for a French Communist, it made no sense at all to the revolutionaries in Indochina. The nationalists there were quick to point out that the true meaning of the Popular Front was that the Comintern was willing to sacrifice Indochina for its own interests. If France was in danger, what better time to make revolution? But the order was firm. Party loyalty held.

Ho Chi Minh, recognizing a sticky wicket when he saw one, vanished from sight, leaving it to others to defend the party line against the nationalists.[4] Le Hong Phong was handed the glory and the burden of party leadership. Phong attended the Comintern's Seventh Congress in July 1935 and (under the alias Hai An) was elected one of the forty-five members of the Comintern Executive Committee. He also received the new party line and following the Congress brought it back to Vietnam, where he encountered stiff opposition to the Popular Front policy from inside the ICP. Through maneuver and purge he managed to eliminate this "lack of conformity"; at an ICP Central Committee meeting in Shanghai July 26, 1936, Phong "pointed out the changes in strategy and tactics and the need for a broad popular front in order to oppose the reactionaries in the colonies, fascism and war. . . . The ICP Central Committee unanimously passed a resolution adopting his views, which was subsequently ratified by the Comintern."[5] The ICP, wearing its Russian straitjacket, as one observer put it, made it through the rest of the decade as best it could.

To maintain perspective, it should be noted that the ICP in the 1930s was never widely influential. French Indochina populations overwhelmingly were politically apathetic and the few politically conscious, at most 10 percent, were divided by contending camps, the camps by factions. Some oppositionists had made ostensible peace with France and milked French colonialism in hidden hatred and contempt. Many intellectuals were in this group. Some were non-Communist nationalists, militant or nonmilitant. Others, while politically conscious, did not commit themselves; these were the famed *attentistes*, or fence-sitters, who probably outnumbered all the other politically conscious groups combined. Finally there were the Communists, both the Trotskyites and the Stalinists of the ICP. Hence the ICP was a minority of minorities. It could mount a few demonstrations and create disturbances (though never so well as the nationalists could), but it could not significantly influence events in Indochina. Small wonder the Comintern paid it inconstant attention.

WORLD WAR II AND ITS AFTERMATH

During World War II Stalin, the USSR, and the Comintern (dissolved in May 1943) were beleaguered, facing the elemental question of survival. Indochina could hardly concern them. Even contact between the Comintern and the ICP was sometimes broken, leaving the ICP entirely on its own.

The war psychologically destroyed the social fabric of French Indochina. The mystique of the French *colon*—so awesome that a handful of French Foreign Legion troops could keep 30 million Indochinese in subjugation with minimum difficulty—was forever shattered by Japanese debasement and humiliation. A newly diminished France was revealed to the onlooking Vietnamese. The image of the French presence, which had long seemed so enduring and unchallengeable, dissolved in the summer of 1945, and when the war ended only the hollow shell of colonialism remained.

The war enabled the ICP to come into its own. The party contributed, modestly, to the defeat of Japan by assisting the winning side. Throughout the war it also continued covert organization building, while its chief revolutionary opponents, the nationalists, either were kept in close check by the occupying Japanese or mistakenly threw in their lot with Japan. The French Surete had decapitated the Trotskyite movement (apparently with secret ICP assistance) at the start of the war, when virtually all of the top Trotskyite leaders were rounded up and shipped off to Madagascar. Thus, although the ICP did not end the war greatly strengthened in absolute terms, it emerged relatively stronger than its challengers. Ho Chi Minh felt strong enough to make a bid for power and launched what was called the August (1945) Revolution to seize control of Vietnam before French colonialism could reinstitute itself. His bid for power, which went as far as it did chiefly because Allied occupiers were operating at cross-purposes, eventually failed and triggered the nine-year Viet Minh War. Unlike Eastern Europe at the end of World War II, where the Red Army installed local communism in power, Ho Chi Minh got virtually no Moscow assistance. Stalin, for whatever tactical reasons, was all too willing to accept and deal with the status quo in both China and Vietnam. It was one more forceful demonstration for Vietnamese revolutionaries of the international Communist movement's unwillingness to risk much or even to sacrifice something in the name of Asian communism. Veteran reporter Harold Isaacs visited Saigon at this time and his conversations with Vietnamese Communists catch the anguish, cynicism, and sense of betrayal that marked their attitude toward the USSR:

> What of the Russians (I asked)? Would they bring any strong
> political support to the Annamite cause? I met no Annamite who
> thought so and I spoke to many Annamite Communists. The
> Annamite Communists, like all their fellow nationalists, suffered
> from a terrifying sense of their isolation. They were unusually

frank and cynical about the Russians. Even the most orthodox among them, like shaggy-haired Tran Van Giau, the partisan organizer, granted that the Russians went in for "an excess of ideological compromise," and said he expected no help from that quarter. "The Russians are nationalists from Russia first and above all." Another Annamite Communist said with some bitterness, "They would be interested in us only if we served some purpose of theirs."[6]

Moscow's interest in Indochina increased somewhat in the immediate post–World War II days because of French developments that related to the colonies. France was moving to the left with a coalition government that included participation by the well-organized French Communist party. For a brief time there was the prospect of a Communist government legally coming to power in Paris. A Communist France would mean a communist Indochina, Ho Chi Minh was told, and he must do nothing to spoil prospects. French sensibilities, so badly mauled by World War II, had to be delicately handled by the party in France, and this meant chauvinistically backing the return of the French *colon* to Indochina. When the French general deplaned in Saigon in September 1945 and declared, "We have come to reclaim our heritage," he was expressing a sentiment shared by most of the French proletariat. Hence word went out from Moscow to the Indochinese Communist party that nothing was to be done that would weaken FCP prospects at home. The Party Central Committee in Saigon was told not to oppose French reoccupation of the city, for to do so would be "premature adventure" even if it occurred in the name of independence; in addition, it would not be "in line with Soviet perspectives."[7]

Harold Isaacs has indicated that he was shown a document dated September 25, 1945, from the FCP headquarters in Paris, that

> advised the Annamite Communists to be sure, before they acted too rashly, that their struggle meets the requirements of Soviet policy. It warned that any premature adventures in Annamite independence might not be in line with Soviet perspectives. These perspectives might well include France as a firm ally of the U.S.S.R. in Europe, in which case the Annamite independence movement would be an embarrassment. Therefore it urged upon the Annamite comrades a policy of patience.[8]

As far as can be determined, the USSR did not mastermind the ICP's August 1945 bid for power and may not even have had advance notice of it.[9] Moscow's initial public reaction was a guarded, vaguely worded endorsement of a victory for anti-imperialist forces. The attempt was conducted in the name of the Viet Minh, a united front, and not in that of the ICP. In an unprecedented decision two months later, the ICP dissolved itself, thus eliminating all superficial evidence of Communist involvement in the new government. Probably Moscow was not prepared to deal with this bold Hanoi effort, for it was the first postwar decolonization attempt. Even if Moscow had wanted to manage the affair, it was not organized to do so. The scene in Hanoi was marked by chaotic, fast-moving events that could not be directed from abroad. In any event, the Comintern had bigger fish to fry in France.

Much later, USSR historians would make a great deal of the August Revolution and imply that the USSR made it possible:

> The Soviet people's great patriotic war (1941–45) gave a great
> spiritual boost to the national liberation movement in Vietnam.
> Victories over Hitlerite Germany and militarist Japan created
> favorable conditions for the August Revolution and the founding
> of the Democratic Republic of Vietnam. . . . The Soviet Union
> gave the Vietnamese people the necessary support in their
> struggle against the French colonialists.[10]

The August Revolution, however, was a bid for power that failed, and that failure became a legacy for the Vietnamese Communists. The USSR did not do in Indochina what it did in Eastern Europe; had it done otherwise, the power bid might have been a success.

The August Revolution is actually a historical fiction in its claims that revolution was achieved and the Democratic Republic of Vietnam (DRV) ensconced in power only later to be evicted by invading French forces. Yet it is clear from interviews conducted by the author among party cadres that this is a myth accepted. The party cadres believe (and this makes the August Revolution important in terms of relations with the USSR today) that the revolution would not have been destroyed had the USSR chosen to block the return of the French military forces— an option, it is held, Moscow easily could have exercised. A second legacy from this period, closer to reality, is the conviction among Vietnamese Communists that the DRV was created largely without appreciable assistance from the USSR.

THE VIET MINH WAR

Relations between the DRV and the USSR during the postwar Stalin years can best be described as publicly noncommittal on the part of Moscow. The character of the relationship reflected the position taken by many West European Marxists, that the Viet Minh struggle against

French colonialism was at best anti-imperialist, but not Communist. At one point, even Communist members in the French cabinet voted to support the war in Indochina. This treatment of Vietnamese Communists by their French comrades derived from the fact that French Communist leaders shared the colonial myth of indissoluble ties binding France to its overseas peoples. They also opposed independence for Vietnam on the grounds that if free it would fall under U.S. domination.[11]

The year 1947 was something of a turning point for the world Communist movement operating in Vietnam and Asia in general. The Comintern, which had been abolished as a World War II concession to the USSR's allies, was reconstituted in November 1947, now as the Cominform (Communist Information Bureau). At its first session Andrei Zhdanov described the DRV as "associated" with the anti-imperialist camp, and he termed the Viet Minh war "a powerful movement for national liberation in the colonies and dependencies." Zhdanov also boxed in the Cominform with the rigid and rather simplistic "two-camp doctrine," under which the Cominform deliberately bypassed what would seem to have been obvious opportunities in Asia.[12]

The Communists were ousted from the French government, and prospects for a Communist France disappeared in the spring of 1947; but Moscow's attention to events in Indochina was not appreciably increased. It focused its attention elsewhere, on China and Indonesia.[13]

Such Soviet-Vietnamese party-to-party relations as did occur chiefly came about at international gatherings such as the Asian Relations Conference in New Delhi in April 1947, a conference called by the Indian Communist Party in 1948, and the important 1948 Calcutta Youth Conference at which the Zhadnov two-camp doctrine was delineated.

State-to-state relations between Vietnam and the USSR came later. The USSR's first official association in Southeast Asia was with Thailand; in November 1946 a diplomatic trade was made: a Soviet Embassy in Bangkok in exchange for the USSR not vetoing Thailand's application for UN membership.

The USSR did not grant diplomatic recognition to the DRV, which had been established in 1945, until January 31, 1950. Even then the timing of recognition aroused the suspicions of the Vietnamese, as it came thirteen days after the People's Republic of China had extended recognition.

Official Moscow histories tend to gloss over the USSR's association with the DRV during the Viet Minh War era, although they do stake a claim for credit in the final outcome: "In January 1950 the DRV was officially recognized by the Soviet Union and People's Democracies and their assistance and support played a major role in Vietnam's victories."[14]

Although the USSR took a minimalist position with respect to the Viet Minh War, and although Hanoi historians today emphasize this fact in the name of self-contained conduct of the war, it is now clear that there was deeper Soviet involvement than was believed at the time. To understand this apparent contradiction it is necessary that we distinguish between open Moscow support of the Viet Minh and Moscow's efforts to ensure that weapons and war materiel got into Viet Minh hands. Public support for the Viet Minh extracted a political price in many capitals, while arms shipments could be covert. Thus Moscow could not openly back the war but it could help fund it if China acted as a conduit—which China was willing to do and which the Viet Minh preferred. When the demands of the Korean War ended, Soviet war materiel but not *Soviet-labeled* war materiel began arriving in volume in Indochina. Even as late as 1953 Moscow was officially denying that any aid agreement with Hanoi existed at all.

There were various reasons why the USSR could not, and did not, openly support Ho Chi Minh and his Viet Minh collaborators. We have noted one—a conflict of interest with internal French developments. Stalin persisted in his continental outlook, opposing "leapfrog communism" as he termed it. Ho Chi Minh was regarded by some in Moscow as too independent, too devious, too likely to become an "Asian Tito." Some observers explain Soviet restraint in dealing with Vietnam as an effort not to intrude into a Chinese sphere of influence. The Chinese at the time did consider themselves the principal patron of Vietnamese communism. Another early reason may have been the influence of the Soviet military, which estimated in 1945 that the Viet Minh had little chance of driving out the French and thus saw no point in being associated with a lost cause; only later in the early 1950s did the Soviet military come to see that possibly the French could be expelled militarily.

All in all it was a strange relationship. An anecdote that offers insight is found in Khrushchev's memoirs. Ho Chi Minh was in Moscow (apparently around 1951) for a meeting with Stalin. During the course of their meeting Ho asked Stalin to autograph a copy of the Soviet magazine he was carrying, *USSR Under Construction*. Stalin obliged and the meeting ended. Stalin then began to worry about the use Ho Chi Minh might make of his autograph, so he sent a KGB agent to Ho's hotel room to steal back the magazine.[15]

Despite his cavalier behavior, Joseph Stalin remains to this day something of an untarnished hero in Hanoi, and his birth date is still observed as a major holiday. None of the vilification of Khrushchev's destalinization has ever found its way into Hanoi party journals. On the 90th anniversary of his birth in December, Stalin was described by

Nhan Dan as a "marvelously noble ideal communist" and was placed on the highest pedestal possible; indeed, he was equated with Ho Chi Minh as a hero worthy of emulation.

In Moscow today, Soviet scholars, if pressed, offer as an explanation for the indifference exhibited during the Viet Minh War that unfortunately the USSR was preoccupied with matters elsewhere, such as Tito, the Greek civil war, and the difficulties in Europe resulting from application of the Truman Doctrine. It is not an explanation the Vietnamese find satisfactory.

Soviet interest in Indochina late in the Stalin period took on a somewhat more detached character even before Stalin's death. This appears to have been a reaction to trends in the region. U.S. influence there was on the rise, often at Moscow's expense, particularly in India and Indonesia, and with respect to SEATO. There began to develop in the Kremlin—not with Stalin himself but with lesser figures waiting in the wings—the view that the USSR's Asian policies had become anachronistic, that a changing world in Asia required reappraisal. Analysis of Asian insurgencies indicated that they often failed and that those that did succeed did not necessarily bring Communists to power. The policy planners in Moscow also undoubtedly were aware of the general climate of left-wing thinking in Asia during the 1950s—specifically, the tendency to view the USSR as a mirror image of the United States, insofar as both were held to be selfish superpowers bent on world domination. Such, for example, was the sense of many speeches at the Bandung Conference in April 1955. For Moscow this sense gave emphasis to the idea that the USSR should establish entry and influence in the region through benign means such as long-term investment of Soviet aid and demonstrations of goodwill. Such thinking in Moscow foreshadowed policies that would appear with the change of guard. For the Vietnamese Communists still locked in their anticolonial struggle—and with Dien Bien Phu still ahead—the trend must have been unconscionable.

In summing up the Stalin years of the Soviet-Vietnamese relationship, it would probably be a mistake to conclude that the association was merely nominal. Certainly relations had a highly negative quality to them, in terms of support not provided and gestures withheld—but this was more than nominal influence. Working backward from later events, we might reasonably conclude that the early relationship was more complex and the early years more formative for both the Vietnamese and the Soviets than once believed. Indeed, the major heritage of this early period for the Kremlin leaders may be the conclusion that their predecessors committed a major historical error in not assigning greater importance and higher priority to Vietnamese affairs and thereby lost several decades of opportunity. For the Vietnamese the relationship in this period began with a condition of bare awareness by Moscow and ended with the mutual perception of many common interests, although it was still one of sharp limits since the USSR had neither demonstrated its reliability nor understood the Vietnamese and their revolution. Worse, from the Vietnamese viewpoint Moscow's interests in Vietnam were almost entirely derivative; hence the actions taken or not taken would be decided by events elsewhere rather than by developments in Vietnam. The Vietnamese leadership hoped and even expected that this situation would change with the advent of Khrushchev, and at first the promise grew—but eventually hope was dashed.

NOTES

1. See Charles B. McLane, *Soviet Strategies in Southeast Asia: An Exploration of Eastern Policy Under Lenin and Stalin* (Princeton, N.J.: Princeton University Press, 1966); Allan W. Cameron, "The Soviet Union and Vietnam: The Origins of Involvement," in W. Raymond Duncan, ed., *Soviet Policy in Developing Countries* (Waltham, Mass.: Ginn-Blaisdell, 1970); Milton Sacks, "Marxism in Vietnam," in Frank N. Traeger, ed., *Marxism in Southeast Asia: A Study of Four Countries* (Stanford, Calif.: Stanford University Press, 1960), p. 96; and J. H. Brimmell, *Communism in South East Asia: A Political Analysis* (Oxford: Oxford University Press, 1959), p. 149.

2. Cameron, "The Soviet Union and Vietnam," p. 178.

3. *Thirty Years* (Hanoi: Foreign Language Publishing House, 1960), pp. 26–27.

4. It was a remarkable absence. Of no other world figure can it be said that his actions for nearly a decade are unknown. It is generally believed that Ho went to Moscow in 1933 (as a lecturer at the Lenin Institute), stayed there until 1938 (with the exception of a brief trip to Macao in 1935 for the ICP First Congress), and then moved to China later in 1938. However, Ho's official biographies and the writings of Truong Chinh and Nguyen Luong Bang—to say nothing of outsiders' accounts—are contradictory on the matter.

5. ICP newspaper, *Dan Chung*, No. 41 (January 3, 1939), quoted in *Vietnam Courier* (February 1984).

6. Harold Isaacs, *No Peace for Asia* (Cambridge, Mass.: MIT Press, 1947), pp. 172–173.

7. John Girling, *People's War* (New York: Praeger Publishers, 1969), p. 18.

8. Isaacs, *No Peace for Asia*, p. 173.

9. See Cameron, "The Soviet Union and Vietnam," p. 171. Cameron concludes that Ho Chi Minh's bid for power was independent of any meaningful contact with Moscow. Indeed, this seems to be the case. In the voluminous revisionist output from Hanoi since 1975, all of which puts a favorable face on any early assistance or support by the USSR, no new credit is given to Moscow; in fact, the August Revolution is still depicted as belonging to the ICP and its Viet Minh alone. The "revolution" failed, of course; the newly created Democratic

Government of Vietnam fled to the bush and began its guerrilla war to oust the French, finally succeeding in 1954.

10. See the speech by CPSU Politburo member V. I. Vorotnikov given in Hanoi on August 31, 1985, published in *Quan Doi Nhan Dan* (Hanoi) (September 1, 1985); JPRS-SEA 85-162 (October 24, 1985).

11. Irvin M. Wall, *French Communism in the Era of Stalin* (Westport, Conn.: Greenwood Press, 1983).

12. Andrei Zhdanov, "The International Situation," in Cominform, *For a Lasting Peace, For a People's Democracy* (Moscow, 1947), p. 2. The "two-camp doctrine" was revised in 1956 at the CPSU's Twentieth Congress. For discussion see John J. Stephen, "Asia in the Soviet Conception," in Donald S. Zagoria, ed., *Soviet Policy in East Asia* (New Haven, Conn.: Yale University Press, 1982), pp. 38–39.

13. Hostilities broke out between the Dutch and Indonesian nationalists in July 1947. The issue came before the UN Security Council and the USSR took over management of the Indonesian cause, consistently supporting it with resolutions and parliamentary maneuvers. The varying interest in Indochina was obviously a function of geopolitics, given that Indonesia is the fifth largest country in the world. The invidious comparison (the USSR and Indonesia versus the USSR and Vietnam) was not lost on the Vietnamese Communist leadership.

14. A. G. Budanov, "Invincible Vietnam," in V. A. Zharov and V. A. Tyurin, eds., *Southeast Asia: History, Economy, Policy* (Moscow: Progress Publishers, 1972), p. 33.

15. See Nikita Khrushchev, *Khrushchev Remembers* (Boston: Little, Brown, 1971), p. 442. At the same time, Khrushchev reports, Stalin ordered a half-ton of quinine (used to treat malaria) to be shipped to Vietnam. It is not clear, however, whether this gesture was related to stealing back the magazine.

Three

THE KHRUSHCHEV YEARS
Opportunity Versus Caution

STALIN, WE HAVE noted, was loath to commit himself in Asia beyond ideological struggle. Nikita Khrushchev moved the USSR to the transworld power level. He was willing and able to leap over the Soviet periphery and seek influence in every quarter of the globe. This shift, from continental to global national interest, underlies most of the USSR's moves in Asia during the next two decades.

For non-Communist Asia the advent of Khrushchev meant a somewhat less paranoid Kremlin. But the USSR remained an ideological oligarchy, now representing new forms of challenge and danger. For Hanoi the change was bound to be an improvement, and Vietnamese Communists sensed that the time of a new relationship with the USSR had arrived. Khrushchev was seen as an ambitious leader who wanted to expel the west from Asia or at least reduce its influence, a goal shared by Hanoi. He wanted to increase Soviet influence in the DRV at the expense of China—a move that, if not overdone, was acceptable to Hanoi leaders. And he wanted more activist policies toward the non-Communist countries of Southeast Asia, about which the DRV was indifferent. In short, the prospect was for a close and profitable relationship. Given such an auspicious beginning it is high irony that relations went full circle. In the end Khrushchev came to be more disliked in Hanoi than any other major Soviet figure before or since.

Khrushchev's appearance on the scene was one of those moments in history that is a conjunction of circumstance and personality. He was, in psychological makeup, totally different from his predecessor, the paranoid Stalin. Khrushchev was a crafty actor and a master dissembler. He came on as a blustering bully, a noisy rocket brandisher whose stock in trade was diatribe, invective, and the ultimatum. But behind this crudity was a cool skilled gambler who measured odds carefully and bluffed well. Much of his rhetoric and shoe banging was the gambler's tactic of psyching out the opposition. Because he was such a competitive gambler, he was constantly tempted to plunge, to risk all on a single move. This kept him always near the edge of danger and once even brought the USSR to the brink of catastrophe. Yet his gambler's instinct seemed to tell him when to quit the game. He made no fatal mistakes.

The circumstance in Asia, in Khrushchev's view, was a changed direction of history. Recent global developments—Soviet success in space, growing U.S. self-doubt—had led him to conclude that the fundamental world strategic balance was shifting. Ventures into Asia could accelerate this, and successes there at the very least could improve the USSR bargaining position when it met the United States at strategic arms limitation talks and in its general pursuit of détente. Projecting an image of a revitalized, more attractive communism would facilitate various external undertakings, boost the morale of the faithful in Asia, and help counter the growing appeal of Maoism.

The bumptious B and K Road Show,[1] as it came to be known, moved into Asia selling open-handedness. Nonaligned and neutral nations were wooed intensively and were told the USSR wanted only to be a good neighbor. Economic and military aid was offered under generous conditions to wean the neutral away from the United States. Ties of all sorts were solicited in the hope that they would reduce U.S. influence. Initially the campaign succeeded, and the Soviet position improved in India, Afghanistan, Burma, and Indonesia. Later it ran into difficulties in part because of the growing challenge by China.

With respect to Vietnam, it is clear in retrospect that Khrushchev's thinking was dualistic. Indochina represented a potential advantage to be exploited, perhaps extensively, but it also was a dangerous quagmire. Opportunism battled caution in Khrushchev's mind, and he seemed to sense intuitively that Vietnam was a place to be conservative in taking risks.

Probably his attitude soon became clear to Hanoi leaders who, as a result, began to suspect he would prove to be an undependable ally. Still, he was an improvement over Stalin's policy of studied indifference. And undoubtedly Soviet diplomats in Hanoi worked to convince the Vietnamese that a new order was in place. Many of Khrushchev's early policies, gestures, and travels were billed in Hanoi as beneficial to the DRV. A better-positioned USSR could be of greater service to Hanoi, it was argued. Khrushchev did provide stepped-up material assistance to the DRV, both economic and military. Soviet officials gave moral and political support to the DRV by taking to such world forums as the UN to defend Vietnamese actions. This helped to confer on Hanoi something it needed badly, a mantle of legitimacy. Although Khrushchev tended to be overly cautious during the last stages of the Viet Minh War, clearly he was an improvement over Stalin in the eyes of Ho Chi Minh.

GENEVA, 1954

It was under Khrushchev that the DRV and the USSR entered into their first joint venture—to this day the most interesting one of all— when they went to Geneva in mid-1954 for the conference that ended the Viet Minh War and arranged for the end of French colonialism in Indochina.

Khrushchev's various new policies in Asia—above all, his involvement in the Geneva negotiations—had the net effect of elevating Vietnam for the first time to the level of true participant in Great Power politics. The changes resulting from the Geneva agreement restructured and deepened USSR-DRV bilateral relations. Each side became more useful to the other, and each also now pursued new and not always compatible sets of national interests. The advantage gained was chiefly that of the DRV, which was finally accepted as a full-fledged member of the socialist community. It even gained some deference because of its key role in the Geneva negotiations.

Given the many thorough works available on this seminal event and its implications, the discussion here can be confined to its meaning for the Soviet-Vietnamese relationship.[2] In general, the Geneva negotiations were complex and marked by cross-purposes, duplicity, and extensive disinformation. Their context that summer was a conjunction of several events: the increasing internationalization of the Viet Minh War itself, the political crisis in Paris, the growing U.S. restiveness about the advances of communism throughout the world, China's elevation from regional to world power, the deep USSR involvement in the German question, and Moscow's efforts to solidify recent gains in the Mideast.

The decision to stage the Geneva Conference appears to have caught Moscow somewhat unprepared. It assembled a hasty private meeting with the Vietnamese and Chinese at which a common strategy was worked out. But the pre-conference maneuvers also involved something of a Sino-Soviet conspiracy against Vietnam. As Nikita Khrushchev wrote:

> Before the Geneva Conference there was a preparatory
> meeting in Moscow. China was represented by Chou En-lai and
> Vietnam by President Ho Chi Minh and Prime Minister Pham
> Van Dong. We worked out the position we would take in
> Geneva, basing it on the situation in Vietnam. The situation was

very grave. The resistance movement in Vietnam was on the
brink of collapse. The partisans were counting on the Geneva
Conference to produce a cease-fire agreement which would
enable them to hold on to the conquests which they had
won. . . .

After one of these sessions in Catherine Hall of the Kremlin,
Chou En-lai buttonholed me and took me into a corner. He said,
"Comrade Ho Chi Minh has told me that the situation in
Vietnam is hopeless and that if we don't attain a cease-fire soon,
the Vietnamese won't be able to hold out against the French.
Therefore they've decided to retreat to the Chinese border if
necessary, and they want China to be ready to move troops into
Vietnam as we did in North Korea. In other words, the
Vietnamese want us to help them drive out the French. We
simply can't grant Comrade Ho Chi Minh's request. We've
already lost too many men in Korea—that war cost us dearly.
We're in no condition to get involved in another war at this
time."

I made a request of my own to Comrade Chou En-lai. "An
important struggle is going on," I said, "and the Vietnamese are
putting up a good fight. The French are taking heavy losses.
There's no reason why you should tell Ho Chi Minh that you
will refuse to help him if his troops retreat to your border under
the blows of the French. Why don't you just tell him a white lie?
Let the Vietnamese believe that you'll help them if necessary, and
this will be a source of inspiration for the Vietnamese partisans
to resist the French." Chou En-lai agreed not to tell Comrade Ho
Chi Minh that China wouldn't come into the war against the
French on Vietnamese territory.[3]

USSR interest in the Viet Minh war, as we have seen, was only
derivative. Geneva offered an opportunity to serve several additional
interests—that is, to weaken France and push it to the left; to undermine
the idea of a European Defense Community; and to advance the
worldwide Soviet campaign of peace and relaxation of international
tensions aimed at undercutting the United States' mutual defense efforts.
The USSR sought an outcome at Geneva that would be at least a victory
of sorts for the Viet Minh, but not one that would reflect favorably on
China, which even then, we now know, Moscow believed must be
contained. The conference was a major power play. The USSR simul-
taneously applied pressure on the Vietnamese, the Chinese, the French,
and the British. The pressure on the Viet Minh was both direct and
through the Chinese. Moscow explained that its purposes were to preempt
U.S. intervention in Indochina (and, by implication, for the Europeans,

to preempt increased U.S. belligerency in Europe) and to reduce world tensions.

China's chief interest, it appears, was to further its "spirit of Bandung" policy of peaceful coexistence and noninterference in the internal affairs of Asian countries.

For Ho Chi Minh and his Viet Minh allies, Geneva was the culmination of a long war in which they now stood bloodied but less bowed than the French. They came to Geneva to witness an end to their war on favorable terms, only to be plunged into involuted European politics. They found themselves sitting with their two fraternal allies on the same side of the table but with differing perceptions and interests. Yet transcendental proletarian solidarity proved decisive in the end. When asked by their Socialist allies to settle for half a victory in the name of Communist solidarity, the Hanoi leaders agreed. They signed the Agreements, with misgivings at the time and later had regrets.

The USSR appears to have benefited most from the Geneva Conference, although the Chinese gained status and prestige. The French, considering that they had lost the war, emerged in a better condition than they had had reason to expect. If it is assumed that the Viet Minh had decisively won—and the conventional view is that since Paris had no stomach for further battle, that was the case—then the victorious Vietnamese were the only losers at Geneva. If, however, the Viet Minh were in worse straits than outsiders realized (and for this contention there is a growing body of evidence), then Hanoi also found the outcome of the Geneva Conference advantageous.

We are not certain even today of all the reasons for USSR caution and its determined pressure on the Vietnamese to accept an unfavorable ending to the war—that is, temporary partition. Apparently the USSR believed that the shaky new government in South Vietnam, under Ngo Dien Diem, would not last out the year and that Hanoi could soon have the South by merely picking up the pieces. The USSR apparently also believed that the United States might intervene militarily if there was no settlement. One explanation offered is that the USSR during the conference reached an understanding with Pierre Mendés-France, the new French premier, that it would facilitate French interests at Geneva in return for French efforts to scuttle the then pending European Defense Community proposal.[4] Although this rather scurrilous charge has never been proved, many Vietnamese Communists later came to believe it, just as they generally came to believe that both the USSR and the PRC sold out Vietnam at Geneva by "not backing Vietnam" and by "talking the French into dividing Vietnam."[5]

Khrushchev later insisted that the Viet Minh were in desperate military straits, virtually unable to continue warfare after Dien Bien

Phu, and that the agreement at Geneva was the best that could be achieved under the circumstances. However, Khrushchev also regarded it as a success, saying bluntly, "At Geneva we succeeded in consolidating the conquests of the Vietnamese communists."[6]

Betrayal of Vietnam, if that is what it was, was not immediately apparent. In the confused year following the end of the Viet Minh War, the DRV and the world awaited the expected collapse of the Diem government. Gradually it became clear that the prospect for the foreseeable future was a divided Vietnam. The DRV turned to the peacetime task of rebuilding the country and launching socialism.

DRV-USSR relations after the Geneva Agreements were somewhat on the cool side. In the year that followed Geneva, the DRV sent a dozen official communications to Moscow, none of which was acknowledged.[7] In July 1955 Ho Chi Minh made what was billed in Hanoi as a triumphant visit to Moscow. Although he had been the DRV chief of state since 1945 and had been in Moscow several times since, he had never been received in that capacity. Now he was greeted with chief-of-state protocol.[8] Soviet welcoming speeches and newspaper editorials acknowledged him properly, if belatedly, as an important world leader. Ho signed several economic assistance agreements, the first in a long series between the two countries. A reciprocal visit to Hanoi by first deputy chairman of the USSR Council of Ministers, Anastas Mikoyan, came in April 1956. A Voroshilov mission, concerned with aid, went to Hanoi in May 1957; a reciprocal visit by a DRV National Assembly group headed by Ton Duc Thang took place a few months later.

However, in late summer 1957, an irritated Ho Chi Minh returned to Moscow, and this time he was all business. Shortly before, the USSR had proposed, apparently without consulting Ho, that both Vietnams be admitted to the United Nations. This would have undercut the legitimacy of the DRV, which maintained it was the only legal government in Vietnam. Ho, in Moscow, objected to this high-handed treatment, and he was successful, for the USSR withdrew its proposal. This was all behind-the-scenes activity; publicly the relationship was fine. Said Ho in November:

> Relations between the USSR and DRV are marked by
> brotherhood and proletarian internationalism as it suits both
> socialist countries. We do our best to improve them. I seize this
> opportunity to thank the Soviet Union for her precious and
> unselfish aid, enabling us to restore the economy and carry out
> national unification.[9]

The post–Viet Minh War years saw the USSR assisting in the economic development of Vietnam (discussed below in detail). The general historical view of relations in this period, taken by Moscow historians, is largely economic:

> Considerable headway was made (in Vietnam) in laying the foundations of socialism. This was done in close co-operation with fraternal countries, including the Soviet Union, which extended and continues to extend large-scale, disinterested assistance and support to the Democratic Republic of Vietnam.
>
> From 1955 to 1965, the Soviet Union and the Democratic Republic of Vietnam signed seven agreements providing for Soviet economic, scientific and technological assistance. Under these agreements the Soviet Union extended credit to the sum of 320 million rubles, or 40 per cent of the total material assistance granted North Vietnam by the socialist countries. 94,500,000 rubles of this is not repayable.[10]

Generally speaking, the last years of the decade were halcyon days in the USSR-DRV relationship. Hanoi was attempting to lift North Vietnam by its economic bootstraps, and Moscow fully supported this "showcase of socialism" effort.[11] Vietnamese determination plus generous USSR aid resulted in significant economic progress in North Vietnam. Had the DRV continued on this course and not decided to unify the country, this sharp upward curve of economic development almost certainly would have continued.

However, in 1959 the Hanoi leadership was seized by the spirit of deliverance of the South and soon became determined to unite the two Vietnams regardless of cost or sacrifice. Initially it hoped to accomplish this through the instrument of French diplomacy, with the French seeing to it that the Geneva Agreements were enforced as Hanoi interpreted them. This was the "peaceful unification" route, which, when judged not possible, was supplanted by the "armed struggle route." The USSR endorsed this policy. For instance, at the Lao Dong Third Congress in 1960, the chief Moscow delegate, CPSU Secretary Nurtidin Mukhitdinov, pointedly listed in his major address the DRV's "two strategic tasks": to carry out the socialist revolution in the North and "to liberate South Vietnam from domination by the American imperialists and their henchmen and bring about unification of Vietnam." He avoided the term *peaceful unification*, which had been standard Moscow public usage up to that time.[12]

The USSR had genuine and in some instances insurmountable problems in dealing with Hanoi, as Khrushchev acknowledged later; these, he said, were due chiefly to Chinese machinations. Throughout his tenure in office Khrushchev was forced to juggle a number of separate objectives involving Vietnam: to prevent China from gaining such influence in Hanoi that it could shut out USSR presence; to shunt off total Viet Cong victory in South Vietnam since that would be seen as a success for China and Chinese thought; to prevent peace and stability in South Vietnam because that would be seen as a victory for the United States; to maintain amicable relations (i.e., coexistence or détente) with the United States; never to behave in such a way as to open himself to the Chinese charge of conspiracy with the United States; and, most of all, to increase Soviet influence in Hanoi.

Increased U.S. efforts to help establish a viable government in South Vietnam at the end of the 1950s required that the USSR begin a diplomatic and political campaign to enhance the DRV position and to deprecate the Government of Vietnam (GVN). Khrushchev and Bulganin went back on the road again, pressing the theme that U.S. assistance to South Vietnam was upsetting the stability of the region and, because it amounted to U.S. aggression, had "grave consequences for world peace."[13] By 1962, the campaign had become a major media event. Touring Bulgaria in May of that year, Khrushchev predicted that Vietnam would become a Korea-type war, which he defined as "a war between capitalists in defense of capitalism against the masses who are certain to win."[14] When a reporter asked if this meant China would enter the Vietnam War, he replied cryptically: "I am like a cavalry man. He has a horse that has a big head. He lets his horse think for him."[15]

Khrushchev's main vehicle in this diplomatic campaign was the mechanism of the International Control Commission (ICC), which Great Britain and the USSR, as conference co-chairmen, had established in Geneva in 1954. In a series of diplomatic notes to London during the year, Khrushchev urged Britain to join in common front opposition to U.S. involvement in Vietnam. The presence of 5,000 Americans in Vietnam, he argued, "was a serious danger to peace and security in Southeast Asia . . . because they are conducting an undeclared war against patriotic forces in South Vietnam who are fighting for elementary human rights and the independence of their country."[16]

If there is an equestrian metaphor here, it is Khrushchev trying to ride two horses at the same time, to achieve détente with the United States and to support the DRV in a war for unification that would mean collision with the United States. This caused USSR policy in Indochina (Laos more than Vietnam at first) to appear erratic and sometimes contradictory. In December 1960 the USSR intervened in the "three princes" struggle for power in Laos[17] on behalf of the Communist-dominated Pathet Lao, chiefly as an investment in goodwill in Hanoi. However, for Khrushchev it proved to be an investment that not only failed to pay much return but also contributed to his growing disillusionment with the idea that great opportunities were present in Indochina. By mid-1964 he appeared willing to wash his hands of truce supervision in Indochina, and even of resignation of Soviet co-chairmanship of the permanent body of the ICC.

DISENGAGEMENT

Khrushchev had always sensed, with a kind of peasant shrewdness, that Indochina was more than met the eye. He saw its danger as a great trap for the USSR.

For this and other reasons, Khrushchev's perspective on Vietnam had begun to change by 1960, imperceptibly at first, gradually with quickened pace. Turmoil in Asia was increasing. Local wars and troubles, in Malaya, the Philippines, Indonesia, and Vietnam, were ushering in a new and dynamic period, and the attendant uncertainty counseled against bold Soviet commitment. The challenge by China was rising. In Hanoi, pressure developed in the leadership to get on with the liberation of the South. The decision to begin armed struggle in South Vietnam was, for Khrushchev, one more potential Asian pitfall. He and others in the Kremlin began to conclude that while their original policy— high posture in Asia—remained essentially correct, it had to be pursued more cautiously, especially in uncertain Indochina. Risks had to be reduced. At the same time, Khrushchev was drifting into serious domestic political trouble.

Originally Khrushchev's goal in Asia had been elemental, to oust the west. Gradually the Sino-Soviet dispute intruded into this effort, complicating, if not displacing it. Khrushchev began to realize that China was his first and most important challenge. His initial response was to attempt to manipulate politics in Beijing and to undercut the Chinese external position, hoping that eventually these moves would bring about reestablishment of the alliance. Some observers believe that near the end of his tenure, Khrushchev schemed to draw the United States and China into war over Vietnam—a ploy that would have forced China back toward the USSR.

By the early 1960s the war in Vietnam had grown increasingly risky; it had also taken on a Chinese dimension. Combat escalated steadily as ever-greater numbers of North Vietnamese regulars were dispatched to the South. North Vietnam began building an air defense system in anticipation of a U.S. air attack, thus imposing on Moscow new and expensive logistic requirements and more deeply involving the USSR in the war. Hanoi's generals in the South employed essentially a Chinese strategy, which meant that if victory was achieved it would be seen by the world as a victory for Chinese thought. Beijing closely identified itself with Vietnam and the war, intimating that it might intervene as it had done in Korea. All wisdom dictated that the USSR reduce its role in Vietnam, not completely but to a safer level.

In the last days of his rule Khrushchev had clearly soured on Vietnam. Some Kremlinologists believe he always had been negative about the Vietnamese. U.S. Ambassador Foy Kohler is quoted as saying from his vantage point in Moscow that his impression of Khrushchev's regard for Indochina was that he wished it would "dry up and blow away."[18] It was not simply that he was skittery about the war and fearful of entrapment; more to the point, it was held, the chemistry was wrong and he regarded the Vietnamese as devious and dangerously crafty in manipulating others.

Precisely how much Soviet-Vietnamese relations had deteriorated in the final months of Khrushchev's tenure is difficult to determine. Many Hanoi watchers contend it was far greater than was realized even later.[19] Jon M. Van Dyke quotes North Vietnamese defectors as having told RAND interviewers in South Vietnam that at one point Khrushchev ordered home all 487 university professors from North Vietnamese institutions of higher education.[20] Trade between the two countries dwindled in 1964, as did official visits. The July 1964 USSR threat to quit the co-chairmanship of the ICC would have meant for Hanoi the loss of its only reliable ally in the post–Geneva Conference diplomatic process and would have seriously undercut DRV legitimacy in international relations. Then, there was Moscow's offhanded response to the Gulf of Tonkin incident (see below).

All this led Khrushchev to two conclusions regarding Vietnam: that competition with China for influence in Hanoi was not a zero-sum game, and that there were (and because of the Sino-Soviet dispute always would be) sharp limits on the amount of control the USSR could hope to exercise over Hanoi. He used a litmus test of loyalty: If the DRV could not be counted as an ally against China, then the relationship should be downgraded.

Khrushchev began moving the USSR from its identification with the Vietnamese Communists' war. Because of the Sino-Soviet dispute (and for other reasons) this had to be done in such a way as to avoid the appearance that the USSR was disengaging. Khrushchev was unwittingly aided by the non-Communist world's mass media. Throughout 1964, the time of the Soviet drawdown, the press in the United States and West Europe offered a steady diet of Moscow reportage about undiminished USSR support for Vietnam and its "just and holy war," together with Cassandra-like predictions that the USSR was about to meet its "sacred duty" and send troops to fight in Vietnam, which would probably touch off a world conflagration.[21] Even a step-up of

U.S. war efforts in Vietnam, such as a naval blockade, "would bring in Red China and Russia."[22] At the same time, the master bluffer in the Kremlin rattled American nerves by suggesting that the relationship with the USSR was in danger. On March 4, 1964, Soviet Foreign Minister Andrei Gromyko handed Ambassador Kohler a diplomatic note warning that "peaceful coexistence with the U.S. was being undermined by U.S. involvement in Vietnam." The USSR also said that its pledge of "all necessary assistance to the DRV . . . remains fully in force."[23]

Hanoi knew none of this was true, but it hardly was in its interest to say so publicly. So it added to the fiction that all was well between the two, insisting that the USSR was unstinting in its support and fully prepared to send troops to Vietnam if Hanoi gave the word.

The private diplomatic sessions between Vietnam and the USSR must have been ugly affairs. The most important of these was held in February 1964. Khrushchev, stung by Hanoi's refusal to sign the limited nuclear test ban treaty (a clear pro-Beijing gesture in his view), had ordered a slowdown of aid shipments to Vietnam. The Vietnamese dispatched Le Duan to Moscow on a fence-mending mission. He was met by Khrushchev's demand that Vietnam take an open stand against China. Le Duan countered with an offer to back two other Soviet moves—both of which had anti-Chinese overtones—in Laos, where the USSR was pressing for an international conference, and in Cambodia aimed at increasing Soviet presence there. The meeting ended inconclusively. Relations were at rock bottom.

The conspiracy of silence continued. Only the Chinese proclaimed the emperor's nakedness, asserting over and over that what was actually taking place in Vietnam was USSR disengagement. Radio Beijing kept up a steady barrage of allegations designed to undercut Khrushchev's credibility and to challenge Soviet integrity and courage.

When the struggles of the Vietnamese and the Laotian peoples grew acute the Soviet policy on the question of Indochina is one of "disengagement." In July 1964 they indicated the desire of the Soviet Government to resign from its post as one of the two cochairmen of the Geneva conference. Soon afterwards when the U.S. imperialists engineered the Bac Bo [Tonkin] Gulf incident Khrushchev went so far as to concoct the slander that the incident was provoked by China.[24]

Moscow's treatment of the Tonkin Gulf incident had particularly infuriated the Chinese. The U.S. air strike on August 5, 1964, was directed against North Vietnamese installations, in retaliation for alleged torpedo boat attacks on two U.S. destroyers. Radio Beijing was scathing in its verbal assault over the incident, while public reaction in the USSR was markedly restrained. Later Moscow shifted to the ingenious explanation that the affair had been provoked by China to embarrass the USSR. While in itself not particularly important, the Tonkin Gulf incident symbolized the new relationship that Hanoi required with Moscow. The nature of the war was changing, as was its image: from bare-footed Viet Cong with their homemade shotguns to Vietnamese Communist armies equipped with the best weapons the Communist world could produce. Technology was making the USSR more important to Hanoi than China. The North Vietnamese High Command was devising a new kind of strategy that attempted to match U.S. technology in terms of weapons and firepower. To succeed it required increased USSR support.

As far as Khrushchev was concerned, however, the policy was disengagement. The subsequent performance was remarkable: Khrushchev engineered a breach of relations that outside observers did not believe; rather, they interpreted the events of the time as some devious shadow play designed to mislead the onlooking world.

What eventually saved Hanoi was Khrushchev's abrupt departure and the advent of a new regime in Moscow determined to rectify Khrushchev's doctrinal errors and policy losses.

It is interesting to speculate on the history of the Vietnam War had Khrushchev remained in power and successfully effected his disengagement policy. There would have been no Moscow bankrolling of the DRV's long war in the South, nor the vitally needed surface-to-air missiles to defend North Vietnam. China was in no position to supply sophisticated hardware even if it had been willing to become military quartermaster for the Vietnamese Communist armies. Possibly North Vietnam would have persevered with its war in the South with whatever war materiel was available. More likely Soviet disengagement would have tipped the factional balance of power in the Hanoi Politburo and put into control that faction advocating pursuit of unification by political *dau tranh* (struggle) rather than by "big unit" or "regular force" warfare. Had this been the case there never would have been a Vietnam War as we experienced it after 1965. Some other quite different form of struggle would have emerged—all of which is interesting to speculate on, but as with all the might-have-beens in history, only a parlor game for historians.

Vietnamese Communists later would argue that Khrushchev, having encouraged them to go to war in the first place (certainly in 1959 he made no effort to dissuade them), then abandoned them. Once more they were left alone to curse Soviet perfidy and to warn themselves never to trust any outsider. It was indeed ironic. Nikita Khrushchev began by breaking the Stalinist pattern of minimal involvement in Asia to win himself plaudits from Hanoi leaders and ended being utterly despised by that same leadership.

NOTES

1. B and K stand for Premier N. A. Bulganin and Party First Secretary Nikita Khrushchev.

2. For a list of these works, see the bibliography in Allan Cameron's *Vietnam Crisis: A Documentary Study*, Vol. 1 (New York: Cornell University Press, 1971), pp. 449–552. See also the study itself and other works by Cameron, probably the most knowledgeable authority on the 1954 Geneva Conference.

3. Nikita Khrushchev, *Khrushchev Remembers* (Boston: Little, Brown, 1971), pp. 442–443. Francois Joyaux, a French historian, has added a good deal to our knowledge of this matter, particularly China's role. He gained access to materials in the French government's archives on meetings and exchanges between Ho Chi Minh and Chou En-lai. See Joyaux, *La Chine et Le Reglement du Premier Conflit D'Indochine (Geneve 1954)* (Paris: University of Paris, 1979). See also Donald Lancaster's *The Emancipation of French Indochina* (New York: Oxford University Press, 1971), pp. 314–336.

4. This allegation was officially denied by France; see *London Times* (June 7, 1954).

5. These phrases were encountered frequently by the author during his interviews with North Vietnamese POWs and Chieu Hoi defectors in 1969 about the Sino-Soviet dispute.

6. Khrushchev, *Khrushchev Remembers*, p. 267.

7. Charles B. McLane, *Soviet Strategies in Southeast Asia: An Exploration of Eastern Policy Under Lenin and Stalin* (Princeton, N.J.: Princeton University Press, 1966), p. 84.

8. In terms of protocol, however, he did not receive as elaborate a reception as had India's Pandit Nehru two weeks earlier.

9. Radio Hanoi (November 6, 1957).

10. V. A. Zharov and V. A. Tyrurin, *Southeast Asia: History, Economy, Policy* (Moscow: Progress Publishers, 1972), pp. 52–53.

11. There was not a great deal the DRV could do to reciprocate. Chiefly, it enthusiastically backed the USSR in the international forum. It also campaigned in support of the USSR's declarations on NATO and its various "peace and security guarantees"; see Vietnamese News Agency (VNA) (December 18, 1957). Premier Pham Van Dong at the United Nations endorsed USSR proposals on disarmament, a halt on nuclear weapons tests, and Moscow's position on the German and Berlin questions; see VNA (November 8, 1960).

12. See VNA (September 1, 1960). Apparently there had been earlier differences between the two over the use of the term *peaceful unification*. When K. Y. Voroshilov, president of the Presidium of the USSR Supreme Soviet, visited Hanoi in May 1957, he lauded *peaceful unification* in his arrival statement (May 20) and, in fact, used the term three times in his five-paragraph message,

according to the TASS (May 20, 1957) account. However the VNA version (May 21, 1957) edited out two of the three references.

13. *Pravda* (February 27, 1962).

14. *New York Times* (May 19, 1962).

15. Ibid.

16. *London Times* (March 17, 1962); similar language was used in the note sent July 3, 1962.

17. For a good discussion of Laos during this period, see Arthur Dommen, *Conflict in Laos* (New York: Praeger Publishers, 1964); and for the USSR role in Laos at the time, see Donald Zagoria, *Vietnam Triangle* (New York: Pegasus, 1967). The second Geneva Conference (1961–1962) dealt with the unresolved problem of Laos left over from the first conference. It attempted to "neutralize" Laos and obviate the conflict among the three principal factions of Souvanna Phouma, Boun Oum, and Souphanouvong as well as among the other major figures at the time, particularly Captain Kong Le and General Phoumi Nosavan.

18. Daniel S. Papp, *Soviet Perceptions of the Developing World in the 1980's: The Ideological Basis* (Boston: Lexington Books, 1985), p. 21.

19. Cameron, *Vietnam Crisis*, p. 36.

20. Jon M. Van Dyke, *North Vietnam's Strategy for Survival* (Palo Alto, Calif.: Pacific Books, 1972), p. 224.

21. *Washington Post* (July 8, 1964).

22. *New York Times* (February 26, 1964).

23. TASS (March 4, 1964).

24. *Peking Review* (November 12, 1965).

Four

ZIGZAG

The Sino-Soviet Dispute

THE SINO-SOVIET dispute[1]—that great multidimensioned face-off between two diverse cultures sprawling together across the Euro-Asian landmass, between two Communist systems divided by communism—truly is one of the far-reaching events in the history of twentieth-century Asia.

The dispute, which now seems as permanently entrenched as any international relations institution ever could be, is compounded of many elements: ideological rivalries, competing civilizations, and orthodox struggles for power and influence.

Because of its many facets and its long duration, the dispute has taken on enormous complexity and over time has been subjected to a wide range of interpretation, particularly from within the region. Our interest here is fairly specific—to understand and appreciate its meaning in terms of the Soviet-Vietnamese relationship.

From the start the dispute had more profound meaning for the Vietnamese Communists than for any other outsider. For them it represented opportunity and benefit, encumbrance and risk. The fact of the dispute touched DRV foreign relations with all countries. During the Vietnam War it largely dictated the kind of strategy that would be employed in the South. Since the late 1960s it has been a central factor in Hanoi's relations with both Moscow and Beijing. And the dispute has permeated the Southeast Asian region, impinging on events and influencing decisions in a half-dozen capitals.

The start of the Sino-Soviet dispute may be fixed at almost any date one chooses.[2] For our purposes it can best be set in 1960, when Mao Zedong's challenge to Moscow's direction of the world revolutionary impulse was frontally counterattacked by Khrushchev in Bucharest.[3] The

51

curtain was torn away, and henceforth the Vietnamese Communists could no longer pretend the dispute did not exist.

Competition between Moscow and Beijing had made Hanoi's dealings with the two countries difficult even before the dispute broke into the open. It had provoked tensions during the Viet Minh War and had triggered unseemly infighting at the Geneva Conference. But in those early days it was more of a nuisance for the Vietnamese Communists, a philosophic abstraction of perhaps doctrinal importance but separate from the material world. They viewed it largely as a spirited ideological tiff laced with certain nationalistic rivalries. Ho Chi Minh persistently shrugged off Moscow's complaint that the DRV was identifying itself too closely with China's hostile behavior. Nor did Chinese criticisms of Soviet policy toward Yugoslavia, the de-Stalinization program, and the strings tied to Soviet aid to China find sympathy or even much interest in Hanoi. Slowly, however, the dispute began to impinge on the DRV economy. Requests to Beijing and Moscow for economic aid increasingly were factored into the quarrel, and the Vietnamese Communists were gradually drawn into the no-man's-land between the disputants.

The Sino-Soviet dispute became central to the thinking of Hanoi leaders chiefly because of the conjunction of two developments: the decision by the Hanoi Politburo to begin "armed struggle" in South Vietnam, and the launching of political campaigns by Moscow and Beijing to enlist the support of Communist third parties in the Sino-Soviet dispute. These developments converted the dispute from a bilateral to a multilateral issue. Slowly it was forced to the forefront of Hanoi's consciousness by events: a change of DRV strategy in the war in the South; U.S. commitment of ground troops to South Vietnam; Khrushchev's "disengagement" moves in Vietnam; rumblings of "cultural" revolution in China; and increased maneuvering by both the USSR and China in Hanoi to secure a position of dominant influence. These developments offered the Vietnamese Communists opportunities, but they also counseled restraint. The resultant dichotomy engendered first uncertainty about the course of the dispute, its duration, and its eventual outcome, and then virtually a state of permanent anxiety. Fruits were to be harvested continually from the quarrel, the Vietnamese Communists knew, but to reach them they had to cross a minefield. Gradually the dispute took on an enduring character for Hanoi: an inextricable mix of opportunism and danger. There was advantage to be gained in it, but there was also the prospect that it could either blow up into a Sino-Soviet war or end in a Sino-Soviet collaboration against the DRV, either of which could ruin unification plans. The leadership quite probably was of two minds: It wanted the dispute to end and was worried that it might.

MEDIATION EFFORTS

Hanoi's initial policy on the Sino-Soviet dispute was to minimize its importance publicly while working behind the scenes to heal the breach. This remains official policy, although today there is no distinguishable difference between the Hanoi and Moscow characterizations of the rift.

Ho Chi Minh's efforts to mediate the dispute began in the late 1950s and continued sporadically until his death a decade later; in fact, they persisted even beyond the grave, since the need to mediate is noted in his last will and testament. Essentially what Ho proposed was an international conference of interested Communist parties to thrash out the problem. He apparently had great faith in the idea that bringing the two disputants together in face-to-face dialogue, under great pressure from friends and allies, could force them to heal the breach or at least paper it over.

During these early years Hanoi officials said little about the rift even privately; and what was said was either bland or obscure. The subject was not discussed in the Hanoi mass media, and in private party meetings an effort was made to be neutral.

Since pragmatism ruled, it probably did not matter much what anyone in the DRV actually thought about the Sino-Soviet dispute. One indication of rank-and-file attitude is found in party lectures on the subject. At the Xuan Mai infiltration training camp outside Hanoi, where PAVN troops destined for duty in the South were indoctrinated, a lecture course was taught called "Contradictions of Communism." It dealt specifically with the Sino-Soviet dispute. An examination of the texts used in the course indicates an effort to maintain balance between the two disputants. But those who took the course said the cadre instructors blamed China more than the USSR for causing the dispute but blamed both equally for allowing it to continue.[4] Probably this same attitude, in a more sophisticated form, extended all the way to the Politburo.

At first, the gestures of mediation were informal, consisting of public and private suggestions put forward by Ho and other DRV officials while visiting Moscow and Beijing. This effort reached its most active level in the period 1963-1964 with a series of demarches.[5] The effort came to nothing, and gradually the expectation, or the hope, that the dispute would end began to fade. It appears that by the mid 1960s the DRV leaders had concluded that, for their purposes, the dispute had become permanent,[6] and it was then that they began to shift from mediation to exploitation.

At all times, early and late, Hanoi officials were determined never to be coerced or maneuvered into alliance with either Moscow or Beijing.

Hence they consistently maintained a bristly sort of independence. Hanoi representatives lectured the two parties frequently at international gatherings, but would take a standoffish position when called upon to align themselves.

This independent posture was seen by many outsiders as the product of a Politburo-level doctrinal dispute between pro-Chinese and pro-Soviet elements. Possibly that notion was encouraged by the Vietnamese themselves. In retrospect this view, which at one time was extraordinarily influential in U.S. government circles, does not appear valid. It was argued that the men of the Politburo could be divided into factions. For instance, Le Duan, a frequent and welcome visitor to Moscow, was regarded as pro-Russian; and Truong Chinh, because of his adopted name (*truong chinh* means long march in Vietnamese, an obvious reference to the great event of the Chinese Communist revolution), was considered pro-Chinese. There was some validity in this analysis: Vietnamese politics, as with all Sinic cultures, is characterized by factionalism, and any policy issue that arises is reflected in factional infighting. To a large extent, however, this "pro-Russian versus pro-Chinese" behavior was an effort to ensure that the DRV would never be co-opted by either disputant.

If the Sino-Soviet dispute ever had been a divisive element in Hanoi decisionmaking circles, it had ceased to be so by the mid-1960s. From then on there were no pro-Russian or pro-Chinese in the Politburo, only pro-Vietnamese members united in dedication to the holy objective of reunification of the fatherland. The Sino-Soviet dispute was treated entirely in terms of serving that objective.

EXPLOITATION FORMULA

By the early 1960s the war in the South dominated Hanoi's considerations, and whatever meaning the Sino-Soviet rift had for Hanoi was in terms of military plans and estimates.

All in all, Hanoi's performance here was masterful. It was continually able to do something no other country could manage (certainly not the United States)—and that was to put the Sino-Soviet dispute to its own use in service of its war. This was no easy matter. Success depended on maintaining a substantive symmetry between the conflicting Soviet and Chinese interests. The basic device employed by Hanoi in this is what might be called the alternating tilt gambit.

This could not be defined a neutralism, for the DRV was never able to hide behind so simple a facade as nonalignment. Neither was it simply even-handed treatment, as outside observers frequently wrote—

a case of walking the narrow line between the two contenders—for in truth there was often no line to walk. Nor was the proper metaphor a man on a tightrope. Rather, as Bernard Fall once remarked to the author, it was a man "walking a straight zig zag through the woods."

The alternating tilt gambit was used chiefly in connection with those doctrinal and policy issues of great importance to Moscow and Beijing. It was made possible because Vietnam was important both as a symbol and in its own right. The DRV would first side with one disputant on some issue—say, the nuclear test ban treaty, the "inevitability" of war, or revisionism versus dogmatism—that clearly put it into one camp. Then, after an appropriate interval, it would come to some gesture or pronouncement that clearly favored the opposite camp. Balance would be redressed, the score again would be tied, and the game of shuttlecock would continue.

Maintaining this parity was a complicated task because various issues had greater or lesser saliency; hence it was not simply a matter of tilt for tilt. Further, the disputants sometimes would shift *their* positions and even reverse them—for example, the positions taken regarding political settlement of the Vietnam War.

Outside observers tended to regard the Sino-Soviet dispute as pure opportunity for Hanoi. As neither party could ever pressure the DRV because of the dispute, and as joint pressure was out of the question, the DRV was free to play one side against the other, milking the dispute for its own advantage. There is validity in this view, but generally it has been overstated.

Although the benefits for Hanoi were considerable, they were limited. For instance, the DRV sought a socialist world united front to support its war effort. This would not have required ending the dispute, but it did mean that the USSR and China would have to agree on common support actions and, specifically, on a single integrated logistics system. Hanoi put the blame for the failure to achieve such an arrangement on both sides, but mainly on the Chinese. A single supply system was proposed by Kosygin during his February 1965 visit to Hanoi. It was rejected outright by Mao Zedong a few weeks later. Moscow would renew the proposal periodically during the next few years, mostly, it seems, to irritate the Chinese. The point is that Hanoi was unable, in this instance, to use the dispute for its own ends; and, indeed, the fact of the dispute prevented the very thing Hanoi was seeking.

Near the end of the war the game began to wear thin—clearly both the USSR and China had wearied of it—but it remained a policy until it foundered in the postwar days.

IDEOLOGICAL INTRUSION

Hanoi's objective in dealing with the Sino-Soviet dispute was to turn it to practical advantage while never being drawn into its maw. This did not mean indifference to the ideological dimension of the quarrel. Indeed, party theoreticians in Hanoi took extraordinarily strong doctrinal stands, expressing themselves frequently and forcefully.

Throughout the Vietnam War, the Vietnamese Communists maintained an ultra-hardline, fundamentalist view of our times, of their enemy in the South, and of the USSR's responsibilities to them. The capitalist world must be destroyed, which could be done only through revolutionary warfare conducted by a unified, centrally directed, international proletariat. Once this notion had been orthodox Marxist-Leninist belief, but by the time the Sino-Soviet dispute reached its boiling point, it was a concept embraced only by the Vietnamese and a few zealots elsewhere. At the same time, Hanoi theoreticians held that internationalism always and everywhere should prevail over nationalistic tendencies. Thus the USSR as well as China were judged, by Hanoi theoreticians, to be guilty of two doctrinal errors.

The first was to put individual national interests over transcendental proletarian solidarity by embracing such pernicious ideas as polycentric communism or the "many roads to communism" idea, which had the net effect of eroding monolithic transnational communism. China (and before it, Yugoslavia) was judged more guilty here, although the USSR was not regarded as entirely blameless.

Anything that questioned or undermined the mystic qualities of proletarian solidarity was regarded as particularly dangerous for Vietnamese communism. Indeed, the history of the movement is one long account of the campaign to blot out divisiveness, splinterism, geographic regionalism and parochial disregard for the center. Ho Chi Minh spent a lifetime trying to weld the Vietnamese Communists into a monolithic whole and keep them there.

In raising the issue of proletarian internationalism[7] or Communist world unity, the Vietnamese threw into the face of world Communist leaders some of the most sacred text of their Marxist catechism, there being nothing holier than workers of the world uniting. Although recognizing the problem of its allies in reconciling patriotism with Communist world obligations, the Vietnamese still treated the matter as a choice between unity and national selfishness. Each Communist nation, large or small, said the Hanoi theoretician, has both national interest and international duty. In dealing with these, the small nation (read DRV) must be free to decide its interest or obligation, which should never be forced on it by a larger nation (read USSR or China).

However, the small nation also has the right to expect support from the big nations. Thus staked out was the claim that the USSR (and China) must support the DRV in the name of international proletarianism but—in the same spirit—may not levy requirements on the DRV, as that would violate the principle of self-determination.

The second doctrinal error was the advocacy of various worthless strategies, such as peaceful coexistence or détente, for use against the capitalist world. These undercut the belief that the only way to destroy capitalism was through unrelieved, uncompromising revolutionary class warfare. Initially the USSR was held by Hanoi to be the lone culprit here, but it soon was joined by China.

At root, particularly for the Vietnamese revolutionaries, was the question of the necessity of war in transforming the world and, within this question, the matter of attendant risk, specifically the risk of thermonuclear war. Orthodox dogma—that is, original Leninism—held that the violence of warfare was inevitable so long as capitalist states remained anywhere on earth, just as violent revolution remained mandatory in overthrowing them. Lenin also believed that war was an integral part of capitalist world competition, but this in itself was not an entirely bad thing because such wars engendered mass discontent, which led to revolution, which would overthrow capitalism. Of course, Lenin had to deal with neither the problem of violence in the form of nuclear war nor the danger that revolution might lead to such a war.

For the USSR, all of this changed with the advent of the atomic bomb. The USSR's position now was that the world should be transformed through the "application of nonviolence" in which "defensive violence" would be used only in cases of "acute struggle." There is much latitude in this position, but it clearly does not extend to risking nuclear war. The DRV (and Chinese) position favored unlimited revolution and unrestricted violence and, while not actually advocating nuclear war, it asserted the need for an offensive state of mind willing to chance nuclear war.

Moscow's advocacy of détente was seen in Hanoi as placing maintenance of world peace above unification of Vietnam, and it meant that the USSR was not willing to support the Vietnamese because it did not wish to risk nuclear war. It was not détente as a danger to the USSR that concerned the Hanoi officials—the Soviets could take care of themselves—but détente as a threat to the DRV. The danger lay in collusion by Moscow against Vietnamese interests. Pham Van Dong would repeatedly express this fear by predicting that "big power détente" would create conditions in which small nations can be "repressed." He would name no names, but his meaning was clear.

Moscow held that the Vietnam War could escalate into world war. The Chinese at the time asserted that this position was simply the result of Soviet fear of U.S. nuclear weapons. The USSR asserted that the only sane way to compete with the United States was through peaceful coexistence and that, given enough time, it would prove a successful strategy. The Chinese position was that peaceful coexistence was a betrayal of Marx and the revolutionary heritage, and that it was self-defeating because accommodation with imperialism merely strengthened it. For Hanoi the test was whether or not détente held out promise for unification.

Emotionally and even logically, the Vietnamese Communists stood closer to the Chinese view—that the hardline no-détente policy was the only proper one for dealing with the United States. Their quarrel with China was over China's failure to follow this logic to its correct final conclusion—namely, that the USSR and PRC should bury their doctrinal differences and help assure victory for the Vietnamese Communists.

The Hanoi leadership viewed the Sino-Soviet dispute in the terms set down by the disputants—and it understood the jargon of their charges and countercharges (revisionism, hegemonism, dogmatism, deviationism)—but for them the more central meaning was that the doctrinal argument was corruptive. All of the respective positions, it was held, represented doctrinal change in one form or another, and change itself represented the ultimate error. Revisionism deliberately called for changed relations among Communist nations; dogmatism, with its confrontational divisiveness, engendered it.[8] For Hanoi planners, any change was disruptive. Externally it threatened supply lines and other kinds of outside support; internally it encouraged factionalism and other forms of enervating divisiveness.

In keeping with the alternate tilt gambit, Hanoi leaders treated the two sinners reciprocally. With China they assumed an anti-détente attitude (which pleased the Chinese) and a pro-unity stand (which did not); with the USSR they voiced support for détente (in certain cases) but refused to accept the Soviet contention that China was the chief cause of disunity. Thus an official Vietnamese visitor in Moscow would endorse détente with respect to West Germany but not with the United States. The same visitor in Beijing would endorse the Chinese call for socialist unity but not the contention that the USSR was the cause of disunity.

Hanoi's stand, being extraordinarily fundamentalist, certainly was not one that could win easy support either in Moscow or elsewhere in the socialist world. It challenged national interests, even nationalism itself. It exhibited a kind of bravado contempt for the universal fear of nuclear devastation. But Hanoi stood its ground. To this day, Vietnamese leaders would like to revert to that primitive communism that pits all of the workers of the world against everyone else. And they are ever ready, eager even, they say, to march to Armageddon with the capitalists.

THE DISPUTE AND THE WAR

Even in its earliest days, the Vietnam War occupied a special place in world communism's affairs, coloring and lending special meaning to all sorts of intracommunist developments, including, of course, the Sino-Soviet dispute. For Hanoi the dispute dissipated the world revolutionary effort and shifted attention away from the main enemy, the United States. Moscow and Beijing both echoed this idea, in charging the other with betraying the Hanoi cause, each asserting that if the cause failed, blame would rest on the other. Thus the dispute was linked to the war.

At first, the meaning of the war in terms of the Sino-Soviet dispute was sharply etched. The issue was Soviet moderation versus Chinese revolutionary irreconcilability. Soon it became more dimensional. After 1965, complexity piled on complexity until the permutations of the dispute over proper strategy and preferred outcome boggled the mind. The Chinese began the war by asserting the correctness of the Vietnamese goal (unification), but by the end of the war they were tacitly opposing it. The USSR began by questioning the wisdom of this goal (as overly ambitious), advocating instead a negotiated approach (that would eventually achieve unification), and it ended by supporting PAVN's go-for-broke strategy. The Chinese initially supported Hanoi's Maoist strategy but later denounced it as being a misinterpretation and misapplication of Mao. The USSR initially opposed Hanoi strategy (chiefly because it was Chinese) and then embraced it (particularly its "fight-talk" tactic) because it lessened risks for the USSR.

The Vietnam War created other paradoxes among Hanoi's two allies. In the early years, China as a regional power was more eager to see a Hanoi victory than was the USSR, whose experience had been that China benefited more than the USSR from regional warfare in Asia. By the end of the Vietnam War these positions had been reversed. China's main propaganda line at the start of the war was that the USSR was plotting to sell out the Vietnamese cause in exchange for gain with the United States. A decade later the USSR was making the identical charge against the Chinese. Late in the war, the Sino-Soviet dispute became intricately enmeshed in the issue of negotiated settlement. However, the original causes (at least the superficial causes) of the dispute had vanished, and the original positions—of selling out to the capitalists and betraying original Marxist doctrine—had been outdated by changed thinking in both camps. The dispute lingered, but not its original rationale.

For the leadership in Hanoi, it became clear after Khrushchev's fall that the new rulers in the Kremlin faced decisions on policy that would have profound effects on Vietnam's fortunes of war. These involved the same two main Soviet policy areas: how best to handle the growing Chinese challenge, and how exactly to define détente with the United States. On one side in the Kremlin were those who wanted to press on with détente even if this meant paying a price in China (and Vietnam). On the other were those who wanted to maintain an essential international proletarian solidarity as a means of countering the Chinese challenge and to allow this objective, which would have meant augmented support for Vietnam, to delimit the pursuit of détente, if necessary.

Within this doctrinal difference was a more specific debate over strategy. In part it turned on the quarrel with China over nuclear warfare and the issue of the United States as a "paper tiger," illustrated by the famous apocryphal exchange:

MAO ZEDONG: The U.S. is but a paper tiger.

KHRUSHCHEV: Yes, of course. But the tiger does have missile claws and nuclear teeth.

In part it turned on a renewed debate among Soviet military theoreticians over the idea of wars of national liberation as well as other "local" (small-scale nonnuclear) wars. Within the Kremlin this debate had a domestic political dimension.[9] Externally it was part of the Sino-Soviet dispute, and, of course, it had relevance in Vietnam.

The basic Kremlin contention held that war of the sort that was developing in Vietnam was feasible warfare and safe even given the existing thermonuclear balance of terror. Such a "genuinely Leninist" view of war was espoused initially by Marshal V. D. Sokolovsky and later by other prominent figures.[10] Out of this purely military concept grew a broader idea, one that fit the Vietnamese concept of *dau tranh* (struggle) in its two manifestations—armed struggle and political struggle. As it finally emerged, the Moscow thesis was expressed thus: First, small-scale local wars, if carefully handled, will not escalate into either world war or big-power confrontation; second, USSR support of such wars is not ruled out by the doctrine of détente. This debate within Kremlin walls had application in Vietnam. Wars of national liberation were designed to be an important and integral part of the Soviet "political arsenal," a stand that remains unchanged to this day. Support of Vietnam's war of national liberation was held to be a *right* on the part of the USSR, whether or not it actually exercised it. Conversely, however, the United States did not have the right to back the GVN since such support would in effect shut the USSR out of the area. At the same time the USSR had the *right* to dispatch troops to North Vietnam to support this war of liberation, but the United States had no comparable right to fund a liberation movement in a Communist country. There was of course no difference of opinion between Moscow and Hanoi on this issue. In retrospect, it appears that Soviet marshals regarded the Vietnam War as both risk and opportunity. The risk was possible confrontation with the United States, and the opportunity was to improve Moscow's strategic and ideological position with respect to China. The important thing was not to get trapped by the war.

Soviet policy during the Vietnam War, as it finally emerged from the debate and the collective leadership process, had three dimensions. First, it was decided that Hanoi would be provided with all the necessary military and economic assistance needed to pursue its war, but that this would be the limit of Soviet involvement. Second, the USSR would continue to deal with the United States by using the strategy of détente, adjusting Vietnamese policy if and when necessary. Third, the USSR would place great emphasis on a negotiated settlement outcome of the war as the best insurance against being drawn further into it (since it could always counter a Hanoi appeal for intervention with a new proposal for political settlement), even though it recognized that this policy would not go down well in Hanoi (as discussed in Chapter 5).

During the Vietnam War many observers contended that the war was regarded by Moscow as the central issue in the Sino-Soviet dispute. Actually it is more correct to say that the reverse was the case, at least for Hanoi—that the dispute was central to the war. The main history of Soviet-Vietnamese wartime relations is the history of Moscow's efforts to gain ascendency over China. Soviet moves in Hanoi were anti-Chinese moves, and if they served Hanoi's war it was largely incidental. The USSR sought to enlarge its ideological sphere of influence (to include Vietnam) and to devise the best strategy for dealing with the United States (including dealing with the United States in Vietnam). The Vietnam War thus was a pawn in a vaster game.

At first the struggle was a silent one, a cryptic anti-Chinese campaign. Moscow still hoped that a complete rupture could be avoided. But the Chinese grew steadily more intransigent. Finally the USSR concluded that the ideological competition with China was now central to its Asian programs. On the heels of this came a second conclusion: that Vietnam was perhaps the best arena in which this battle could be fought.

Chinese dealings with Hanoi during the war years were never skillfully handled. Perhaps the Chinese simply did not care to be clever. In any event, China frequently was uncooperative with the DRV in its conduct of the war and at times seemed to be an outright saboteur of the war effort.

China never accepted the Vietnamese posture on the Sino-Soviet dispute. If Vietnam was not against Moscow, it was against China. This adamant attitude continued throughout the Great Proletarian Cultural Revolution, although Beijing was so often preoccupied then that it failed to take advantage of anti-Soviet opportunities in Hanoi. Early and late China refused the Moscow (and DRV) call for united action, including the demand for a joint or coordinated military supply system for the DRV, which hurt China badly in Hanoi. The USSR subsequently maintained that the Chinese refusal was responsible for the decision of the United States to intervene with ground troops in Vietnam and for the bombing and air strikes in North Vietnam. Had China agreed to a common front, the Moscow argument runs, there would have been no U.S. involvement:

> In 1964, the U.S. warmongers had drawn up plans to expand the war against the DRV in order to win the war in Vietnam. However, the Pentagon was dreadfully afraid of the recurrence of a situation like the Korean War, during which the two nations—Soviet Union and China—joined efforts to repulse the United States. Therefore, the U.S. political task first of all was to make sure of China's stand.
>
> The Bac Bo Gulf incident in August of 1964 is an example. The United States spread a rumor, claiming that DRV torpedo boats had attacked U.S. warships. It thus started its first bombing of DRV territory. From secret Pentagon documents made public last summer, we see that Washington had carefully studied China's stand before it adopted this step to expand the war in Indochina. . . .
>
> In February 1965, when Soviet Chairman of the Council of Ministers Kosygin visited the DRV, he exchanged opinion[s] with the Chinese leaders on the situation in the Indochina peninsula. The Soviet side had taken the initiative in putting forward a proposal that the DRV, China, the DPRK and other socialist nations issue a joint statement exposing the acts of U.S. aggressors. However, Mao Tse-tung opposed the joint efforts by socialist nations to resist imperialist aggression.
>
> It was made clear later that he had already told U.S. political critic Snow, when interviewed in January 1965, about China's stand if the United States intensified its aggression against North Vietnam. He had promised the U.S. embassy that China would not participate in the war, so long as the United States did not attack China.

Taking note of this clear statement, the U.S. warmongers felt they were then free to act, and that they would be able to intensify the air bombing on the DRV at an appropriate time.

In early February 1965, South Vietnamese patriots attacked a U.S. air force base in Pleiku. The Pentagon regarded this as an excuse to intensify air bombings of the DRV. At the same time, large numbers of U.S. troops landed in South Vietnam in direct participation of the war against the troops of the National Liberation Front. . . . (Thus) Peking severed its ties with the socialist community and refused to take concerted actions. First of all it refused to take concerted actions with the Soviet Union and other socialist nations and took the path of colluding with U.S. imperialism and betraying the interests of the national liberation movements.[11]

Hanoi's 1979 *White Book* on Chinese-Vietnamese wartime relations was even more specific about Beijing's repeated refusal to accept the "united action" concept:

On February 28, 1965 [the Chinese] rejected the Vietnamese draft of February 22, 1965, for a joint statement by the socialist countries condemning the United States for intensifying its war of aggression in South Vietnam and for unleashing a war against the Democratic Republic of Vietnam.

In March 1965, they rejected the Soviet proposal that the parties of the Soviet Union, China and Vietnam meet to discuss joint action in support of the Vietnamese people's struggle. . . .

In April 1965, on two occasions, they rejected the Soviet proposal for joint action . . . (and) rejected the Soviet proposal to set up an airlift via China and build airfields on Chinese territory to defend the Democratic Republic of Vietnam.

In February 1966, Chairman Mao Zedong rejected the idea of creating a united international front in support of Vietnam as suggested in the course of the high-level Sino-Vietnamese talks.

In March 1966, Chairman Mao Zedong again rejected the suggestion for the founding of a united international front.[12]

Chinese intransigence reached its highest point in early 1967, if Soviet claims are to be believed. During this time, hardly a week went by without a Soviet accusation: that Soviet shipments were being delayed; that Soviet specialists en route to Hanoi were being pulled off trains or otherwise delayed or harassed; that Soviet surface to air missiles transiting China were being unloaded for disassembly and copying; that some equipment such as planes was being stolen outright.

There was a basis in fact for the charges. Zhou Enlai in September 1967 acknowledged that trains and military warehouses in China had been looted of supplies destined for Vietnam.[13] However, China, while admitting sabotage of the Vietnam War, took the general tack that whatever it did was in the DRV's best interests. Its argument was based on the idea that massive aid shipments to Hanoi would so increase the Soviets' leverage that eventually Moscow would control the DRV. Then it would sell out Vietnam and force a settlement acceptable to the United States. Said Radio Peking at the time: "Present Soviet leaders have proved to be incurable revisionists . . . arrogant power politicians and chauvinists whose aim is to rule the world in partnership with the American imperialists."[14]

To shut China out of Southeast Asia would not be in Hanoi's interest, and China meant to prevent this even if Hanoi did not understand the wisdom of its actions. In curtailing overland shipments, China may have hoped to force the USSR to do more ocean shipping that in turn would lead to a U.S. naval blockade of Vietnam and present the USSR with the unenviable choice of confronting the United States or abandoning Vietnam.

Chinese sabotage, of course, was rich grist for the Moscow propaganda mill, and the most was made of the theme that China refused to join a common support effort for Vietnam. This castigation is typical:

> The Chinese leaders have categorically refused to undertake concerted measures with the Soviet Union and the other socialist countries in providing support to the Indochinese people's struggle. Moreover, the Peking leaders have also persisted in slandering and attacking the Soviet Union and other fraternal socialist countries. All their sordid activities are aimed at tearing the peoples of the Indochinese peninsula away from their loyal friends and allies, the Soviet Union and the other socialist countries, and at weakening the anti-imperialist forces. Clearly, such a policy only benefits the imperialists and runs counter to the common objective of the communists and progressive forces which calls for united action in the struggle against imperialist aggression. This common objective is explicitly set forth in the appeal adopted by the 24th CPSU Congress. The appeal said "Let the universal movement for the cessation of imperialist aggression in Indochina, for the withdrawal of all the troops of the United States and its allies, for the implementation of the lawful rights of the peoples of Vietnam, Laos and Cambodia to be masters of their land, spread and become stronger."[15]

Hanoi may have been able to fault China's ideological line on joint support ventures, but not its ideological line on the war itself. The

Chinese position here, at least initially, was rock hard and totally pro-Vietnam.

The essential Beijing doctrinal stand early in the war was this: The Vietnam War is a crusade that must be supported by Communists everywhere, even if this means war with the United States (should it choose to intervene). The United States is a paper tiger that can be defeated. Implacable militancy is required. Offers of political settlement should be rejected out of hand; there should be no interim dealings with the United States of any sort. The USSR errs in its pursuit of détente, which is a betrayal of Vietnam for it abandons all out class warfare.

In psychological or emotional terms the Vietnamese empathized far more with this Chinese position than with Moscow's rationalizations about the benefits to all of détente with the United States. One should battle the devil, not sup with him, held the Vietnamese. But they also realized they could ill afford such emotional indulgence—even if the Chinese could.

The Chinese distinguished sharply between the two Communist forces warring in Vietnam—the North Vietnamese and the National Liberation Front (NLF) in the South. The USSR did not. Initially the Chinese held that the NLF by itself could win its war—victory being defined as a monopoly of political power for the NLF without direct involvement by either the DRV or outsiders. This could be done by employing the Maoist doctrine of people's war. For the Chinese the important thing was not only a victory for the NLF but a victory by means of people's war strategy and in no other way. The beginning of the end of full Chinese commitment to the Vietnam War came with the DRV's decision to begin dispatching large numbers of PAVN troops to the South in late 1964, regarded as an abandonment of people's war strategy.

The Chinese posture with respect to the Vietnam War was cleverly rationalized: They *could* not intervene because they *ought* not intervene. The argument ran like this: The Vietnamese Communists must fight a Maoist people's war because only this strategy will deliver victory. The most important rule in people's war is that it must be fought by the people themselves and not by outsiders. By definition the Chinese excluded themselves from participation in the war.

When the nature of the war changed in early 1965, from revolutionary guerrilla war to what Hanoi generals call regular force strategy war, the Chinese took an ever more critical attitude toward the *way* the Vietnamese were fighting. The rupture over strategy became total with the publication of Lin Biao's *Long Live the People's War* in August 1965. In blunt terms Lin Biao implied that the Vietnamese now were breaking

all the basic rules of people's war. In the 1968 Tet offensive, when
North Vietnamese Defense Minister General Vo Nguyen Giap lost 70,000
of his best troops in the streets of South Vietnam's cities, one could
imagine Lin Biao paraphrasing the remark of the French general watching
the charge of the Light Brigade: "It is magnificent. But it is not the
People's War." To his Chinese critics General Giap probably would have
replied that technology—the helicopter, massive fire-power, instant communications—had revolutionized warfare and that to fight the Americans
with the tactics used by the Chinese against the Japanese in the 1930s
would mean certain defeat. Increasingly in the late 1960s, the Chinese
tended to take the position that it was not for them to tell the Vietnamese
how to conduct their war, but since they ignored Chinese advice they
had to assume full responsibility for their actions and the eventual
outcome. Thus, when Xuan Thuy went to Paris in 1968 to begin talks
with the Americans and South Vietnamese, the Chinese asserted that
this was a mistake that would come to nothing, but also that it was a
North Vietnamese decision.

In this way the Chinese avoided being drawn into the quicksand
of the war and could always maintain a maximum choice of options.
They could, if they ever chose, intervene massively or if necessary
disengage entirely. If the Vietnamese Communists lost the war no stigma
would attach to China because it could point to Hanoi's failure to follow
China's advice.

Hanoi's characterization of this behavior—particularly since the
end of the war—is total perfidy. The Chinese were untrustworthy and
undependable; they change friends like one changes underwear, said
Vietnamese Ambassador Nhuyen Co Thach at a Colombo press conference
in May 1979.

In retrospect, it appears that the meaning of the war for the Sino-
Soviet dispute was this:

1. The USSR had much to gain by Vietnamese Communist victory
   and, once victory became a realistic possibility, did everything
   it could to ensure it. Moscow was not willing to pay the price
   of ruined détente with the United States, but it was never
   obliged to face that unpalatable choice.
2. China by 1970 did not want the Vietnamese Communists to
   achieve a clear victory, partly because of the growing Hanoi-
   Moscow closeness and partly because it probably would have
   meant Vietnamese control of all Indochina. The residual Chinese
   interest in the war was validating the abstraction called people's
   war, and with Mao Zedong's departure that purpose diminished.

However, China could not bring itself to take those actions that would have prevented decisive victory by North Vietnam.

3. Both Moscow and Beijing looked on the war from their vantage point as major powers with global interests, each at all times asking in what way the war served it. Their common interest was that the other should reap no benefit, regardless of the war's outcome. Probably the Vietnam War worsened Sino-Soviet relations; possibly it merely demonstrated how incompatible the USSR and China had been all along.

A common view at the time, in McLuhanese terms, was that the war was cool for the USSR, hot for China; a nuisance for the USSR, an imperative for China. The USSR, it was widely held, had little to gain in a clearcut Hanoi victory because it would also be seen as a Beijing victory; however, it did have much to gain from an indeterminate ending, such as a standoff followed by some sort of political compromise involving Moscow participation. Soviet officials were quoted as expressing the private hope that the war would end in a draw. On the other hand, it was commonly held that China was psychologically committed to the war and that a defeat of the Vietnamese Communists would be a catastrophe for Beijing. Possibly these propositions never were true or were true for only brief moments.

THE DISPUTE TODAY

The Sino-Soviet dispute for Hanoi has lost all of its original meaning as well as most of its wartime utility. In deciding to choose sides, and in opting for the USSR, Hanoi has redefined the dispute as simply a struggle against Chinese hegemonism.

Hanoi's victory in war had a profound effect on both the dispute itself and on each of the two disputants. The Chinese badly miscalculated the ultimate outcome of the war. They had anticipated that the United States would stay the course but would not be able to win in decisive terms; hence what would eventually emerge would be some sort of permanent standoff, much as happened in Korea in the early 1950s. Probably they also calculated that South Vietnam would eventually move to the left to a more neutral or nonaligned posture. Thus China could expect reasonably stable relations with all four countries in Indochina as well as dealings with each on a bilateral basis. All of these estimates proved wrong, leaving China in a highly untenable position in Indochina. For Moscow, as discussed in detail later on, Hanoi's military victory in South Vietnam was a matter of unalloyed elation. The USSR had gotten on the right track early, by anticipating a final

Hanoi victory months before the Chinese made such a determination, and by pouring in support and making lavish promises for the future. Victory found the USSR's position in Hanoi as favorable as China's was unfavorable. This trend—up for the USSR, down for China—continues to the present. Today the USSR is Vietnam's most supportive friend while a full-scale cold war rages with China.

In a sense China holds the United States to blame for the outcome of the war. Mao Zedong observed to a West German ambassador that "the Americans were never serious about the Vietnam War; otherwise they would never have left after only 50,000 casualties." From Mao's view, and the Chinese sense of magnitude being what it is, this is a plausible conclusion (although the ambassador thought Mao was being sardonic). If "only" 50,000 casualties changed a U.S. policy, then the United States could not have been serious about the war in the first place. Mao had depended on the United States to forestall a Hanoi-dominated Federation of Indochina, and the United States had disappointed him.

The *manner* in which the war ended was an influence on Chinese radicalism, which in turn affected the Sino-Soviet dispute. Earlier radicalism—the dogmatism charged by Moscow—gave way to a more moderate stance. The Cultural Revolution, nearly the ultimate in radicalism, had created a weakness that endangered China. Ideology had become suspect in the face of the growing demand for economic progress. So China abruptly changed course. This change was facilitated by— and to a certain extent was attributable to—the way the war ended. China's previous behavior had been in part a product of its perception of the United States as an enemy, in turn a heritage of the Korean War. Ignoble U.S. disengagement from Vietnam in 1973, and the spectacle of the United States standing by doing nothing in 1975 while the tank-led North Vietnamese Army thundered south, undercut the image of fanatic U.S. imperialism. This U.S. behavior convinced the Chinese, as nothing else ever could have done, that the United States was not China's mortal enemy perpetually dedicated to its destruction. It was perhaps the final irony of a long ironic war.

We now know that Sino-Vietnamese relations were never as warm or harmonious as we believed them to be in the late 1950s and early 1960s. We also know that the downturn that ended with a rupture three years after the end of the war began much earlier and became much more serious than was apparent at the time. The Chinese attitude began to change in the late 1960s, partly owing to the shift by China from regional to world power with its attendant change in national interests. Whereas it once was in China's interest that the United States be expelled from the region, it now served China better if the United States remained as a counterforce to the USSR. China was also alarmed by the quantum jump in Vietnamese geopolitical strength and influence, and by the new power balance it faced as Hanoi began to tilt toward Moscow. All of China's calculations for Southeast Asia had been upset.

Today China regards Vietnam as a regional challenger—which means it is more than a Moscow surrogate—and it expects that Hanoi's expansionism as "the little hegemonist" will continue regardless of the future of Vietnamese-Soviet relations. Nor does China consider Vietnam to be a simple Moscow satellite, although it certainly believes Vietnam will remain a dependent client state for the foreseeable future. Sino-Vietnamese rapprochement would require that Hanoi distance itself somewhat from Moscow, that it ease its efforts to dominate Kampuchea and Laos, and that it stop its mistreatment of ethnic Chinese in Vietnam. The present poor Sino-Vietnamese relations have not come by the choice of either party so much as they have resulted from blunder, chiefly that of the Hanoi leadership. As noted earlier, studies based on interviews with Vietnamese on the general subject of the Sino-Soviet dispute strongly indicate that most Vietnamese believe that in the long run Vietnam simply must get along with China. Its neighbor is too immense and too close ever to permit permanent confrontation. Sooner or later a workable relationship will be established. The problem is to find some face-saving formula for rapprochement. Hanoi's present leaders probably will not be able to find one, but a new leadership can, and probably will.

Most observers, including this author, assume that eventually the Sino-Soviet dispute will burn itself out, but that even when it does, China and the USSR will continue to compete with each other for influence in Indochina. Thus, when the dispute as it now exists does end, a struggle for power among the three—Vietnam, China, and the USSR—will continue.

Hanoi suffers great anxiety over the possibility of a Sino-Soviet rapprochement, or at least professes such anxiety. Any move by either party, even meetings called at the deputy foreign ministry level to discuss outstanding problems, will bring a high-level Hanoi official flying in to Moscow seeking reassurance. China lists Moscow's backing of the Vietnamese occupation of Kampuchea as one of the "three obstacles" to improved Sino-Soviet relations (the other two being Soviet occupation of Afghanistan and the large numbers of Soviet troops along the China-Mongolia border). As China gives every indication of holding the line here, markedly improved relations with the USSR are unlikely in the foreseeable future.

Hanoi's concern is probably justified, however. An end to the Sino-Soviet dispute would allow greater latitude for both Moscow and Beijing in dealing with Vietnam and possibly could result in their joining forces in a way that would be detrimental to it.

NOTES

1. The standard works on the Sino-Soviet dispute include those by Allan Cameron, William Griffith, Edward Crankshaw, Robert Rupen, and Donald Zagoria. For writings on the dispute and Vietnam, see P. J. Honey's *Communism in North Vietnam: Its Role in the Sino-Soviet Dispute* (Cambridge, Mass.: MIT, Center for International Studies, 1963); W. R. Smyser, *The Independent Vietnamese: Vietnamese Communism Between Russia and China, 1956–69* (a condensed version of Smyser's Ph.D. dissertation published by the Ohio University Center for International Studies, Southeast Asia Program, 1980); and Eugene Lawson's *The Sino-Vietnamese Conflict* (New York: Praeger Publishers, 1984), also based on the author's Ph.D. dissertation). In addition, see Douglas Pike, "The Impact of the Sino-Soviet dispute on Southeast Asia," in Herbert J. Ellison, ed., *The Sino-Soviet Conflict: A Global Perspective* (Seattle: University of Washington Press, 1982).

2. Most writers establish the year as about 1958 or, at the latest, 1960, when Moscow called home its corps of military and economic aid advisers in China. Some refer to 1956 as the start. Mao Zedong, in interviews with Edgar Snow and others, implied it began about 1949.

3. The dispute was officially put before the world Communist leaders with Khrushchev's pyrotechnical attack on China and Peng Chen's bristly counterattack at the Third Congress of the Communist party of Romania in June 1960. For a good account of this matter, see Edward Crankshaw's *The New Cold War: Moscow vs. Peking* (New York: Penguin Books, 1963), Ch. 10.

4. This information was generated in interviews conducted by the author. Unfortunately, much of the data was destroyed by a fire in the U.S. Embassy in Saigon in the late 1960s; those research materials that were saved are now in the Indochina Archive at the University of California, Berkeley.

5. A good example of the effort to end the rift is found in the Lao Dong Politburo statement of February 10, 1963; it lists the major issues involved and concludes with a call for a "socialist summit" to resolve the problem. The text is contained in Honey's *Communism in North Vietnam*, pp. 181–185. Also typical of the Hanoi position at this time is General Vo Nguyen Giap's article "On Internal and International Unity," in *Nhan Dan* (February 21, 1963).

6. Realization may have been a slow process, but we need to fix the time more precisely. I am inclined to think that this conclusion was drawn in the months following Khrushchev's fall, when his successors brushed aside Ho's renewed mediation efforts. But not until after the death of Mao did it become evident that Mao's successors had little interest in ending the rift.

7. Proletarian internationalism among European Communists was a code word for Moscow control; it was not used as such in Hanoi.

8. There were two forms of revisionism evident to the theoreticians in Hanoi: (a) the revisionism that reinterpreted Marx and Lenin and was simply

a form of heresy, and (b) the revisionism that rejected the current official interpretation of Marxism-Leninism in favor of a return to the original interpretation. In Hanoi both were condemned, but the measurement was the degree to which either betrayed the ideals of world revolution in the name of national interest by the USSR (or China).

9. As the idea of wars of national liberation gained in fashion in Moscow at about this time (early 1960s), it was seized upon by the Soviet marshals (whom Khrushchev called "the metal eaters") as a way to increase military appropriations and gain new Soviet influence externally. Eventually, the issue became one of the crowbars that pried Khrushchev out of office. Officially the idea of wars of national liberation remains operative in Moscow, although Soviet commentators now tend to finesse the issue when questioned about it, saying that wars of national liberation primarily meant wars against colonialism and that no colonies remain in existence today.

10. See Marshal V. D. Sokolovsky, *Voennaya Strategiya* [Military Strategy] (1962), in addition to later revised editions in 1963 and 1964; in the daily newspaper *Red Star* (1964), and in the monthly journal *Military Thought* (1964).

11. "U.S. Intensification of Its Aggression Against Viet-Nam and Peking's Double-Faced Tactics," Radio Moscow (January 10, 1972).

12. Smyser, *The Independent Vietnamese*, p. 24.

13. *Asian Notes* (November 23, 1967).

14. Radio Peking (June 20, 1965).

15. Radio Moscow (December 26, 1971).

Five

HANOI AND MOSCOW AT WAR

THE VIETNAM WAR was the seminal event in the history of Soviet-Vietnamese relations. The war, then the effects and aftermath of the war, have dictated day-to-day relations and have imprisoned the two countries in an association that future historians may judge not in the interest of either.

As an exercise in historical speculation one can credit (or blame) the Vietnam War for a whole series of events and conditions outside the borders of Indochina. It can be hypothesized that the Vietnam War:

1. brought about the downfall of Nikita Khrushchev, thereby touching off a prolonged succession crisis in the USSR (this was the result of Khrushchev's weak response to the Gulf of Tonkin incident, which made him appear indecisive in the Kremlin corridors of power and was used by hardliners to undermine his political base);
2. politically destroyed a president of the United States, Lyndon Johnson, and ushered in a decade of social trauma that, in effect, became an American cultural revolution;
3. triggered the Great Proletarian Cultural Revolution in China (seen as a power struggle between Mao and those challengers who wanted to end the Sino-Soviet dispute and take common action with the USSR against the United States in Vietnam; according to this thesis Mao saw that he had to move quickly to rid himself of his rivals before the Vietnamese situation made it impossible for him to avoid joint action with the USSR— hence he launched the Cultural Revolution);
4. convinced Indonesian Communists that the time had come to make their bid for power, which they did, and subsequently the Indonesian Communist party was emasculated;
5. very nearly precipitated a Sino-Soviet war;

6. made complete and enduring the dispute between China and the USSR, which, had there been no Vietnam War, would have healed long ago; and

7. assured the swift economic development of Japan and the non-Communist states of Southeast Asia by providing a security shield that allowed them to ignore temporarily the regional balance of power politics and funded their economic takeoff by pumping in vast amounts of offshore U.S. procurement money.

In actuality, of course, each of these momentous events was the product of a host of historical forces, and each was too complex to have had a single cause such as the Vietnam War. Still it is fascinating to speculate what would have been their history had there been no Vietnam War.

The Vietnam War itself began in the late 1950s. If a precise date is needed, May 1959 is as appropriate as any. That was the month in which the Fifteenth Plenum of the Lao Dong party met in Hanoi and ordered the start of armed *dau tranh* (struggle) in the South in the name of unification of the two Vietnams.

Soviet-Vietnam wartime relations can be divided into three phases: (1) from the start of the war until October 1964, (2) from October 1964 to February 1968 (the Tet offensive in South Vietnam); and (3) from February 1968 to the end of the war in April 1975. During the first phase, as we noted in the previous chapter, the association began on a high note and then declined precipitously at the end of the period. In phase two, the Khrushchev-ordered disengagement was halted and relations improved slowly and cautiously. After 1968 the relationship grew more intimate, although not necessarily more harmonious or more reliable for either party.

TURNAROUND

The nadir of the wartime relationship was reached in early 1964. Khrushchev's agonizing reappraisal and Hanoi's growing disillusionment collided in Moscow in February 1964 at a ten-day meeting between the DRV delegation (headed by Le Duan) and Khrushchev along with other high-level Soviet officials. Both sides set forth their respective grievances, which were then discussed item by item. Le Duan tried to patch up the Sino-Soviet dispute; Khrushchev demanded that the Vietnamese openly side with the USSR against China. Neither side got what it wanted. The Hanoi press (February 15) published what it implied was a joint communiqué, but was not; it was the first time the two Communist parties had met officially and not issued a joint communiqué. Hanoi's communiqué declared that during the meeting "opinions were exchanged, frankly and usefully . . . (because) in spite of the existence of divergences in the international communist movement, exchanges of view between parties are necessary."[1] The point could hardly have been expressed in bleaker terms.

The year 1964 saw a reduction in Soviet economic aid to the DRV along with a decline in Soviet exports to Vietnam. Shipments of Soviet heavy machinery and construction equipment in 1964 dropped 30 percent from 1963, which in turn had been down 20 percent from 1962.[2] At the same time, there was a steady warming in Hanoi's rhetoric about China. Foreign diplomats in Hanoi at the time say official public hostility for Moscow was scarcely contained.

This deterioration of relations halted abruptly with the departure from power of Nikita Khrushchev. He was deposed on October 13, 1964, by a task force of conspirators headed by Leonid Brezhnev following a complex political battle in the 170-man Central Committee[3] from which emerged rule by quadrumvirate: Brezhnev, Alexi Kosygin, Mikhail Suslov, and Nikolai Podgorny.

Hanoi's first acknowledgment was symbolic. The November issue of the party journal, *Hoc Tap*, was delivered to Hanoi bookstores on October 10; on October 14 all copies were pulled off the racks and replaced with a new edition. Excised out was an article by Hong Chuong, "Long Live the Soviet Revolution," a veiled attack on Khrushchev for what he had done to the spirit of that event, replaced by a neutral statement on the October Revolution by Le Duc Tho. Premier Pham Van Dong flew at once to Moscow for a "private briefing." In November Hanoi staged a "solidarity conference" between Vietnamese and Soviet academics. The Kosygin new year greeting, dated December 30, 1964, promised "all necessary aid" for the DRV in its struggle.

What could be called the start of full and intimate wartime relations came on February 7, 1965, the day the United States began sustained bombings and air strikes in North Vietnam. It could be argued that the proper date was the previous October, when Khrushchev was ousted, or December 1964, when the Hanoi High Command ordered a change of strategy in the South—from revolutionary guerrilla warfare to big-unit, high-technology warfare, the kind of combat possible only if backed by the armament factories of the USSR. But February 7 seems most appropriate since, until that day, the USSR's commitment to the war was still open-ended. The Kremlin leadership had already indicated to the DRV that Khrushchev's disengagement policy would be reversed, but policy options remained with respect to the war. After February 7, and following subsequent developments that month, the USSR was increasingly locked into an association in which policy choice was reduced either to full support or to total breach.

The kind of leadership that emerged in the Kremlin during the subsequent war years, collective leadership, by its nature tended to lack certitude. Khrushchev's replacements were aged bureaucrats of limited capacity for whom a succession crisis was always imminent, and they were plagued by the ghost of Stalin. The party bureaucracy, saddled with a stale and defensive ideology, was going through something of an identity crisis, and it became fashionable at the time to ask whether the USSR would last until 1984. The economic scene was beset by growing demands from the civilian sector and by a slackening growth rate. Alienation was high among the system's technocrats, who ran much of the internal machinery. Tension in the system was constant because of the cold war with the United States (particularly given its fresh memory of the Cuban missile crisis), an inability to settle the Sino-Soviet dispute, the Czechoslovakia syndrome, and poor party-to-party relations in many countries. Such was the context in Moscow.

Although the new leadership was determined to reverse disengagement from Vietnam, there was no quick plunge into new policy. Certain decisions were taken with respect to the Soviet quartermaster role, such as Soviet-provided air defenses, but for the first few years the relationship did not change appreciably.

It is still not clear exactly how supportive the USSR was during this period. Most observers believe that until 1968 Moscow was only reluctantly helpful. It is known that each military aid program was carefully negotiated and that supplies were categorized by the USSR to distinguish those for use in the North and in the South. Moscow was quite generous in supplying air defenses for the North but niggardly with arms for the South, such as crew-served weapons. Apparently this policy was based on the Soviet estimate that the war in the South could not be won and, hence, that support effort was something of a waste. This assessment changed in the aftermath of the 1968 Tet offensive when, for the first time, Moscow realized a Vietnamese Communist victory in the South was a possibility.

The Kremlin's dealings with Vietnam, of course, were conducted in a broad context. In particular, Moscow did some policy experimentation in the region. Relations with China worsened, but there was little the USSR could do about them. Existing governments in Southeast Asia appeared to be fairly durable, with some moving to the left. Late in the decade the USSR began a renewed effort to penetrate the region. Soviet diplomatic, naval, commercial, and cultural activity—sheer Soviet presence—increased steadily and at times even dramatically. Yet the effect was mostly motion without movement, and little was translated into clear Soviet advantage. Only later would a breakthrough come.

Early in this period DRV attitudes toward the USSR were not dissimilar from those of previous years. Hanoi wanted to be faithful to the "Rome of communism" but found it difficult because of Moscow's behavior. It regarded the USSR as the model for economic development and decisionmaking. Gradually, however, this sense of identification began to erode, and DRV leaders increasingly began to identify themselves with the Third World.

THE YEAR 1965

It was one of those rare years in history that witnesses a whole range of events that prove to be watersheds or historical landmarks.[4] For the USSR and Vietnam, 1965 was the most fateful single year in their relationship. During 1965 the battleline in the Sino-Soviet dispute was clearly drawn for Hanoi; the parameters of DRV logistic dependency on the USSR were fixed; and opportunity bloomed for the USSR to exploit Hanoi against China as a propaganda vehicle throughout the world. The basic psychological content of the Soviet-Vietnamese relationship also was established, and those fundamental attitudes and behavioral patterns—Vietnamese distrust and dissatisfaction stemming from unwanted dependency and Soviet puzzlement and irritation at Hanoi's cool reception of what Moscow perceives as supportive gestures—endure to this day.

By early 1965 the Communist military campaign in the South was being sharply intensified. North Vietnamese regulars were joining the PLAF[5] and moving down the Ho Chi Minh trail through Laos—which meant that country was being drawn inexorably deeper into the war. The smell of victory was in the air for Hanoi. In its 1965 New Year's Day official message it was stated flatly that victory would be achieved within twelve months.[6] Many observers in the South, including some in the U.S. Embassy in Saigon, regarded this to be a realistic estimate.

The Kremlin's assessment of the region as the year began appears to have been threefold: The Chinese intransigence that now dominated Soviet policy in Asia (and Vietnam) increased and became protracted; the regional balance of power in Southeast Asia was stable for the moment and ASEAN governments were reasonably durable; and the Vietnamese Communists were doing well militarily, which almost certainly would mean increased U.S. intervention. Probably the Kremlin's anticipated long-range scenario for Vietnam, assuming increased U.S. military involvement, was this: First would come a sharp military struggle that eventually would end in stalemate, neither side being able to prevail;

then would come some form of negotiated settlement; following the settlement there would be a drawdown of U.S. military forces from Indochina, though not complete disengagement; and the GVN would begin to drift toward the left. At the time this was the conventional "pessimistic" view of the outcome of the war held by most observers (the "optimistic" view being that the South Vietnamese and their allies would prevail decisively).

In this context, then, the Kremlin began to devise and advance its new policies in Vietnam and in Asia in general. The initial changes were mostly cosmetic. Kosygin, the careful cadre and true *homo sovieticus*, always much concerned with form and propriety, moved to put the Moscow-Hanoi relationship into neat order. Meanwhile, Brezhnev took to emphasizing the strategic importance to socialism of the Vietnamese struggle. As Brezhnev's political strength was drawn from military and party-military connections, he could not, as could Khrushchev, treat Vietnam as strategically insignificant.

An important first order of business was to disavow what had never been officially enunciated policy—Soviet "disengagement" from Vietnam. Presumably this was done through private assurances, for nothing was said on the matter in *Pravda*. The Chinese alone, as usual, sought to keep the record straight: "The new leaders of the CPSU came to realize that it was no longer advisable to copy Khrushchev's policy of 'disengagement' in its totality. So they switched to the policy of involvement, that is, of getting their hand in."[7]

In February 1965 Kosygin made his historic mission to Hanoi to negotiate and sign a defense pact. It was the start of a Soviet-Vietnamese military association that has become today an alliance in all but name.

Kosygin stopped in Beijing and made a very public appeal for a "united action" policy on Vietnam—that is, for joint and coordinated Sino-Soviet military assistance to Hanoi. He was unsuccessful. Then he went on to Hanoi, where the mission was met at the airport by 10,000 cheering Vietnamese. With Kosygin were Yuri Andropov, then a CPSU Central Committee secretary; V. V. Kuznetsov, USSR first deputy foreign minister and former ambassador to China; and three top military officials: M. Vershinin, the commander in chief of the air force and deputy minister of defense; Colonel-General E. Loginov, minister of civil aviation and a former head of Aeroflot; and Colonel-General G. S. Sidorovich, deputy chairman of the State Committee of the Council of Ministers for Foreign Economic Relations and specialist on Soviet military aid.

The official agenda of the five-day meeting (February 6–10) contained three items: Soviet military aid to the DRV, Soviet economic aid to the DRV, and the Sino-Soviet dispute. At the end came a nine-point joint communiqué, the key points being as follows:

(3) The Soviet Government again confirmed it would not remain indifferent to the safeguarding of the security of a fraternal Socialist State and would render the necessary assistance and support to North Vietnam.

(4) The two Governments reached proper agreement on the steps to be taken to strengthen the defensive potential of North Vietnam and agreed to hold regular consultations.

(5) The Soviet Union fully supports the South Vietnamese people's just heroic struggle for independence, democracy, peace and neutrality waged under the leadership of the National Liberation Front. . . .

(8) The two Governments declared that they will continue to fight tirelessly for strengthening cohesion between fraternal Socialist countries on the basis of Marxism-Leninism.

(9) The unity of the Socialist camp and the international Communist movement is an imperative condition for the victory of the working class in the struggle against imperialism and for peace, national independence, democracy and Socialism.[8]

Subsequently, the joint communiqué was treated by the USSR as a binding defense pact. It was duly ratified by the CPSU Central Committee on March 26, 1965.

At a mass rally on February 7, Kosygin pledged Soviet support for North Vietnam, "if aggressors dare to encroach on her independence and sovereignty." He added: "The Soviet Union will not remain indifferent to the destiny of a brotherly Socialist country and is ready to give North Vietnam all necessary assistance."[9] Kosygin's remarks were made a few hours prior to the first (February 7) U.S. air strikes. At a Soviet Embassy reception on February 8, Kosygin condemned the "blatant attack" on North Vietnam by U.S. planes and added, "Our international duty is to increase and consolidate the strength and national defense potential of the Socialist community."[10]

The airs strikes into North Vietnam apparently were coincidental and not timed by the United States as a message to Moscow. The press treatment around the world, of course, was that Kosygin had been "bombed by the Americans." All things considered, Kosygin's public response was relatively mild. The action, he said, violated the rules of the cold war between the United States and the USSR, a legalistic tack that infuriated the Chinese.

The policy on the Vietnam War unveiled by Kosygin during this trip continued essentially unchanged through the next ten years. Moscow would supply the Vietnamese Communists with all necessary war materiel, either from its own stocks or those obtained from East Europe. It would support any negotiated settlement acceptable to Hanoi. It would carry on a psychological warfare campaign to discourage U.S. escalation of the war and generally to villify the United States worldwide. Above all, it would use the war to seek ideological advantage over China, in Vietnam and throughout Asia.

This is not to say that Moscow's view of the war was always a confident one, or that its policies were consistently unambiguous. Soviet officials had the same problem other leaders have had: to chart the course of the war, anticipate its eventual outcome, and act accordingly.

In Hanoi, of course, there was relief that the USSR again was *engaged*, even if for less than admirable motives. The North Vietnamese knew full well that the chief Soviet purpose was to counter China. This meant that the USSR remained on the defensive in Hanoi, and with the Asian left in general. The Chinese continued to blacken Moscow's image by stressing the paucity of its aid to Vietnam and the timidity of its behavior. Beijing also charged that the USSR was a "war broker" in service to the United States. Most telling, perhaps, was the Chinese charge of Soviet racism, that Moscow sent only money whereas if it truly cared for its "yellow brothers" it would send troops. Repeatedly Beijing employed the theme that the USSR was without integrity and merely sought to "buy" Vietnamese goodwill rather than earn it. Probably the Hanoi Politburo shared this view to some extent. North Vietnamese cadres interviewed by the author in the South in 1969[11] tended to describe Moscow's assistance in unflattering terms. The USSR was acting correctly, but for the wrong reasons. The cadres believed that the USSR was *obliged* to assist because if it did not, it would lose all influence among the progressives of the world. They also contended that the USSR was in direct competition with China over war strategy and that the USSR could not allow Maoist doctrine to be proved successful. If this were to happen, they said, it would forever establish the superiority of Maoist thought, the efficacy of Mao's brand of war of national liberation, and the correctness of Mao's doctrine of controlled brink-manship against paper tigers, all of which would demonstrate the bankruptcy of Soviet thought. To counter the appealing Chinese strategy, this line of reasoning continued, the USSR sought by its presence, and with the kind of military hardware it put into the hands of the Vietnamese Communists, to lead them to root their strategy in technology, enmeshing them in a kind of combat that only the USSR could equip and supply.[12] This interpretation may not have extended to the Hanoi high command. But it is clear that the Hanoi leadership reasoned that the USSR was involved in the war because of the Chinese challenge.[13]

In the spring of 1965 the USSR launched a major worldwide political warfare campaign in support of the Vietnamese Communist cause. It was a classic textbook case of the art of disinformation. Built on the universal fear of nuclear war, the dominant theme was that unless the United States immediately reversed its policy in Vietnam and disengaged, the USSR (or, it was sometimes suggested, China) would dispatch troops to Vietnam, leading to superpower confrontation and horrendous carnage if not World War III. Much was implied, little was asserted. It was a campaign at the subliminal level, strumming nerves and raising the anxiety level of the Americans and their close friends. It was a whole-cloth propaganda campaign. We now know that neither the USSR nor China had any intention of dispatching troops into the war in South Vietnam. All the world could hear, however, was the drum-beat cacophony from Moscow:

- Kosygin, on February 16, warned the United States that North Vietnam raids could trigger World War III. "The situation is increasingly serious. . . . The USSR will not leave the DRV standing alone."[14]
- "The unheard of U.S. aggression in Vietnam may flare into the flame of a big war," said Marshal R. Y. Malinovsky, the Soviet defense minister on February 22.[15]
- Said Kosygin on February 27: "The Vietnam War will spread beyond its present boundaries unless the U.S. halts its aggressive actions."[16]
- The USSR has a diplomatic campaign to get three countries into war; China will enter the war if the bombing does not stop.[17]
- On March 23, Brezhnev hinted that Soviet volunteers might be sent to Vietnam. At a Red Square rally he said many Soviet citizens had offered to fight in Vietnam.
- The March 23 headline of the New York Times read: "Brezhnev Hints Force for Hanoi."[18]
- On March 25 Reuters reported that "China today offered volunteers for Vietnam."
- Soviet General Alexei Yepishev said on April 5 that "thousands of Soviet people, the personnel of whole units, have declared their readiness to go to Vietnam as volunteers to fight."[19]
- A TASS communiqué dated April 18th indicated that if the Vietnam War continued, "The USSR in case of necessity and given an appeal by the DRV, will consent to the departure for Vietnam of Soviet citizens who expressed a desire to fight."[20]
- Kosygin, on April 19, declared that continued U.S. bombing and air strikes in North Vietnam might lead to "retaliation in kind."[21]
- American academic Hans Morgenthau stated that "having just returned from Moscow I carry with me [a] major impression . . . the likelihood of Soviet military intervention."[22]

- American financier Cyrus Eaton visited the USSR in May and said he had been told in confidence by the Kremlin leaders that "the Vietnam War could escalate at any moment into world war."[23]
- A more or less flat prediction that the USSR would enter the Vietnam War came from academic Richard Hudson following his return from a two-and-a-half-week tour of the USSR in the spring of 1965.[24]
- Drew Pearson on June 2 predicted that the USSR would enter the Vietnam War. So did Marvin Kalb in a CBS television news broadcast on the same day.
- The *Washington Post* headline of June 18 read: "Moscow Hints of Supplying North Korean Troops for Vietnam."[25]

It was full scale psychological warfare. The USSR canceled the Moscow appearance of Mary Martin and her cast, who were on a world tour with the musical *Hello Dolly*. American youths serving as guides for a U.S. art exhibition in Leningrad were heckled daily by hired hoodlums for being "Vietnam liars." All in all, a most impressive demonstration of Soviet agit-prop cadres at work.

Lost in this Cassandra outpouring was the ever-present reality that there would be no intervention—a reality that went unnoticed even when asserted by credible sources. At the United Nations, Soviet delegates scoffed at the idea of imminent war. Private assurances in the Moscow diplomatic circle were common. They even appeared in the Soviet domestic press. *Pravda*, which discussed the subject frequently, stated explicitly there was to be no Soviet troop involvement in the Vietnam War. The rationale offered was that a war of national liberation was an internal affair that must be conducted by those wishing to be liberated. Outside fraternal brothers could supply assistance but could not and should not take part in combat. To send in troops, *Pravda* argued, would be tantamount to "forcibly imposing one's will upon other peoples."[26]

To its credit the U.S. government was not rattled by this campaign. It took measure of the Soviet-Vietnamese relationship and concluded early on that there was no prospect of Soviet troop intervention. However, throughout the war there were continual reports of Soviet participation in the fighting in Vietnam. For instance, the *London Daily Telegraph* (January 11, 1966) asserted that Colonel Gagarin, the cosmonaut, "publicly admitted" that Soviet troops were fighting in Vietnam. Reports continued on the imminent departure of such forces. General Alexei Yepishev, chief of the Main Political Administration of the Soviet Armed Forces, in April 1966 declared: "Thousands of Soviet people, the personnel of whole units, have declared their readiness to go to Vietnam as volunteers to fight for the freedom of the much-suffering Vietnamese people."[27] Reports from Bonn, West Germany, claimed the presence in North Vietnam of 200 East German missile experts who "wear Russian uniforms and speak Russian and man anti-aircraft missiles around Hanoi."[28]

Near the end of 1965 the Kremlin began to suggest to North Vietnam that there might be other limits to Soviet involvement. The Alexander Shelepin mission to Hanoi in December 1965 stressed the need for joint socialist world efforts to fund the Vietnam War, which was becoming increasingly expensive. This was in part an anti-Chinese gambit, but Shelepin indicated the USSR was interested in common funding even if China did not participate. Clearly he wanted other socialist nations to pick up part of the bill. Shelepin also advanced what appeared to be a sharpened political settlement offer. It was portrayed in some diplomatic quarters as a Soviet ultimatum to Hanoi: Negotiate or no aid. This was not the fact, but it suggested to Hanoi leaders that the USSR was increasingly serious about negotiations and that they must therefore be careful in handling the matter. It was necessary for Hanoi to reject the Moscow proposal because, although it offered a detailed mechanism for a political settlement, it relegated unification to the category of problems to be settled at some later date. That, of course, was unacceptable to Hanoi. It may be that Shelepin and the Kremlin leaders expected a rejection but still regarded their proposal as a useful way of suggesting limits of Soviet commitment.

In sum, the year 1965 established the outline of the USSR-DRV relationship, which was to remain essentially unchanged for the next ten years. If Soviet partnership was judged less than adequate, and such was the view in Hanoi, it was the perception that shaped Vietnamese attitudes toward the USSR throughout the war and in turn became the legacy of the postwar relationship.

DIFFERING OBJECTIVES, CONTENDING STRATEGIES

The Soviet-Vietnamese association during the Vietnam War, as is often the case with allies in wartime, was a relationship divided by common purposes. What made it so exceedingly complicated was the fact of the continuing Sino-Soviet dispute.

Moscow and Hanoi, of course, had their separate national interests, which automatically meant differing (if not conflicting) policy objectives along with alternate (if not contending) strategies to achieve respective goals. The USSR, as a superpower, had national interests everywhere; these were complex, often difficult to manage; hence Moscow was constantly obliged to balance its interests in Vietnam with interests elsewhere. Hanoi faced no such complexity. It had a single purpose, the holy crusade to unite North and South Vietnam under its banner, and a single criterion for USSR relations, to ensure continued support of the cause.

Throughout the war, Soviet policies were cast ambiguously. There is little indication that the USSR was confident it knew the direction events would take. Nor was there ever a clear definition of Soviet purpose. As Donald Zagoria neatly expressed it (in a conversation with the author), policies were more clearly defined in terms of what Moscow sought to avoid rather than what it sought to gain. It sought to avoid entrapment; it sought to avoid the unexpected; it sought to avoid the unknown, which could become an entanglement. The USSR held the war at arm's length, always treating gingerly any decisions concerning it. It could, and did, accept as appropriate the DRV goal of unification but seemed to doubt that this could be achieved.

Hanoi's strategy to achieve unification passed through several stages. Its initial strategy of revolutionary guerrilla war employed what is called armed *dau tranh* and political *dau tranh*, the hammer and anvil that would destroy the enemy.[29] The organizational instrument employed was the united front—one of the great political inventions of the twentieth century—named the National Liberation Front (NLF) of South Vietnam. The NLF was to oust the existing South Vietnam government, form its own provisional government, and then merge with the North in unification. This required that Hanoi keep the NLF on short rein to prevent repetition of the Viet Minh War experience, in which it won the war and lost the peace. The Hanoi leadership was determined that the independent-minded southerners in the NLF would never get an opportunity to go their own separate way.

With the arrival of the Americans and other foreign troops to aid the GVN cause, the strategic problem faced by Hanoi came to be seen as two-staged. First, the U.S. and foreign presence had to be eliminated, either forced out or induced to leave. Then the southern opposition to unification—mainly the South Vietnamese in the GVN, but also certain elements in the NLF—has to be overcome. The stated DRV position on U.S. departure—which the USSR was obliged to echo—was not simply that the United States must quit Vietnam but that it must do so in such a way that opposition by the remaining Vietnamese would be impossible. In effect, Hanoi's price for allowing U.S. withdrawal was that the Americans had to unilaterally disarm South Vietnam on their way out. That was the meaning of the constantly reiterated DRV position that peace could come to Vietnam only if the United States withdrew all of its military and civilian personnel *and* all U.S. military materiel. The war, of course, was being fought by the GVN almost entirely with U.S.

weapons and hardware. There was no ambiguity in Hanoi's position here—nor in Soviet support for it—for DRV representatives asserted the demand daily at the Paris talks; but somehow the qualification of unilateral disarmament never registered with observers around the world, who heard only the cry for peace.

The Kremlin's estimate throughout most of the war years apparently was that neither decisive victory nor decisive defeat for Hanoi was probable. Rather, there would be an indeterminate outcome that might eventually lead to unification. Rather deft footwork was required, therefore, to position the USSR so as to prepare it for either contingency. Moscow supported the Vietnamese Communist cause by funding the military campaign to achieve unification; but it also maintained a position favorable for a negotiated settlement in which unification would be postponed, perhaps indefinitely. Some have argued that the difference in objectives between Hanoi and Moscow lay in the fact of war; that is, the Vietnamese Communists wanted *war* to achieve unification while the USSR simply wanted *warfare* that bled the United States, bogged it down, and ruined its image around the world.

As the war dragged on, Hanoi leaders increasingly came to regard the Sino-Soviet dispute as a major impediment to victory. A visceral reaction developed, first ill-concealed irritation, eventually scarcely contained outrage—a fact never appreciated by outsiders. This sour wartime view of the disputants is implied in some of the writings at the time and by the behavior of the DRV leaders at Hanoi diplomatic functions. It is found most clearly in the testimony of prisoners and defectors held in the South. The author spent much of the summer of 1967 in POW and *Chieu Hoi* (literally, "open arms") camps in South Vietnam interviewing North Vietnamese cadres about the Sino-Soviet dispute. The opinion held by the 100 or so individuals interviewed was consistent: Neither China nor the USSR was supporting "the revolution" to the extent they should. Such support as that made available was for the wrong reason. Vital weaponry was withheld. The overriding point these cadres made was not how much China and the USSR had done for Vietnam but how much they had not done. This complaint of inadequate commitment was expressed by all without significant deviation. It led to the inescapable conclusion that the same perception, in somewhat more sophisticated form, extended upward to the Hanoi Command and the Politburo itself.[30]

It is difficult to track the strategic thinking of military analysts and others in Moscow at the time, or to determine their evaluation of events and trends during the course of the war. It is not even certain that the military institutes in Moscow made much serious effort to monitor the war, a conclusion supported by subsequent Soviet military behavior in Afghanistan and elsewhere.

The absence of data may be due to the natural lack of candor in USSR military writing. In part, it is certainly due to the influence of ideology. For instance, in Soviet doctrinal writing on the war it is consistently argued that Chinese troop involvement would be a strategic error, despite the fact that at times it would have made sense militarily. The difficulty in exploring what might be called the Soviet military science view of the Vietnam War is that there is no great body of published military writing dealing specifically with the strategy and tactics used by Hanoi. Almost all discussion is cast in the general context of wars of national liberation. There is an enormous amount about this subject published in Moscow, some of it applicable to Vietnam, some not—but one can never be sure whether a Vietnam application is intended.

Hanoi military writers went along with the idea of treating the Vietnam War and wars of national liberation as somewhat interchangeable, although they probably regarded this parallelism as contrived and artificial. Today the approach permits them to claim extensive Soviet interest and support, since they can link everything written on wars of national liberation to Vietnam. An early example is the treatment afforded the Lao Dong party's 1959 decision to begin armed *dau tranh* in the South. A year after the decision was made, a Communist Parties Conference in Moscow produced a statement endorsing the idea of wars of national liberation. The Hanoi media chose to interpret the statement as an endorsement of the Lao Dong party decision: "The (Moscow) statement clearly points out that the colonialists will never grant freedom to colonies, never voluntarily quit the countries they are exploiting. It also points out that the people should wrest independence by appropriate means, peaceful or otherwise."[31] Actually the Moscow statement does not endorse the Lao Dong decision; nor does it endorse a war of national liberation for Vietnam. It does not even mention Vietnam by name.

Soviet thinking about insurgencies was not nearly as advanced as that of the Chinese. Soviet military advisers in Hanoi had the advantage of not having brought with them a great body of guerrilla war dogma and were therefore free to agree with Hanoi strategists if they chose to do so. Even so, there were doctrinal problems. For the most part these turned on the relationship between armed and political *dau tranh*, which for the USSR involved supplying necessary military hardware. The proper balance between armed and political *dau tranh* had to do with allocation of resources such as war materiel and manpower, and with military priorities. The two basic options always were either emphasis on armed *dau tranh* (which could be guerrilla warfare or regular force warfare) or emphasis on political *dau tranh*, which involved a mixture of violence (politics with guns), proffered political settlement, and protracted conflict. Initially the USSR stressed political *dau tranh*, then switched to greater use of armed *dau tranh* after the 1968 Tet Offensive. Political *dau tranh* would be less costly for the USSR, but not if it meant fifty years of protracted conflict. Soviet strategists may have concluded that armed *dau tranh* in net terms was cheaper. Or it may be that they became convinced of the efficacy of the Vietnamese strategy, in which case their earlier doubts were overcome.

China's strategic advice was more extensive and more complex. Its basis was that the Vietnam War was unique, quite distinct from earlier limited wars. Vietnam was fighting a "people's war," which meant it must be fought in certain ways. A basic principle of people's war was that the people themselves were the instrument of war, meaning that victory would come through proper organizational, motivational, and mobilizational efforts, which had to be made by the people themselves and not by outsiders. Such a doctrine, of course, gave the Chinese maximum flexibility: They could dispatch as many troops as was in their interest and fall back on people's war doctrine argument if they chose to hold them back. The Chinese troops that were sent to Vietnam served Chinese domestic transportation needs almost exclusively. The only rail connection between China's remote Yunnan province and southern Guangxi province was the railroad line that ran through northern Vietnam. To keep this line open the Chinese had, at the height of the war, assigned some 60,000 troops to Vietnam, almost all of them railway maintenance and storage personnel or anti-aircraft crews defending the railway marshaling yards.

I have never found plausible the frequently encountered assertion that the DRV did not want Chinese troops in the war because once in they would refuse to leave Vietnam. A contrary case can be built, that the DRV in 1965-1966 schemed to entrap the Chinese into the war but that the Chinese understood the game and refused to play it. In retrospect, it is clear that China saw Vietnam as a trap and had no intention of repeating its Korean War mistake. However, to this day the opposite perception—what might be called the Fulbright Red Hoard intervention myth—persists among Americans.

There is considerable irony in the changing wartime postures of China and the USSR. Early in the war China called for a clearcut Hanoi victory with no partial solutions or anything that smacked of *status quo ante*. Only a doctrinally pure resolution of the struggle would reassert the validity of people's war. Moscow on the other hand seemed amicable to any outcome that would leave the USSR in a preeminent position in Vietnam. By the end of the war China was almost desperately hoping for stalemate while the USSR, smelling the blood of total victory, urged the Vietnamese forward. Initially China wanted no political settlement of any sort, whereas the USSR held that such an arrangement would be a useful way station en route to the ultimate goal of communization of Indochina. By the end of the war these two positions had been reversed. At the start of the war China hoped that the United States would be driven from the region, its credibility as a dependable, effective ally destroyed. By the end of the war the Chinese were hoping that some U.S. presence would remain. Initially the USSR hoped to see the United States discredited in Indochina but not expelled, for that would leave the field to the Chinese; this view changed when the USSR realized it might be able to replace both the United States and China.

If the DRV's bilateral relation with the USSR during the war generally progressed from poor to good, the relationship with China was a steady downhill slide. Just as we now know that the Sino-Soviet dispute began earlier and went deeper than the world realized at the time, so too did the Sino-Vietnamese split. In the 1950s there were difficulties, but they were well papered over. By the mid-1960s the divisions had become serious. Near the end of the war, in the early 1970s, it was clear that China did not want a decisive Hanoi victory. However, it was never able to bring itself to do those things that might have prevented this outcome, inhibited as it was by the Sino-Soviet dispute.

If we are to believe an angry General Vo Nguyen Giap, China collaborated with the United States against North Vietnam throughout the war:

> The Chinese government told the U.S. that if the latter did not threaten or touch China, then China would do nothing to prevent the attacks (on Vietnam). It was really like telling the United States that it could bomb Vietnam at will, as long as there was no threat to the Chinese border. . . . We felt that we had been stabbed in the back. . . .
>
> Later when the U.S. began systematically to bomb North Vietnam, the Soviet Union proposed to send air units and missile forces to defend Vietnam. It was the Chinese leaders that prevented it from doing so.
>
> We had to resolve the situation in a way which would not affect our war of resistance against the Americans. For this reason we could not publicly denounce the Chinese, nor could we reveal the Soviet proposal. . . .
>
> After Nixon signed the Shanghai Communique, this showed that the Chinese leaders were clamoring for an American presence in Southeast Asia, even in South Vietnam.

When we recount all these events and link them to the war
in the southwest [i.e., Kampuchea] we can see the treachery of
the Chinese leaders.[32]

China's attitude toward the Vietnam War can be summed up thus:
It wanted the Vietnamese Communists to win (and, more than the
USSR, believed ultimately they would win), but it also insisted that the
war must never endanger China. This meant the DRV must never do
anything that could provoke a Chinese confrontation with the United
States. China stood willing to supply all *necessary* military and economic
aid to North Vietnam—the quarrel here being over what was necessary,
which in turn was a reflection of conflicting military doctrines. China
did not want to get entrapped in the war and consequently preached
the sermon of self-reliance inherent in the Maoist concept of revolutionary
guerrilla war. Although it would not admit to this, China also was
governed by a sense of its own limits of power, realizing it was able
to control neither the DRV nor the course of the war. The Chinese (or
at least Mao Zedong) wanted to prove the superiority of the people's
war doctrine. Finally, the touchstone for Chinese policy throughout was
the Sino-Soviet dispute. If forced to choose between the war and its
own interests in the dispute, it invariably chose the latter. Such is
approximately what a Chinese historian speaking candidly would say
about the Chinese role in the Vietnam War. A Vietnamese historian
would probably agree basically with this but would describe the fundamental Chinese orientation as being a mix of ideological commitment
and selfish pursuit of Chinese national interest, the latter dominating;
that despite considerable assistance,[33] Chinese aid always was conditional
and never certain; and that the Chinese did not actually care deeply
about the Vietnamese unification cause but, instead, were moved chiefly
by their hostility toward the USSR.

The respective Chinese and Vietnamese perceptions can be refined,
and the major fundamental contradictions that characterize Sino-Vietnamese wartime relations can be isolated.

First, the DRV wanted, and China did not, a Communist world
united front on Vietnam. This did not necessarily require an end to the
Sino-Soviet dispute, but it did call for agreement on the basic course
of action and a single logistic system.

Second, the DRV wanted, and felt it had the right to, total Chinese
commitment, which it never got. It never got infantry troops nor the
volume of aid it felt it needed. Chinese support was always reserved
and consistently used as a bargaining device in the Sino-Soviet dispute.
During the Cultural Revolution, when aid from China dwindled because

of internal preoccupation, DRV leaders were furious over what they considered to be Mao's mad irresponsibility.

Third, the DRV wanted to take high risks to win the war, including moves that could endanger China such as the use of Chinese combat troops, or at least a large Chinese backup force in North Vietnam.

Finally, there were sharp differences over strategy, turning on the proper balance between armed struggle and political struggle in terms of resource allocation, priorities, and primacy of emphasis. China, in Hanoi's view, perceived three possible strategies open to North Vietnam: protracted conflict/people's war strategy; political settlement strategy (more correctly, political-diplomatic struggle strategy); and big unit warfare strategy. The Chinese advocated the first of these, Hanoi believed, because it was closest to orthodox Maoist thinking, because it minimized the risk to China, and because it was the least dependent on Soviet arms factories. China did not object to the second strategy in principle, only to the fact that extensive Soviet diplomatic effort would be required for it to work. The third strategy, of course, had to be built around Soviet aid, which made it unacceptable. The Chinese began the war advocating the first strategy but gradually shifted to the second, chiefly because it was the only feasible alternative to the third strategy (which the DRV embraced after 1968) that would forge a bond of dependency between Hanoi and Moscow.

BIG-UNIT WAR YEARS (1966–1973)

Soviet-Vietnamese relations during the heart of the war—the period between the arrival of U.S. combat troops and the Paris Agreements—became something of a roller coaster ride for the North Vietnamese. The war increased in intensity and magnitude, inexorably drawing in the USSR. Military shipments increased. Talk of a negotiated settlement fluctuated. The USSR became in effect a co-belligerent, even suffering some casualties; Soviet officials much later said "more than a few hundred" Soviet citizens died in Vietnam during the war.[34] *Krasnaya Zvezda* (Moscow), in an article dated December 11, 1967, noted that Soviet military instructors occasionally operated side by side with North Vietnam missile men.[35] There were persistent reports of Soviet military officers making clandestine visits to South Vietnam. A PLAF defector named Bui Cong Tuong told the author (in November 1970) that in April 1967 a Soviet general and four other military observers had landed by submarine in Kien Hoa province and for four hours had visited Cho Thom village (Mo Cay district), which was the home village of Mrs. Nguyen Thi Binh, the NLF chief negotiator at the Paris talks. The fact that Caucasians had been to the village was later confirmed in interviews with villagers, but neither the nationality of the five nor the fact that they came by submarine was ever established. Tuong said that prior to the arrival of these people, the PLAF had built an elaborate fake "regimental headquarters" in the jungle to impress the Soviet visitors.

During much of 1967, Moscow's attention to the war seemed to stray, in part because of problems arising in the Mideast, although there is no reason to believe this had any serious impact on Hanoi's conduct of the war. There was increased interest from Moscow during and after the 1968 Tet Offensive, then the Soviet war spirit clearly began to wane. By 1971 the Moscow mass media was no longer describing the war as a heroic and glorious fraternal enterprise nor welcoming the opportunity for the USSR to meet its destiny. Rather, the war became an obligation, the USSR's "necessary duty." Illustrative of the more sober attitude is this *Pravda* commentary:

> The fraternal peoples of the Soviet Union and Vietnam are linked
> by relations of friendship and cooperation which are based on
> unity of objectives, common ideology, and on principles of
> socialist internationalism. The Soviet Union, loyal to its
> international duty, has given and is now giving the DRV all-
> round support and assistance both in peaceful economic building
> and in the rigorous military ordeals.[36]

Hanoi leaders were aware that the USSR (and China) might tire of the burden of war, and concern grew that the two might not be held in an alliance of close support. Hanoi long had been forced to suffer Soviet experimentation with détente; now China was moving down the same road. This situation represented both a psychological danger (Hanoi abandoned by its two allies) and a material threat (a U.S.-engineered cutoff of military and economic aid): "The U.S. aims to achieve a compromise [deal] with big powers [USSR, PRC] in an attempt to make smaller countries [DRV] bow to U.S. arrangements."[37]

The Americans, said Hanoi, spray the "toxic gas of chauvinism abroad to play socialist countries one against the other," and it was now reaching "opportunistic heads" in Moscow and Beijing.[38] Hanoi's ultimate fear was that circumstances would combine in such a way that both the USSR and China would find it in their respective national interests to pressure North Vietnam into a settlement that did not yield unification.

The Soviet Union, after the U.S. "opening" to China in 1971, attempted to pressure Hanoi into signing a Treaty of Friendship and Cooperation, which would clearly be anti-Chinese. But Hanoi had still not given up on China, and the effort failed (it did, however, succeed seven years later). The meaning of the U.S.-China rapprochement, said Moscow, was that the Chinese, having failed to provoke the United States into war against the USSR, was now attempting to instigate one through manipulation. Moscow also asserted publicly that some secret agreement had been reached between the United States and China concerning the Vietnam War. The Americans' move added new fuel to the fire of the Sino-Soviet dispute. Increasingly, it seemed to Hanoi, the USSR was becoming preoccupied with other matters. It was attempting to improve its relations with Indonesia. It was engaged in a spirited diplomatic competition with the Chinese in Eastern Europe. There was a step-up of Soviet activity in the Mideast and the start of the Soviet naval build-up in the Mediterranean and Indian Oceans. Soviet diplomats were everywhere in Asia attempting to sell the Brezhnev Asian security concept. At the same time, Moscow assured Hanoi that it was not losing interest in the war and would never allow its other interests to betray Vietnam. The USSR realized its vulnerability here and feared that the Chinese could use the situation to improve their position in Hanoi. High-level Soviet officials were sent in a steady flow to North Vietnam to assuage anxiety; most important of these was president Nikolai Podgorny (October 1971), the highest-ranking Soviet visitor since Kosygin in 1965.

The last year of full-scale war in Vietnam—1972—was a difficult one for Soviet-Vietnamese relations. That was the year of the Easter Offensive by the North Vietnamese forces; the year the United States mined the waterway channels of North Vietnam and began intensive air strikes on the DRV transportation system; and the year of the negotiations that led to the Paris Agreements. It was a vastly changed scene, one that loosened Hanoi's hold on the USSR.

Part of the changed scene was Richard Nixon as president of the United States. His views had long been known in Hanoi as well as in Moscow, and only he, of all U.S. presidents involved in Vietnam, was considered to be a true Vietnam War hardliner. Lyndon Johnson, regarded by many Americans as a super-hawk on the war, was never seen as such in Hanoi. The North Vietnamese evaluation of Nixon stemmed from the 1964 presidential election (Lyndon Johnson versus Barry Goldwater), which was seen as a test between hawk and dove in which Johnson, the dove, won. Nixon's campaigning on Goldwater's behalf and his statements on the war during the next four years made it clear to Hanoi that Nixon was as hawkish as Goldwater, and also more clever. Today Hanoi officials probably would judge Richard Nixon to have been the most formidable foe of all the U.S. presidents they have faced.

Nixon's trip to Moscow in May 1972 shocked the North Vietnamese, even though they knew of it in advance. Nixon's visit to Beijing the previous July had been an enormous affront for Hanoi—certainly it is rare for the hated leader of a hated enemy country to be received as an honored guest by one's close ally—but the Vietnamese leaders considered this the sort of perfidious behavior to be expected from the Chinese. For Moscow to embrace Nixon was much more grievous. It was also hypocritical, for the USSR had vehemently denounced the Chinese for inviting Nixon to Beijing. Nor were the Hanoi leaders mollified by Moscow's rationale: that some good would redound to the DRV from the Nixon trip to Moscow. Members of the Nixon delegation in Moscow were told privately by their hosts that Soviet and Vietnamese officials had exchanged heated words over the invitation. The Vietnamese sharply criticized the USSR the day Nixon arrived, characterizing the invitation as "setting national interests against the interests of world revolution . . . seeking to serve their own [Soviet] national selfishness."[39]

The Americans, meantime, were attempting to pressure the USSR on the Vietnam War. President Nixon, on May 9, 1972 (this was at the time of the People's Army of Vietnam [PAVN] Easter Offensive), said the USSR must "choose between détente with the U.S. and support of Hanoi's full-scale aggression in the South," adding that the United States and the USSR were on the threshold of a new relationship but further progress was blocked by Hanoi's intransigence. Thus, he firmly linked the Vietnam War with improved U.S.-USSR relations. The Nixon view was that the USSR should not be free to provide military assistance to its ally for the purpose of taking over a U.S. ally. The rule in the big-power game, he indicated, was that one big power can help an ally improve its defenses but not to launch invasion.[40] Earlier the linkage approach had been used by Henry Kissinger in his April 1972 trip to Moscow. Kissinger indicated that progress on détente depended on a satisfactory outcome of the war. The USSR countered with the proposal that the United States and the DRV should return to the conference table for private (i.e., secret) talks; and that if the United States agreed, the USSR would see to it that the DRV attended. The bargain was struck, but Moscow then discovered it could not deliver Hanoi. Rather than sending negotiators to Paris, the North Vietnamese responded by launching the biggest military assault of the war, the 1972 Easter Offensive.[41]

It later became clear that General Giap had expected the Easter Offensive to break the back of South Vietnam's defenses and begin an unraveling process within the GVN that would inevitably lead to a North Vietnamese victory. The Kremlin marshals may have agreed with this assessment; certainly it was the kind of military assault the Soviet Army would have launched. However, the Easter Offensive failed not because Moscow was found wanting but because the South Vietnamese outfought the invaders from the North.

In the last months before the Paris Agreements (February 1973), as the war was winding down but with delay after delay, the USSR grew increasingly weary of the whole business. It reacted with remarkable calm to the U.S. mining of Haiphong's waterways, which marooned ten Soviet freighters in the harbor. It even displayed some public impatience with North Vietnamese behavior. The result was that for the first few months after the Paris Agreements were signed, a distinct coolness permeated Soviet-Vietnamese relations.

POLITICAL SETTLEMENT

Soviet-Vietnamese relations involving negotiations to end the war, as with all of the contending parties, existed in a world of their own. The decade-long history of this effort is a record of tangled duplicity and cross-purposes, of false starts and dead ends, of tortuous rhetoric and obscure semantics, of dissembling and self-serving hypocrisy. In retrospect it is clear, as it was clear to a few at the time, that a true political settlement—that is, one involving a genuine compromise—was never possible. North Vietnam wanted unification under its banner and South Vietnam did not. Wherein could there be a compromise? The *act* of negotiating, of course, was an acceptable tactic—Hanoi strategists called it the "talk-talk, fight-fight" tactic—because it was an integral part of political *dau tranh* strategy.

However, Hanoi's memory of betrayal by its allies at Geneva in 1954 was undimmed, and the Politburo was determined never again to trust the fate of unification to the conference table. Most observers in Paris seemed unable or unwilling to recognize this fact and over the years persisted in reading into DRV moves forthcoming behavior and a conciliatory attitude where none existed.

Hanoi's refusal to accept a political settlement was not the result of rigid unreasonable stubbornness in the Vietnamese character or some fanatic intransigence. It was simply a product of Hanoi's objective—unification. Some goals in warfare are given to negotiated compromise. Conflict over political power and control of territory are, at least in theory, negotiable, as these can be shared or divided. But unification by its very nature was an indivisible objective. A settlement short of unification would have been accepted in Hanoi only if the alternative was annihilation. Hence a genuine settlement, involving compromise, never was in the realm of reality.[42]

The USSR early in the war was manifestly uninterested in any sort of political settlement, perhaps because of Communist world politics or because it was thought futile to try to persuade the North Vietnamese to accept a settlement short of unification. In any event Moscow simply echoed the DRV's hostility to the idea. Later it grew more interested, but even then was constrained, being locked into Hanoi's no-negotiation position. The Sino-Soviet dispute played a part; initially China strongly opposed negotiations, probably one reason the USSR publicly toyed with the idea. Many Americans at the time demonstrated a peculiar naivete about Moscow's stance on a negotiated settlement; or perhaps it was a case of wishful thinking, an attribution to the Soviets of a willingness to help the United States end the war on favorable, or at least acceptable, terms.

The subject of negotiated settlement was of course discussed frequently during the war by the USSR and the DRV. The first serious discussion, in 1964, involved an initiative from the United Nations. Secretary General U Thant sent a message to Ho Chi Minh suggesting that Ho and U.S. officials meet privately in a session that U Thant would arrange. Probably U Thant sent the message at Moscow's suggestion. Ho Chi Minh replied that he was willing to meet. As the DRV since 1958 had been highly antagonistic toward the UN,[43] Ho's affirmative reply was probably the result of Moscow pressure. U Thant's efforts got nowhere, however, for the United States rejected the proposal.

A case can be made that in February 1965 the USSR mounted an eleventh-hour effort to interest the DRV in a political settlement. It was at this very time that the Americans were making their fateful decision to send ground troops and planes into the war. Although it cannot be documented, some observers believe that the purpose of Kosygin's February 1965 mission to Hanoi was to head off such a decisive development—not, as it was officially explained at the time, "to strengthen the defense capacity of the DRV." While Kosygin was in Hanoi the Americans bombed North Vietnam, but he and the Soviet mass media publicly downplayed this provocative act. Such would hardly have been his reaction had he come to arm North Vietnam for war; it was very much the behavior of one who has come in search of a way to head off the impending escalation of war. What lends credence to this thesis is that it was learned much later that the Hanoi Politburo was beset at the time by serious apprehension over the military devastation about to be unleashed on the DRV. The leaders were uncertain, if not badly divided, as how best to cope with the threat. Some in the Politburo—Pham Van Dong is believed to have been among them—advocated the endorsement of a Soviet exploratory effort to determine the U.S. price (i.e., what it would require from North Vietnam) for not dispatching combat troops to South Vietnam or beginning air attacks on the DRV. This was opposed by hardliners who, according to this interpretation, engineered the NLF attack on the U.S. installation in the southern highland town of Pleiku that triggered the retaliatory U.S. airstrike on the North and foreclosed the option of sounding out the Americans. If ever there was an opportunity during the war—and probably there was not—to settle it through negotiations, it was in early 1965.[44] Later that year Moscow suggested to France that an international conference on Vietnam be staged. At the same time, the USSR began acting as an informal conduit between Hanoi and Washington over a U.S.-initiated effort to get the DRV to stop supporting the NLF in South Vietnam. Nothing came of either of these ventures. In November the subject of negotiated settlement was again taken up in Moscow discussions with Premier Pham Van Dong, Party Secretary Le Duan, and General Vo Nguyen Giap. Soviet officials suggested that at the very least the DRV should clarify its policy on a political settlement beyond the vague position outlined in the DRV's Four-Point peace plan of April 1965, which merely called for an end to hostilities to be followed by talks. The USSR also urged Hanoi officials to be more receptive publicly to the idea of negotiations, whatever the actual policy might be. At the DRV's insistence, the USSR agreed not to engage in bilateral discussions with the United States on ending the war, a proposal given some currency at the time.

During the next three years, until the Paris talks began in 1968, Soviet commentators suggested from time to time that negotiations be inaugurated. The sense of these comments seemed to be that a bold, Soviet-led initiative would somehow start a chain reaction that would end the war. Much of the private discussion between the two nations throughout the war concerned the possibility of negotiations in exchange for a halt to U.S. air attacks on North Vietnam. The USSR later claimed that an agreement on this had been worked out between the DRV and the USSR in 1967, but that it was subsequently sabotaged by China.

The DRV's decision to go to Paris and begin talks with the United States[45] appears to have caught the USSR off guard, even though Hanoi had been intimating interest for several months.[46] The Kremlin moved quickly to shift from its cool attitude toward talks to full endorsement,[47] and during the next few weeks it assisted in making the protocol arrangements in Paris.

At the same time the USSR began a series of spoiling gestures aimed at the emerging temperate mood. War shipments, Moscow announced, were to be increased. Soviet diplomats at the UN began arguing the Vietnamese Communist cause in excessively shrill terms. The Soviet press gave increased prominence to American critics of the war, such as Robert Kennedy and William Fulbright, apparently in an effort to raise the antiwar temperature in the United States. The Moscow press began attacking President Johnson with personal invective, something not done before. All of this seemed calculated either to restrict U.S. freedom of initiative in negotiations or to reduce the chance of their success. Possibly Moscow was not sure it wanted a settlement of the Vietnam War.

After the Paris talks had been under way for a year or so, there began to develop among respected Kremlinologists in the West the belief that Soviet leaders were changing their view of the Vietnam War, that they were moving toward the conclusion that the USSR no longer had much to gain in support of this costly venture, and that the continuation of the war chiefly served China. The reasoning went like this: The war is useful as it serves to tar the image of the United States and as a symbol of USSR solidarity with world communism that prevents others from turning toward Chinese leadership. Both of these objectives have been accomplished. The war is very expensive. The USSR has gotten out of it all that is possible. Now it should seek an end. Further, there is the ever-present threat of Soviet-U.S. confrontation. Finally, continued war will polarize the region, driving all of Southeast Asia into the arms of either the United States or China.

The Soviet thinking coincided with, or was a result of, several other developments. North Vietnam's spirit and determination were flagging. Factionalism was rising in the Hanoi Politburo. China was coming to view negotiations with interest for the first time. The United States was putting "linkage" pressure on the USSR to contribute to ending the war.

By mid-1972 the DRV bluntly acknowledged it was beleaguered. *Nhan Dan* complained that both the USSR and China were "big powers that have succumbed to the Machiavellian policy of reconciliation with U.S. imperialists . . . who are now attempting to lure us into the path of compromise."[48]

By late 1972 the chief issue in negotiations at Paris had become the division of political power in South Vietnam and specifically the future of Nguyen Van Thieu and his government. Moscow began asserting rather authoritatively that if Thieu himself would depart, Hanoi would accept a three-way power sharing arrangement in the South (i.e., the GVN, the People's Revolutionary Government (PRG), and the so-called Third Force). It was apparently during the Podgorny visit to Hanoi in June 1972 that this proposal was thrashed out. Hanoi, under pressure, accepted this risky road to unification after first extracting from the USSR a promise of lavish postwar economic aid. On this basis events moved ahead at the conference table. In the subsequent negotiations Hanoi lost on the Thieu departure, but it won a more important point:

that there need not be withdrawal of PAVN troops from the South. It was a compromise solution neither side liked.

How much Soviet coercion was involved in getting the DRV to sign the Paris Agreements is still unclear. The prevailing view—that Moscow first opposed negotiations, then came to favor them, then forced Hanoi into line—greatly oversimplifies a highly complex situation. Soviet attitude was a major factor in Hanoi's decision. But there were other factors as well: the demonstration of "smart" bombing in December 1972 (a destructiveness the PAVN High Command did not realize was possible); the growing stability of the GVN; the success of the Vietnamization (U.S. withdrawal) program; war weariness in North Vietnam; factional and doctrinal disputes within the Hanoi Politburo; the sheer cost of the war; and finally the prospect of achieving unification through political *dau tranh* strategy.

Whatever else they were, the Paris Agreements were no victory for Hanoi, and were certainly not regarded there as such. The Agreements did leave DRV military forces intact in the South, a situation that at one time would have been considered an enormous advantage. But no longer could that alone compensate for the fact that the Agreements did not displace the South Vietnamese government, either institutionally or in terms of power holders. Originally, in the mid-1960s, Hanoi in seeking its goal of unification faced both a major impediment (the presence of U.S. military forces) and a minor impediment (the socio-political institutions of the South Vietnamese government—minor because the GVN at that time was as close to being a nongovernment as is possible and still remain in business). By 1973, however, the relative weights of these two impediments had been reversed. The GVN had strengthened itself immeasurably, and at the same time the ARVN-PAVN balance of forces was more or less equal. Thus it was no longer Hanoi's chief objective simply to get the Americans out. Now it was to weaken and debilitate the GVN. In the Hanoi view, as the Agreements did not accomplish this, they did not significantly advance the cause of unification. Some of Hanoi's friends argued that the Agreements created conditions that would eventually debilitate the GVN and thus lead to unification. But the Politburo had been down that road before—in 1955— and was highly pessimistic about the new arrangement. At best for Hanoi, the Paris Agreements held out future promise.

The DRV signed the Agreements because at the time it could not do otherwise. It signed because of military punishment, having been badly mauled in the 1972 Easter Campaign, and it needed a respite from warfare. It signed because of Chinese defection and Soviet pressure. When it did sign it was with a mental reservation—that as soon as possible, probably by 1976, it would return to full-scale war. It hoped it could still count on Soviet assistance.

THE END OF THE WAR

Time suddenly slowed in Indochina in the months following the signing of the Paris Agreements. The war took a quantum drop in level of combat. It became a low-grade form of violence, a cease-fire "war of the flags," what could loosely be called politics with guns. It was an ambiguous situation and a period of constant maneuver for all parties.

Soviet policies and actions in Indochina in this twilight period between the withdrawal of U.S. troops (1973) and the collapse of the South Vietnamese government in 1975 largely were by-products of the Sino-Soviet dispute and the changed triangle of relations among the USSR, China, and the United States. As U.S. troubles in Southeast Asia multiplied, Soviet interest in the region increased. The watershed here appears to have been 1973. Leonid Brezhnev, for instance, in one year reversed the ratio of his activities—meetings and visits—in Asia. In 1972, the ratio, Asia to non-Asia, was 1:2; in 1973 it was 2:1. President Nixon declared 1973 the "Year of Europe"; Brezhnev in effect declared it the "Year of Asia."

The Soviet assessment of the Indochina scene in the spring of 1973 was that there would be a marked reduction but not a total cessation of military activity for several years; that in effect a military standoff would prevail; and that there would be a political imbroglio among the three contending elements—the DRV, the GVN, and the PRG/NLF—which would remain locked in a struggle that each could survive but none could dominate. This was also the conventional wisdom of most observers at the time.

Probably the USSR did not want immediate decisive Vietnamese Communist victory but preferred and expected a transitional period of stalemate during which Hanoi's forces would gradually undermine the non-Communist South, slowly attaining the superiority required to seize total control. Some observers believe that Moscow favored this scenario because of past experience. (Stalin did not want a quick victory by the Chinese Communists after World War II, preferring a phased victory.) A slower unfolding of events in Indochina would have given the USSR ever-increasing influence and added Hanoi dependency, whereas a quick victory could have meant greater Vietnamese independence subsequently.

Hanoi's intentions were reasonably clear at the time, and they have been confirmed by PAVN generals in their postwar memoirs. The Vietnamese Communists were exhausted by the eight years of war during which they suffered ghastly casualties. The party's cadre structure was in disarray. There were serious shortages of men and supplies, the result of heavy losses during the last (Easter 1972) campaign. Time was needed to re-equip and retrain, and to restore psychic energies. In short, these were all the reasons Hanoi had signed the hated Paris Agreements in the first place.

Word went out to the faithful in North and South Vietnam: Victory is not lost, only postponed; local military actions are permissible if not too costly; attention must be paid to recruiting, training, and resupply efforts. In early 1974 agit-prop cadres began telling PAVN troops at indoctrination sessions that a general offensive was being planned for sometime in 1976. It was billed, like earlier campaigns (the late 1965 campaign, the 1967-1968 Winter-Spring Offensive, and the 1972 Easter Campaign), as the decisive battle of the war. Throughout 1974 all of the orders and directives out of Hanoi and down the chain of command in the South were consistent with this general instruction: Hold, resist, build, prepare for 1976 and the final battle.

This plan levied new logistic requirements on the USSR, which obliged by dispatching vast new quantities of military and economic assistance. Major construction began on the Ho Chi Minh trail through Laos.

In late 1974 PAVN units in South Vietnam received orders to conduct a limited military campaign in Phuoc Thanh province north of Saigon. The plan was to capture the northern half of the province. Within a few weeks, by early January 1975, all of the province had fallen, much to the surprise of both Hanoi and Saigon. A second limited campaign was ordered in the Central Highlands, centering on Banmethuot. The South Vietnamese Army had advance information about this attack and prepared for it. But its defenses quickly crumbled and the town was captured. As it turned out, Banmethuot was the last true battle of the Vietnam War. The South Vietnamese Army, which had stood and fought under far worse conditions in the past, from then on hardly fought at all. Soon, the command structure was in such disarray that the army was unable to fight. On April 30, a Soviet-made tank crashed through the ornamental gate in front of Independence Palace in Saigon. The Vietnam War was over.

In the final three months of the war, the USSR had to move smartly to keep abreast of the rapidly changing situation. Its calculation that the post–Paris Agreement period would be a time of strategic stalemate had gotten it into trouble. For instance, it had advised the Khmer Rouge in Cambodia to negotiate a settlement with the Lon Nol government, but this was advice that proved wrong. Soviet thinking in the last months of the war was better than that of the Chinese, however. By early January 1975 the USSR had concluded that the Vietnamese Communists were going to win and win quickly, something the Chinese failed to see for at least another month. The USSR adjusted its behavior accordingly while China lost precious weeks clinging to its earlier estimate of indeterminate stalemate for an indefinite period. The result was that the USSR emerged into the postwar world in Indochina in a far better position than China.

SUMMING UP

Soviet policy during the Vietnam War was an equal mixture of pragmatic international politics and judicious commitment. Soviet behavior in Vietnam was opportunistic, wary of confrontation or entrapment, conservative in taking risks, and continually plagued by ideological dilemmas. It is now clear that USSR behavior throughout the war had much less certitude than seemed at the time.

In general, however, the USSR managed its affairs well. It was on the winning side when Hanoi achieved decisive victory. But even had there been a compromise settlement, which Moscow long considered the more likely outcome, it would have been in equally good shape. It managed to support the war fully—indeed, made it possible—without causing a confrontation with the United States. For Moscow the arrangement proved ideal: it funded a war against the United States yet remained only an adversary, not an enemy.

The war served Moscow well in several respects. It vilified the United States worldwide and badly tarnished its image; it kept the United States occupied, making anti-Soviet moves elsewhere less likely; and for years it sabotaged improvement of U.S.-Chinese relations.

Most important for the USSR, the United States never played the Soviet card in the war, never seriously addressed the fact of Soviet participation. In retrospect it is difficult to reconcile the USSR's enjoyment of a détente relationship with the United States while financing a war *against* the United States. It is equally difficult to decide whether this was successful Soviet diplomacy, inexplicable U.S. shortsightedness, or simply cross-purposes at work. The USSR wanted the United States to be bogged down in a land war in Asia, and it wanted détente. It got both because the United States never forced it to choose between the two. As if by tacit agreement, both sides kept the two issues in separate water-tight compartments. The result was a remarkable spectacle—the United States and the USSR locked in an eight-year proxy war during which their relationship was more amicable than either before the war or after.

Perhaps the most difficult judgment to make on the wartime relationship of the USSR and the Vietnamese has to do with the amount of control Moscow could exert over Hanoi decisions. There were, and still are, two schools of thought on this matter. The first, which might be called the European orthodox diplomacy school, held that the USSR obviously had enormous influence in Hanoi: The USSR was large and the DRV was small and dependent, so how could it be otherwise? The USSR might not have chosen to use its leverage, but there was no question that leverage existed. The second might be called the school of Asian mentality. It held that the first school's reasoning was correct for nineteenth-century Europe but not for twentieth-century Asia. Moscow's influence in Hanoi, it held, was dissipated by the stubborn Vietnamese notion of *doc lap* (independence); by ideological mandates imposed on the USSR as world leader of Marxism; by internal politics in the Kremlin; and, most of all, by the fact of the Sino-Soviet dispute. All of these combined to create a condition in which the USSR could exert no real influence on issues considered crucial by the DRV—for example, a negotiated settlement of the war short of unification.

Publicly the USSR never said much about its influence in Hanoi. But in private talks with the Americans and others during the war, its diplomats and leaders insisted that the USSR did not have the leverage the Americans assumed it had. Over and over they would assert: We cannot control the North Vietnamese; they will not take our advice on many issues; and if we cut off aid in an ultimatum, they will get what they need from China or do without. Late in the war (circa 1972), Soviet diplomats, still speaking privately, argued that the top Kremlin leaders, such as Brezhnev, were attempting to get Hanoi to settle the war on terms acceptable to the United States; but they could go only so far in this effort because of opposition by Kremlin hardliners. The argument was that U.S. toughness, such as mining Haiphong harbor, weakened Brezhnev's hand.

The DRV, of course, enjoyed a certain latitude of action because of the Sino-Soviet dispute and because Vietnam was such an important symbol in the world Communist movement. It was able to control decisionmaking strategy and largely determine the course of the war by presenting Moscow (and Beijing) with only two choices: Accept Hanoi's policies, or disengage entirely. Perhaps it was bluff, but Hanoi consistently got away with it. Only early on had Soviet disengagement ever been a real possibility—as Khrushchev had sought this end—but later in the war it was impossible for Moscow.

If the PAVN High Command generals in Hanoi could be persuaded to speak candidly about the USSR and its role in the Vietnam War, what would they say? Probably they would make the following points:

1. Throughout the Vietnam War (or the Vietnam Revolution as the North Vietnamese would term it), the progressive forces in Indochina had the right to claim total commitment from the

USSR, but they never got it. Moscow policy with respect to the war was a mixture of ideological posturing and selfish pursuit of national interest.

2. Despite large quantities of war materiel sent by Moscow, it was never as much as it might have been, and not always the right weapons or war materiel. In critical moments, when Hanoi needed material or psychic support the most, Moscow temporized or hedged its response.

3. The USSR never truly *cared* about the Vietnamese Communist cause. It supported this cause for the wrong reason: because of its dispute with China. When it had to choose between serving Vietnam and serving its interests in the Sino-Soviet dispute, it unhesitatingly chose the latter.

4. If the truth be known, the *USSR* was a paper tiger. It had an unrealistic sense of the limitations of its own power and was excessively fearful that PAVN's major military offensives might somehow draw it into war with the United States. The Vietnamese Communists were willing to take high risks for the cause, whereas Moscow always treated that cause as a trap.

5. In short, Moscow never was staunchly in the forefront of the Vietnamese Revolution. That forever will remain its final unforgivable sin.

Despite the USSR's reservation—which in Moscow is privately put down as ingratitude on the part of the Vietnamese—Soviet handling of the Vietnam War was a clearcut success, one of its few in Asia in recent years. Communist victory in Indochina may have been a product of U.S. irresolution or loss of will, but it also was a victory for the USSR.

Given its return, the USSR had invested a great deal of money and effort; and the question at the end of the war was, What would the USSR do with its investment? Would it build on it in an orthodox diplomatic manner, seeking to serve normal Soviet interests in the area? Or would it seek, with the Vietnamese, to establish a regional empire under Soviet tutelage?

NOTES

1. VNA (February 15, 1964).

2. Total Soviet exports to Vietnam in 1964 were 11.2 million rubles, down from 19.2 million rubles in 1983. There was a rise in one commodity, petroleum, which increased from 91,800 tons (3.7 million rubles) in 1963 to 101,000 tons (4.1 million rubles) in 1964. DRV exports to the USSR remained about the same:

31.3 million rubles in 1964 versus 31.8 million rubles in 1963. See *Vneshnyaya Torgovlya* (Moscow), No. 10 (1965), pp. 3–6.

3. Officials in Moscow in late October were showing East Europeans a list of "29 Khrushchev shortcomings," presumably the reasons for his ouster. See *New York Times* (October 30, 1964). It is interesting to note that Khrushchev's Vietnam policy was not on the list.

4. These events include cultural revolution in China, the development of the bomb in China, the end of the Sukarno era in Indonesia, the Singapore-Malaysia separation, U.S. troops to the Dominican Republic, the Soviet spacewalk and the U.S. Gemini flight, President Johnson's war on poverty, the Watts riots and the Selma civil rights march, the deaths of Winston Churchill and Albert Schweitzer, and the Queen's reception of the Beatles.

5. By PLAF I mean the People's Liberation Armed Forces—that is, the army of the National Liberation Front of South Vietnam—as distinguished from the People's Army of Vietnam (PAVN) or the army of the Democratic Republic of Vietnam or North Vietnam. Note that this PAVN buildup in the South preceded the United States' decision to send ground troops to Vietnam.

6. Radio Hanoi (January 1, 1965).

7. See the commentary entitled "How Low Can They Sink?" in *Jen-min Jih-pao* (Beijing) (December 23, 1965).

8. TASS (February 10, 1965).

9. VNA (February 11, 1965).

10. Ibid.

11. The United States was apparently indifferent to the fact that Kosygin was in Hanoi. The chronology of events was this: At 2 A.M. February 7, 1969, PLAF forces attacked the Pleiku airfield in South Vietnam, wounding a number of Americans and damaging aircraft. President Lyndon johnson ordered retaliatory air strikes on North Vietnam military installations near Dong Hoi, carried out later the same day, and on the PAVN communication center at Vinh the following morning. The Kosygin mission left Hanoi February 10. It has been suggested by P. J. Honey and others that Hanoi officials ordered the Pleiku raid in the hope that U.S. retaliation strikes would occur during the Kosygin visit.

12. See *SRV Foreign Ministry White Book on China* (Hanoi, 1979) for discussion of this view.

13. Meanwhile, the Chinese played into Soviet hands by sabotaging Soviet freight trains transiting China en route to North Vietnam. This began in early 1965, became fairly commonplace during the Cultural Revolution, then tapered off. The first incident, it appears, occurred in early March 1965, when sixteen boxcars of small arms and four passenger cars with Soviet advisers were stopped at the Sino-Soviet border. After a day of protests by Moscow, four freight cars were permitted through, but eight freight cars along with the four passenger cars were turned back. Apparently the Chinese concern was not the hardware but the personnel, inasmuch as the Chinese thought a Soviet expeditionary force of 20,000 advisers was on its way to North Vietnam—and this they wanted to prevent.

14. *Washington Post* (February 17, 1965).

15. *New York Times* (February 23, 1965).

16. *New York Times* (February 28, 1965).

17. *Washington Post* (March 24, 1965).

18. *New York Times* (March 23, 1965).

19. *New York Times* (April 18, 1965).

20. TASS (April 18, 1965).

21. TASS (April 19, 1965).

22. *New Republic* (May 1, 1965).

23. *New York Times* (May 24, 1965).

24. Richard Hudson, "Warning From Moscow," *War-Peace Report* (June 1965).

25. *Washington Post* (June 18, 1965).

26. *Pravda* (October 27, 1965).

27. *London Times* (April 5, 1966).

28. *Sunday Times* (London) (May 1, 1966).

29. See Douglas Pike, *PAVN: People's Army of Vietnam* (Novato, Calif.: Presidio Press, 1986), for a full explanation of the *dau tranh* strategy.

30. Ibid.

31. See VNA (December 12, 1960); see also *World Marxist Review* (December 1960).

32. Miguel Rivero, *Verde Olivo* (Havana) (February 10, 1980).

33. Today there is total depreciation of Chinese military assistance in the writings coming out of Hanoi. But these are not necessarily to be believed.

34. This point was made by an authoritative source in private conversation (1982) with the author in Moscow. Most of these casualties, he further indicated, were at SAM sites hit by U.S. air strikes. Apparently there were also a number of Soviet casualties on the Ho Chi Minh trail.

35. Also in North Vietnam were some 3,000 military technicians, some of whom were assigned to maintenance of the more complex military equipment; others were instructors.

36. Vadim Nekrasov (deputy editor of *Pravda*), "The Demands of the Times," *Pravda* (October 15, 1971).

37. *Nhan Dan* (May 21, 1972).

38. Ibid.

39. *Nhan Dan* (May 24, 1972).

40. Linking détente with the Vietnam War was not a new idea for Nixon. In March 1968, before he was president, Nixon wrote a speech calling for such linkage. The speech was to be given on April 1, but on March 31, when President Johnson dramatically announced his decision not to run for reelection, Nixon canceled the speech. The text had already been released, however.

41. Undoubtedly Moscow knew of this impending attack—the Batitsky mission to Hanoi in February certainly dealt with it—but the USSR was unable (or perhaps unwilling) to dissuade the North Vietnamese.

42. There was, at least in theory, a scenario that would eventually lead to unification of North and South Vietnam. It posited a slow (ten- to twenty-year) and gradual voluntary coming together of the two Vietnams, first into a

loose confederated arrangement, then—say, by the year 2,000—into a full federation, which would be satisfactory to the Hanoi leadership by that time. The idea is explored in Pike, *War, Peace and the Viet Cong* (Cambridge, Mass.: MIT Press, 1969).

43. This is the case in part because the DRV simply distrusted international organizations on the grounds that they were controlled by the superpowers, and in part because of UN efforts to mediate an end to the Korean War. Throughout the Vietnam War the DRV rejected, usually in scathing terms, any suggestion of UN involvement. The Hanoi press deprecated the UN in every way it could. The United States had no more faith in UN peacemaking abilities than did Hanoi, which is the chief reason it rejected the U Thant overture. For further discussion see the author's *War, Peace and the Viet Cong*, pp. 423–424.

44. See Allan Cameron, "The Soviet Union and Vietnam: The Origins of Involvement," in Duncan's *Soviet Policy in Development Countries* (Waltham, Mass.: Ginn-Blaisdell, 1970); Zagoria's *Vietnam Triangle* (New York: Pegasus, 1967); and Jon Van Dyke's *North Vietnam's Strategy for Survival* (Palo Alto, Calif.: Pacific Books, 1972) for further discussion of the USSR's negotiated settlement moves.

45. This decision came on April 3, 1968, and followed President Johnson's March 30th speech in which he proposed talks, halted the air war in North Vietnam, and announced his political retirement.

46. DRV Foreign Minister Nguyen Duy Trinh, in keeping with DRV diplomatic practice, chose an unlikely venue to signal a basic change of DRV policy on settlement of the Vietnam War—a toast at a banquet for some visiting Outer Mongolians. For years the DRV's position was that there could be no negotiations with the United States until that country stopped all acts of war *against North Vietnam and South Vietnam* (a phrase that was used repeatedly). In Trinh's toast to the Outer Mongolians, he said that the DRV was willing to begin negotiations provided the United States halted "all acts of war *against North Vietnam*," but he said nothing about acts of war against South Vietnam. Obviously this meant that talks could begin if U.S. air strikes and bombing of North Vietnam ceased even while the war in the South continued. The signal, however, went unnoticed in Washington.

47. Actually, neither the DRV nor the USSR introduced any substantive changes into the negotiations. Hence Radio Moscow was able to rewrite its commentaries overnight simply by taking out the phrase *negotiated settlement fraud* and replacing it with *people's peace proposal*.

48. DRV Minister of Foreign Trade Phan Anh in an interview with *Aziya Afrika Segodnya* (Moscow, March 1972).

Six

SOVIET-VIETNAMESE ECONOMIC RELATIONS

ECONOMIC RELATIONS BETWEEN Moscow and Hanoi over the years have amounted largely to travel down a one-way street: Many rubles have gone in, but few have come back. The USSR and China supplied the Viet Minh with money and weapons, although it is difficult to sort out their contributions because much of the USSR assistance was funneled through China. In the Vietnam War, the USSR and China began as co-equal suppliers of military assistance to the DRV, but the burden gradually shifted to the USSR and became increasingly expensive. The USSR supplied economic aid to the fledgling DRV in modest amounts in the 1950s, but by the end of the Vietnam War it was providing about 80 percent of the DRV state budget. In the post–Vietnam War era, Moscow's economic and military assistance steadily increased as did Vietnamese dependency on this aid. This condition continues today. Since the early 1980s, however, the economic relationship of the two has taken on a new and more complex character. These themes are traced throughout this chapter.

THE VIET MINH WAR

As noted earlier, Stalin made no commitment to the Viet Minh struggle against the French in terms of official endorsement or political or diplomatic support. This led some observers to conclude that the USSR was indifferent to the outcome of the war and provided no significant support for Ho Chi Minh and his followers. Others concluded that Moscow did little because the war was being funded adequately by China. These erroneous interpretations have been reinforced over the years by official Hanoi fiction about the nature of the struggle: that it was a self-contained battle fought without significant outside assistance. This myth is perpetuated by Hanoi today in part because it does not

106

want to make a liar out of earlier Moscow claims that the USSR was not associated in a material way with the Viet Minh War, and in part to escape acknowledging a debt of gratitude to China. Because of the current bad relations with Beijing, early Chinese support is now totally deprecated in Hanoi. For instance, General Hoang Van Thai, in writing about the Viet Minh War, recently declared: "We used only 3,600 rounds of artillery at Dien Bien Phu and if we'd used Chinese tactics would have lost the battle."[1]

Viet Minh forces from the start of the war received important military assistance from the outside. Most of it came either from China or from the USSR through China; to separate the two historically would be virtually impossible. The important point for our consideration here is that while the USSR found it impolitic to support the war publicly, it could and did see to it that war materiel got to Vietnam. The difference was one between avowed support that would have cost the USSR diplomatically and gun-running that served the same purpose. Within the Kremlin, justification for the shipment of arms to Indochina could be found on several grounds: making mischief for the imperialist world in general and the Franco-American alliance in particular; as a response to Chinese insistence that Moscow act fraternally; or simply to bleed and weaken France. Covert military aid would accomplish these interests as effectively as military aid openly delivered, and it would be more acceptable to the Viet Minh.

In the early days of the war, the Viet Minh units consisted chiefly of armed propaganda teams. These were small in size, operating from home villages and not expending much ammunition or military supplies; what was needed could be taken in raids on French outposts. As the Viet Minh forces developed, logistic needs multiplied and outside assistance increased correspondingly. Communist victory in China vastly improved Viet Minh prospects, and when the Korean War turned into a stalemate (mid-1951) a dramatic increase in Communist war shipments to Indochina became possible. Some 200 Molotova trucks, the Chinese said later, began a "red ball" express from the Canton docks to the Vietnam border, where the war materiel was turned over to Viet Minh porters. Another 300 trucks served the Kunming–Phong Tho route supplying Viet Minh forces in northern North Vietnam. This permitted Viet Minh fire power to be steadily enhanced until, battalion for battalion, the Viet Minh matched the French, making decisive victory on the battlefield possible for the first time. The three Viet Minh regiments at Dien Bien Phu were almost completely equipped with Soviet weapons, including 300 crew-served artillery pieces. Most of the trucks and almost all of the communication equipment used in the last two years of the war were Soviet made. In all, this military assistance supplied by the USSR must have totaled at least a billion dollars.

Throughout, however, the USSR did not acknowledge its involvement in the Viet Minh War. As late as May 1953, Moscow was still officially insisting that it provided neither military nor economic assistance to the DRV.[2] Technically, perhaps, this was true. The aid was given to China, which gave it to the DRV. One result of Moscow's public position was that among rank-and-file Viet Minh, there never was much knowledge about the true source of aid; hence the Chinese tended to get more credit for their support than they deserved.

A further difficulty presents itself in any attempt to assign credit for military assistance in the Viet Minh War. Some war materiel that went into Vietnam from China was U.S. made, captured in Korea, seized earlier from the fleeing Chinese nationalists, or even made in the USSR.[3] Of the Soviet made weapons that turned up in Vietnam, some had previously armed Chinese forces fighting in Korea and some had been diverted from the Korean War after they were no longer needed. Thus any attempt to determine the source and specific history of any one piece of war equipment was difficult at the time and impossible today. It is equally impossible to fix with any precision the total amount supplied by the two allies. The important point, however, is that the USSR was involved in a collaborative effort to ensure that the Viet Minh forces received virtually all of the military hardware they could absorb.

An interesting, if somewhat quixotic, account of Soviet military assistance to the Viet Minh was provided in the memoirs of a Soviet citizen who served in Indochina:

> Of an older yet very valuable vintage of (Soviet) specialist in Vietnam are those Russians who learned Vietnam and its ways and language in the 1940s and 1950s and who in fact are veterans of the jungle warfare of the remote time. Such a man is Platon Skrzhinsky, forty-four, a native of the Ukraine now residing in Moscow. After the Second World War he enlisted in the French Foreign Legion. But when the French shipped his unit to Saigon, Skrzhinsky made lans to desert. It took him a year to establish contacts with the guerrillas. In his new Vietminh ranks he found other deserters from the French: one Australian, two Germans and several Algerians. He received a Vietnamese name, Truong Thanh, meaning Loyal One. He married a native girl, and they had a baby. By 1950 he commanded a guerrilla artillery unit. He returned to Moscow in 1955, with his six-year-old Vietnamese daughter. Anya. For nearly ten years he had been employed as an editor with Radio Moscow, helping with

broadcasts in Vietnamese to Southeast Asia. Present day survivors of such desertions from the French Foreign Legion (in Moscow) include a Pole, a Czech, and an East German. Most of this romantic group may still be used for whatever training advising or interpreting is required in connection with Vietnam.[4]

EARLY ECONOMIC AID

What might be called the first flag flying or deliberately visible USSR economic assistance for the DRV came in late summer 1954, when the Soviet freighter Akhan Zhensk arrived off Vietnam to begin services as a passenger vessel under Operation Exodus, the great Vietnamese population transfer arranged at Geneva earlier in the year. Nearly 1 million North Vietnamese moved to the South, and some 100,000 were transferred from the South to the North, many of them aboard the Akhan Zhensk.

Formal overt economic assistance by the USSR began with the signing of the first Vietnam-USSR Non-reimbursable Economic Aid Agreement on July 18, 1955. It was renewed every year until 1985, when it was replaced by a long-range aid arrangement. The original date is still observed each year in major ceremonies in Hanoi.

Under the first agreement, the USSR promised to assist the DRV in about 90 projects, some 25 of which could be classified as major. These included the Hanoi Machine Shop No. 1, for manufacturing tools and farm implements (opened in 1956); the Tin Tuc tin mine; the Lao Cai apatite mine (fertilizer raw material); the Vinh and Lao Cai Electric plants; the Haiphong Fish Cannery (3,000 tons per annum); the coal mines at Hon Gai, Cam Pha, Ha Tu, Deo Nai, Mong Duong, Thai Nguyen, and Cao Son; dredging of the Haiphong harbor; tugboats for harbor use; and tea-processing plants at Phu Tho and Ha Giang.

The total cost of these projects at the time was estimated by outsiders to be about $100 million; Soviet commentary indicated that the USSR's initial aid came to 400 million rubles, a figure that did not include the cost of some 1,000 Soviet technicians and specialists sent to Vietnam (electrical engineers, construction engineers, and tea and cotton production specialists) or various educational services.

D. Stevanovskiy, writing later in *Selskaya Zhizn*, described the early economic ties as follows:

A DRV Party and Government delegation headed by Ho Chi Minh visited our country in July 1955. Documents were signed which marked the beginning of trade and economic cooperation between the Soviet Union and Vietnam. The Vietnamese people received all-around assistance which enabled them to overcome the grave consequences of the resistance war against the French in a short time and create the preconditions for restoration and development of the national economy.[5]

This Hanoi version of the early years was also written later:

It is noteworthy that during the 1953–59 period, North Vietnam with Soviet assistance built and put into operation 45 industrial enterprises and projects. The Soviet Union provided great assistance to Vietnam in training technicians and skilled workers. During the 1955–60 period 1,400 Soviet specialists worked in Vietnam training thousands of skilled Vietnamese workers. During the same period, thousands of young Vietnamese men and women were trained at universities and vocational schools in the Soviet Union. These were initial and very important steps in building the foundations of USSR-SRV [Socialist Republic of Vietnam] cooperation.[6]

The economic aid to the DRV in the early years (i.e., 1955–1964) amounted to about 7 percent of the total aid granted by Moscow to the Socialist countries. This was only about 10 percent of the aid granted by Moscow to non-Communist developing countries.

Soviet economic assistance to Vietnam over the years may be divided into four types: (1) commodity aid, such as food or petroleum; (2) capital or "central plant" investments, such as textile factories or water conservancy projects; (3) services, such as technical assistance by advisers and specialists or schooling for Vietnamese; and (4) military assistance.

Initially most assistance was emergency commodity aid. Then it shifted to capital investment, until about 1965, when military assistance and economic aid in direct support of the war effort came to dominate. There was a return to capital investment in the first few years after the end of the Vietnam War, but when the Vietnamese economy sank into stagnation there was a shift to commodity aid. In the 1980s capital assistance again returned to prominence.

Soviet aid over the past three decades has represented the bulk of all outside assistance to the DRV, ranging from about 55 percent to 90 percent of the total in any one year. Until the end of the Vietnam War at least one-third of all Soviet assistance was termed nonreimbursable—that is, *gratis*. Such aid is no longer granted in this category, although from time to time Moscow writes off various loans to Vietnam, which amounts to the same thing.

Commodity aid, the first type of assistance to go to North Vietnam after the end of the Viet Minh War, began a few weeks after the signing of the Geneva Agreements with a shipment of some 170,000 tons of Burmese rice, which the Soviets had bartered for cement and which was needed to head off starvation in North Vietnam. A year later came 9.9 million yards of cotton and synthetic cloth, 1,000 tons of wool yarn, pharmaceuticals, and newsprint. In 1957 the USSR granted 47 million rubles in a long-term loan for the purchase of ferrous metals and chemicals for fertilizer. During the next decade there were additional shipments of commodity items, chiefly wheat and petroleum, which, while significant, did not match the shipments from China. In the early years at least 20 percent of the rice eaten in North Vietnam came from the rice fields in the Chinese provinces adjacent to the DRV—some supplied as economic assistance but most of it sold. During the Vietnam War years, Soviet commodity aid was mainly food, petroleum, chemical fertilizer, and pesticides. Such aid continues to the present.

The second category of Soviet aid, capital investment, began with the July 1955 aid agreement involving a grant of 400 million rubles, 75 percent of which was for capital investment projects (the remainder for commodity aid). In addition, the USSR sent some 1,000 technicians and specialists to North Vietnam to replace the departing French in coal mines and factories, and undertook the training of some 10,000 Vietnamese in the USSR.[7]

Hanoi later described this first aid agreement as a

> manifestation of a new type of relationship, one of disinterested
> mutual assistance among fraternal socialist countries based on
> genuine proletarian internationalism. . . . [It was] help for our
> country to overcome the serious consequences of the nine year
> resistance war against the French and create the necessary
> material base for restoring and gradually developing production,
> especially in agriculture.[8]

This capital investment involved 45 separate projects, the most important of which were electric power, mining, heavy industry, and light industry associated with agriculture. As listed by Hanoi, these projects included

> construction of 150 factories and industrial plants, establishment
> of dozens of collective farms and the opening of several technical
> schools. From 1955 through 1961 this aid amounted to 309
> million rubles and involved 30 industrial enterprises; four
> thermoelectric and two hydroelectric power plants at Vinh and

> Lao Cai with substations and high-tension lines which increased
> total drive power production by 20 percent; two coal mine
> enterprises (the Lang Cam and Hong Gai collieries); the Tinh
> Thuc tin mine; the Lao Cai apatite mine; the Phu Tho tea
> processing plant and the Haiphong Canned Fish Factory. The
> Hanoi Mechanical Engineering Plant was equipped by the USSR
> to make 400 types of machine tools which now accounts for 13
> percent of the nation's total production of machine tools. . . . We
> also received 18 ton bulldozers from the USSR. . . . The
> equipment for ten (wired) radio relay stations. . . . In the
> agricultural field the USSR thus far has given us more than 1,500
> types of agricultural machines; 23 tractor centers; equipped 29
> state farms; and helped set up ten mineral and lumber
> exploitation sites. The USSR trained Vietnamese cadres in the
> USSR and built for us an institute of agriculture and forestry and
> a polytechnical college.[9]

An additional capital investment agreement was signed in 1957 under which the USSR loaned the DRV the equivalent of $100 million to modernize several DRV coal mines, build a fish refrigeration plant, and enlarge electric power plants.

Interest in Vietnam's oil potential began early. The Soviet Ministry of Geology sent a team to North Vietnam in late 1958 to conduct a two-year exploration study. This was followed by test well drillings, the first of which occurred in early 1960 in Thai Binh province. The work was halted during the war.

The third type of assistance, personal services by advisers, and education and training of Vietnamese either in Vietnam or in the USSR, has always constituted an important Soviet contribution to the economy of North Vietnam. Probably it predates other types of aid; as early as 1951, a small group of DRV cadres went to the USSR to study Soviet agricultural methods for a year. Based on scattered Hanoi press reports, it is probably safe to say that 7,000 Vietnamese from the DRV studied at least briefly in the USSR in the 1950s. The educational service activity was formalized on March 7, 1959, with the signing of the DRV-USSR Treaty on Scientific and Technological Cooperation. There have been many such treaties since then. It is claimed that between 1952 and 1980 "three Ph.D.'s, 2,000 MA's and thousands of technicians were trained in the USSR."

The cost of economic assistance in those initial years—that is, until 1961—has been variously estimated from an improbable low of $130 million to a high of $900 million. The spread of estimates is the result of tabulation or exclusion of grant aid, which is free, and of credit aid, which is supposedly a loan to be repaid but is often subsequently

TABLE 6.1
Soviet trade patterns (in millions of rubles)

	Soviet Exports to DRV	Soviet Imports from DRV
Trade average for 1959-1962	R 31.8	R 21.3
Trade average for 1963-1966	R 55.7	R 28.3
Trade average for 1967-1970	R 153.3	R 16.7

Source: M. Trigubenko, "The Soviet Union's Trade and Economic Cooperation with Vietnam," Far Eastern Affairs (Moscow), No. 4 (1983).

written off. Chinese assistance during this period is even more difficult to calculate, but it appears to have been about 20 percent greater than Soviet assistance.

The late 1950s also saw the beginning of a modest amount of trade between North Vietnam and the USSR. What was called a Reciprocal Commodity Delivery protocol was signed in Moscow on May 5, 1956, arranged by then DRV Minister of Commerce Pham An. Under this protocol, the USSR agreed to buy from Vietnam all of the goods it produced for export that it could not sell elsewhere—about $5 million worth. A DRV-USSR Trade and Maritime Navigation agreement was signed in Hanoi on March 12, 1958 (and is renewed annually), extending most-favored nation status in commerce and navigation. To facilitate the shipment of goods the first direct Moscow-Hanoi railway (via China) was opened on June 5, 1956. And Ho Chi Minh signed the first formal DRV-USSR trade agreement in Moscow on July 18, 1958.[10]

Early trade consisted chiefly of Soviet trucks, tractors, industrial equipment, textiles, pharmaceuticals and consumer goods in exchange for lumber, rubber, tobacco, seafood, tea, coffee, fruit, spices and small amounts of minerals. The average trade imbalance for the period 1955–1958 was about two to one against the USSR; Soviet exports averaged about 6.2 million rubles per year and Vietnamese exports to the USSR averaged about 3.3 million rubles.[11] As indicated in Table 6.1, the balance improved during the early 1960s, then swung heavily to the USSR.

During the Vietnam War, trade in the usual sense of the term between North Vietnam and the USSR was virtually nonexistent. It was resumed after the war, as discussed below.

In 1960 the DRV launched its first Five-Year Plan (1961–1965), an ambitious undertaking built around Soviet capital investment. A DRV-

USSR Five-Year Assistance Agreement was signed in Hanoi on December 23, 1960,[12] to fund nearly 100 projects, about half of which could be called major. These included the Uong Bi Thermoelectric plant north of Hanoi (30 Soviet engineers and technicians assigned); development of the coal mines at Van Dau, Ha Tu, Coc Sau, and Deo Nai; the Lao Cai apatite mine and the Tinh Tuc tin mine; the Lam Thao superphosphate plant; the Cam Pha mine equipment factory; the Uong Bi electrical equipment factory, the Dong Anh electrical supply company, and the Tac Ba electric wire manufacturing company; Haiphong oil storage facilities and the Bai-Chay-Phu Ly oil pipeline; Hanoi Machine Tool Factory No. 1 and the Cam Pha Engineering plant; medium- and short-wave radio transmitters for Radio Hanoi; the Hanoi automobile repair plant; and tobacco, tea, coffee, and cotton projects on 37 state farms. Lesser assistance included technical journals, blueprints and specification drawings to facilitate manufacture of machine tools, electrical equipment, automotive accessories, chemicals, and building materials. In December 1960 there was also a gift of US$5 million in medical supplies.

Outside estimates of the cost of assisting the first Five-Year Plan range from US$50 million to US$108 million. The USSR fixed the cost at 101 million rubles, of which about 60 percent was *gratis* and the remainder a loan (later written off).

An auxiliary agreement of the Five-Year Plan was signed September 15, 1962, for the DRV agricultural sector, which in economic terms is more important than the industrial sector. This involved an estimated $41 million for water conservancy; the purchase of tractors, water pumps, and agricultural machinery and equipment for the state farms; assistance in developing animal husbandry and the production of industrial crops (such as rubber, lacquer, ramie, and kenaf); and the construction of several agricultural technical centers and colleges. Under the same agreement the USSR sent medical teams to combat malaria, trachoma, and tropical diseases. In November 1962 work began to modernize and triple the handling capacity of the DRV's major port of Haiphong. The harbor was dredged, reinforced concrete deep-water wharves were constructed, warehouses and repair shops were added, and modern loading equipment was installed.

The DRV's 1961–1965 Five-Year Plan, by all evidence, progressed well in the first two or three years, and the prospect was for fast-paced DRV economic development. Then came the fateful decision to begin armed struggle in the South. Economic resources were diverted away from the plan, and by 1965 it was in shambles.

Soviet economic aid during the later Vietnam War years (1965–1975) was entirely geared to keeping the North Vietnamese war support system operating. Transportation and communication facilities were enlarged and repaired after bombings. Shortages due to wartime re-location were replaced from Soviet stocks. Construction work only replaced losses from the air war, with no significant nation building during this time. The result was that North Vietnam emerged from the war in the same stage of economic development it was in when the war began. (See the appendix at the end of this chapter for the available data on wartime economic assistance.)

The Kosygin mission to Hanoi in February 1965 (discussed below) renegotiated outstanding loans, reassigning some of the funds so as to put greater emphasis on industrial activity to support the war. Economic discussions continued throughout the next few years. Kosygin returned to Hanoi in February 1966, and Ho Chi Minh had been in Moscow earlier for the April 23 CPSU Congress and economic talks. Le Duc Tho and Hoang Van Hoan led separate economic missions to Moscow in the summer of 1966. Le Thanh Nghi was there in September 1967 to sign a new economic aid agreement under which the USSR would supply North Vietnam with metal-welding machine tools, electric motors, steel and engineering handling equipment, farm machinery, and fertilizer. The aid agreement the following year (signed in December 1968) called for the USSR to supply North Vietnam with additional electrical power and electrical distribution facilities, mining equipment, machine tools, railway construction machinery, excavators, metal, railway rolling stock, bakeries, and pasta production and tea processing facilities. Similar agreements were made annually throughout the war.

Le Duc Tho signed an aid agreement in Moscow on July 14, 1968, under which the USSR agreed to support directly the DRV's annual budget. The details of this agreement were never released, but it is believed that by 1970 the USSR was funding 80 percent of the North Vietnamese state budget.

By the 1970s, USSR assistance to the DRV was diverse and voluminous:

> Soviet built enterprises in Vietnam account for 75 percent of the coal being produced; one third the electric power produced and all the tin mined. Engineers have reconstructed the port of Haiphong. . . .
>
> Work on the design and construction of coal mines is being done by 140 Ukranian mining specialists; 60 engineers and technicians are working at hydro-electric stations. . . .
>
> The USSR is supplying Vietnam with fertilizer, pyrites, various metals, agricultural machinery, industrial equipment, motor vehicles, oil products, foodstuffs and clothing and fabrics, totaling 220,000 tons (July to September 1971). . . . Cargo delivered to North Vietnam from Soviet ports in the Far East

totaled 350,000 tons; North Vietnamese cargo carried in Soviet
vessels to third countries totaled 200,000 tons (in the same July–
September 1971 period). . . .

In addition to military supplies the Soviet Union has given
the battling DRV all around economic aid . . . in the
constructions of 45 industrial enterprises and other projects. The
most important of these are the Thach Ban Hydroelectric power
station, the Uong Bi thermal electric power station, the Vang
Danh and Mong Duong coal mines, coal pits, a plant for the
production and repair of mining equipment in Campha, a power
equipment repair shop, plants for the production of cutting
instruments and bearing repairs, means of communication, a
bakery plant with a capacity of 50 tons of baked goods daily,
and a number of other food industry enterprises.[13]

MILITARY ASSISTANCE

The first post–Viet Minh War military aid from Moscow for the
DRV that the author has been able to document is the dispatch to
Vietnam in 1957 of an unspecified number of USSR Army officers as
faculty advisers in PAVN artillery and engineering schools.[14] PAVN's
needs at the time were of the palace guard type—that is, military
hardware to maintain the regime in power. However, almost everything
required had to be imported, as there were no arms factories in North
Vietnam. During the 1950s a small but steady flow of such military
hardware came in from the USSR and a somewhat larger flow from
China. The war in the South had begun in 1959 but did not initially
levy much demand on the USSR as quartermaster as activity in the
South chiefly consisted of mobilization rather than combat; in any event,
strategy called for the southern forces to be self-sustaining and to capture
what they needed from the enemy.

All of this changed when the nature of the war changed in 1965—
because of a new Hanoi strategy, the arrival of U.S. ground troops in
South Vietnam, and the advent of air war in North Vietnam. Great
logistic demands were now imposed by Hanoi on Moscow, and the
response was forthcoming.

The seminal event in the USSR's wartime support of the DRV was
the Kosygin Mission to Hanoi in February 1965. The meeting, we now
know, was devoted chiefly to planning overall war strategy and to
determining Hanoi's future military needs for which the USSR would
be responsible. It was a detailed study and included the contribution
of several key Soviet military officials who were part of the delegation:
General Yevgeny Loginov, Soviet minister of Civil Aviation; Marshal

Konstantin Vershinin, chief of the Soviet Air Force; General Georgy Sidorovich; and the future Soviet leader, Yuri Andropov.

The Kosygin Mission had profound historical meaning beyond the fact that it arranged for the USSR to fund the DRV's war. In effect it authorized full-scale protracted conflict, because without USSR commitment, Hanoi leaders could not have embarked on the course that they did.

Specifically the mission accomplished the following: It fixed the volume and kind of military assistance that the DRV could expect from the USSR. It underwrote the Vietnamese economy to the extent that the USSR in effect agreed to subsidize the DRV state budget to permit conduct of war in both the North and the South. And it renegotiated, consolidated, and reconfirmed past economic agreements, adjusting them to wartime requirements.

Unofficially at the time it was reported that the Kosygin Mission committed itself to an initial military aid program of about 1 billion rubles.[15] The DRV's public description of the mission's work was laconic. Said VNA: "There was unanimity about the measures to be taken to strengthen the defense potential of North Vietnam."[16]

In mid-April came a follow-up military aid mission by the Vietnamese to Moscow, headed by General Vo Nguyen Giap, with Le Duan and Foreign Minister Nguyen Duy Trinh. The three spent a week in discussions with Brezhnev, Kosygin, and Alexander Shelepin. This was followed by an aid mission under economic czar Le Thanh Nghi, resulting in a supplementary aid agreement signed by the two sides on July 10, 1965.

Military shipments resulting from the Kosygin and Giap missions began at once. By September Kosygin could report to the CPSU Central Committee Plenum that "we have already supplied North Vietnam with a considerable amount of weapons and military equipment. Our policy is to continue to render North Vietnam all the assistance, material and political, that it needs."[17]

By December the Soviet Defense Ministry's newspaper, *Red Star*, was reporting that the "rockets and fighters made by the Soviet people are guarding the skies of North Vietnam."[18] That month Le Thanh Nghi returned to Moscow and on December 21, 1965, the two sides signed their annual aid and trade protocol for 1966, about which *Pravda* said:

> The aid given by the Communist Party, the government, and the people of the Soviet Union to the Vietnamese struggle is a great inspiration to the people and gives them immense strength in the fight against American aggression and for deliverance of the homeland. The signing of the present agreements on economic

and other aid between our countries is valuable support and assistance in the struggle of our peoples and makes a positive contribution to the strengthening and development of the fighting solidarity between our countries in the common revolutionary cause.[19]

Radio Moscow and *Komsomolskaya Pravda* throughout January and February 1966 noted that North Vietnam was receiving weapons, aircraft, rockets, and anti-aircraft weapons with radar guidance systems. This is a typical report: "The Soviet Union is faithful to Vietnam in its international duty. . . . The world knows all about USSR's help . . . up-to-date weapons, aircraft, rockets and munitions and other equipment necessary to strengthen Vietnam's defensive power."[20]

The emphasis in such reportage was on the defensive character of the weapons. Radio Moscow said North Vietnam was receiving "all they ask for" in war materiel and noted that PAVN now had Soviet-made surface-to-air missiles, quick-firing self-tracking anti-aircraft weapons and supersonic interceptor fighter aircraft.[21]

The CPSU in March 1966 sent private letters to Communist parties in Western Europe describing the Soviet aid to Vietnam during 1965:

The Soviet Union delivers to the DRV great quantities of armaments, including rocket installations, anti-aircraft artillery, aircraft, tanks, coastal artillery, warships and many other items. In 1965 alone weapons and war material to the amount of a half billion rubles was sent to North Vietnam. Moreover, North Vietnam received aid in training of pilots, rocket personnel, tank and artillery specialists. Our military aid is given to the extent regarded necessary by the Vietnamese leaders themselves. Large military and material assistance is also given by the USSR to the National Liberation Front of South Vietnam.[22]

Moscow press discussion of the USSR's state budget in late 1966 indicated that defense expenditures had increased from 5 to 15 percent and attributed the increase to the Vietnam War.

Hanoi was particularly circumspect in acknowledging the military traffic, especially in the early years of the war. This bland 1967 treatment by Le Thanh Nghi is typical:

In our present fight against the U.S. imperialists we have an extremely big rear—the socialist camp. . . . The Soviet Union has been assisting us relentlessly and in every way, materially and morally. . . . Thousands of Soviet technicians assist us in building and developing our economy. . . . The USSR has provided us with the necessary war means to defeat the U.S. aggressors.[23]

Gradually the press treatment by Hanoi and Moscow became more explicit. An August 1971 TASS report revealed that new agreements had been signed

> to strengthen the defense capacity of North Vietnam . . . and greatly increase [shipment] of rockets, radar equipment, jet aircraft, anti-aircraft weapons and thousands of Soviet military experts to help Vietnamese soldiers master military techniques. . . . Vietnam [is being] supplied with petroleum products, transport means, arms, ammunition, and other military supplies necessary for developing the DRV's economy and to strengthen its defense capability. . . . Essential armaments, ammunition, and other military supplies, the basis of the DRV air defenses, came from the Soviet Union. Soviet instructors help Vietnamese fighting men undergo training in the Soviet Union's military schools. As foreign observers and military specialists acknowledge, the Soviet Union's support is one of the most important factors.[24]

After the war the USSR was even more specific:

> In their [DRV] struggle against U.S. aggression . . . the Soviet Union, loyal to its internationalist obligation, provided Vietnam with unlimited assistance in combat equipment. . . . Modern rockets, fighter planes, artillery pieces, tanks, other technical equipment for war, ammunition, fuel and food supplies were continuously shipped from the Soviet Union to Vietnam. Everything needed to hit back at the enemy was continuously shipped from the Soviet Union to Vietnam. Soviet military experts in battle positions in Vietnam and in Soviet military academies helped train Vietnamese citizens as command cadres and military experts.[25]

The military aid supplied North Vietnam by the USSR during the war was not exactly generous, but essential needs were met. Hanoi's war would have been impossible without it, for it had neither tank factories nor the capability to make howitzers, missile launchers, or even rifles.

Vietnamese Communist forces during the war were supplied with the best of Soviet military technology. The commonly held image of barefoot guerrillas fighting with homemade shotguns was as false as the notion that North Vietnam lay as helpless as Ethiopia in 1938 before incoming bombers. The air defenses used by North Vietnam during the war were vastly superior to any ever previously seen in action, including those of London and Berlin during World War II. There were some 6,000 anti-aircraft weapons ranging from 37mm to 100mm scattered across North Vietnam, as well as 35 SA-2 surface-to-air missile (SAM) batteries (with six missile launchers per battery) and 15 SAS-3 batteries (with five missile launchers per battery)—a total of about 250 missile launchers. PAVN had other tactical missiles, such as the heat-seeking rocket known to be so deadly to helicopters and low-flying aircraft.

Soviet build-up of the DRV air defenses began in late January 1965. The first surface-to-air missiles with Soviet technical advisers arrived in February, the same month that the United States began its systematic bombing and air strikes in North Vietnam. A crash military supply program was launched following the Kosygin and Giap missions (February and April 1965). As a result, some 500,000 tons of war materiel arrived in North Vietnam in 1965; 1.5 million metric tons (mt) arrived in 1966, followed by 2 million mt in 1967. The number of radar-controlled anti-aircraft weapons rose from virtually nothing in mid-1964 to 1,500 by mid-1965 and 6,000 by October 1966. Thirty SAM batteries, manned by Vietnamese with 4,000 Soviet missile advisers and technicians, were operational by the end of 1965. In the first three years of the war the USSR shipped some 10,000 "barrels" to Vietnam—that is, 120mm and 140mm rockets; 120mm and 160mm mortars; and artillery up to the 152mm weapon, which has a ten-mile range. Several hundred fighter planes were also delivered (MIG 15s, MIG 17s, supersonic MIG 21s, and, later, the more advanced MIG 21C and MIG 21D), along with a few Ilyushin 28 twin-jet tactical bombers, although these never saw action. For ground use and the major offensives of 1967-1968, 1972, and 1975, the military supplied T-54 and PT-76 tanks, AK-47 and AK-57 automatic rifles, machine guns of various calibers (at least a half-million total during the war), helicopters, military trucks, and vast quantities of sophisticated communication equipment. The USSR's response to the military failure suffered by Hanoi in the 1968 Tet Offensive was to announce a 20 percent increase in military shipments to North Vietnam. Soviet oil tankers, including the famous long-serving SS Poti and SS Kostroma, for years plied the route from "mother Odessa" to Haiphong. The USSR supplied all of North Vietnam's petroleum during the war.

In terms of sheer volume (i.e., tonnage off-loaded at Haiphong), the peak of USSR military aid shipments was July 1969. In the years before, since 1965, deliveries had risen rapidly; after 1969 they slowly began to decline. The type of military hardware being delivered also was changing, from small arms and light weaponry to the heavier and more expensive type of armament. Much of this was air power. The PAVN Air Force MIG inventory tripled in three years from mid-1967 to mid-1970, increasing from about 80 to about 336 (including the 111 planes lost during this period). The first shipments were mostly MIG 15s and 17s; by 1970 they were mostly MIG 19s and 21s.[26]

As 85 percent of the hardware being delivered in the later years of the war was of the more sophisticated type, most came from the USSR and East Europe; China was simply unable to provide such aid. Simpler war materiel, such as uniforms, small arms, and so on, did continue to come from China, however.

As North Vietnam's productive capacity and manpower were diverted to war needs, the country became more and more dependent on the USSR and China for civilian goods and services. Commodity aid shipments increased steadily as a result. Two Le Thanh Nghi missions to Moscow in 1968 (May and November) negotiated supplementary aid agreements for large quantities of food, fuel, and transportation equipment; steel and ferrous metals; chemical fertilizers; and military equipment to replace depleted stocks. By the end of the war the USSR had built or rebuilt 420 major industrial factories or enterprises, had helped expand the northern road and railroad system, had made a major contribution to keeping DRV agriculture going, and was supplying Hanoi with everything from circus equipment to voice teachers.

During the war a steady stream of Vietnamese traveled to the USSR for military training and civilian technical schooling. Air cadets were trained in MIGs and Czech L-29 Delfins at the Soviet Air Force Academy at Bataisk.[27] Future railroad engineers went to the Institute of Railroad Transport Engineers in Moscow and prospective sea captains to the Maritime Engineering School in Odessa. The prewar level of training had been about 1,000 Vietnamese per year, but during the war it rose to about 10,000 Vietnamese at any one time for training, scattered among some fifty Soviet cities. At the same time there was a flow of Soviet specialists and technicians to the DRV. They served some eighty enterprises and included geologists, animal breeders, engineers, machine tool workers, and steel makers.

Moscow provided other services. USSR agents in Hong Kong and in the South Vietnamese black market purchased some half-million dollars worth of piasters a week for use by the NLF in South Vietnam and Cambodia.[28] Two electronically laden Soviet trawlers stationed themselves four miles off the runway at the U.S. Air Force base on Guam, monitoring take-offs of the B-52 missions to Indochina and radioing data to Hanoi. In 1970 the USSR began propaganda broadcasts to U.S. servicemen in South Vietnam—in English and laced with

American slang. A typical broadcast would urge these servicemen to take a rest and recreation trip outside Vietnam, and then desert:

> Don't forget that certain people in the States are waiting for the
> day when you get back. . . . The only way of making sure is to
> go the other way from Vietnam after your six day leave. You
> guys are really rotting in the jungle while some people are
> raking in the dough back in the states. . . . Go on, boys, keep
> on fighting. Go ahead, keep on dying![29]

Another broadcast told the story of a GI who decided to go AWOL while in a Tokyo hotel swimming pool. "Geez! In Vietnam we had to swim in bomb craters," the alleged GI is quoted as saying. "Damn this war!" Said in another broadcast: "Every GI in Vietnam dreams of returning to his hometown in the USA and quite a number would like to do something about it." Said in a third: "All that has to be done is to take part in the struggle against the Vietnam War. Go AWOL often. Violate traffic rules. Grow long hair. Do everything that will give the Army a reason to discharge you."[30]

Moscow also pressed for greater war contributions from East Europe, particularly after 1968. It is estimated that of the military assistance provided in the period 1969–1973, about 25 percent came from East Europe, chiefly Czechoslovakia and East Germany.

Moscow's total expenditures in the Vietnam War can be variously calculated, with different totals struck.[31] By one reliable estimate that takes into account all direct and indirect costs (1960–1975), the total is $8 billion. Based on a formula derived from comparative production costs—that is, from the cost of the goods and services had they been purchased in the United States—the total is somewhat higher, about $11 billion for ten years (1965–1975). The most conservative total for USSR military aid in the period 1965–1975, using a purchasing power formula, is $3.6 billion. The general range accepted by most U.S. government analysts is around $5 billion, a figure the author also accepts.

In comparative terms it is clear that the USSR's contribution to the Vietnam War in one year, 1968, exceeded the cost of its support of the Communist side throughout the entire Korean War. Assuming the $5 billion figure, military aid from the USSR to the DRV from 1965 to 1975 accounted for about 20 percent of the military aid it provided worldwide. And it represented one-third of its military aid to non-Communist countries during the period. It is probably a safe estimate that Soviet aid represented about 65 percent of the total received in North Vietnam during the war (with 25 percent coming from China and 10 percent from Eastern Europe).

A constant major problem concerned assured delivery of war goods a third of the way around the world. Overland shipment across the USSR and through China required tedious and time-consuming cargo transfers at Zabaykalsk, the transfer point south of Irkutsk, or at Druzhba, Kazakhstan, or Naushki in Mongolia because Chinese and North Vietnamese rail systems could not accommodate Soviet boxcars.[32] Goods then went to Vietnam via the Nanning-Hanoi and Kunming-Hanoi railway lines, or by truck along the eight major roads from China to North Vietnam. Most Soviet-made goods came overland in the early years. There were natural delays and slowdowns due to the vagaries of the Chinese railway system. Deliberate disruption and sabotage also occurred. When this problem first began to develop in 1967, the DRV pushed through an agreement under which it and not China took delivery at the Sino-Soviet border and arranged onward transportation, thus reducing (though not eliminating) disruption. It should be remembered that this agreement was written during the Great Proletarian Cultural Revolution in China, when Beijing had lost considerable administrative control in the provinces.

One North Vietnamese cadre told the author of a 1966 incident he witnessed whle working in a Hanoi freight yard. A train from China arrived, and the engineer said that fifty miles from the Vietnam border the train had been stopped by Chinese provincial troops who removed crates of new rifles and replaced them an equal number of crates filled with worn-out rifles that had been received from the USSR fifteen years earlier. In another instance, People's Liberation Army (PLA) technicians learned that a new-model surface-to-air missile was passing through China; they arranged for the train to be stopped, removed the missile, disassembled it for copying, reassembled it, and sent it on to Vietnam (however, they reassembled it incorrectly—hence the clear evidence of tampering). When Hanoi complained about these incidents, the Chinese either blandly denied all or offered the explanation that the USSR was cleaning out its military warehouses and shipping obsolete and worn-out material to North Vietnam.[33]

The USSR complained publicly of this "lack of cooperation" by China, of "obstacles placed in the way of the transit of Soviet goods across Chinese territory to Vietnam . . . [and] provocations against Soviet personnel who cross China on their way to Vietnam."[34] When nothing came of these complaints, the USSR cut back on the number of land shipments. From 1965 to 1970 the percentage of total Soviet goods to Vietnam passing through China dropped from 80 percent to 50 percent, then to 25 percent by 1975. Some observers at the time believed the Chinese hoped their sabotage would cause more Soviet aid to go the sea route, thus forcing the United States to blockade North Vietnamese ports (as with Cuba in 1962), which in turn would provoke a U.S.-USSR confrontation. Chinese harassment did somewhat reduce the quantity of USSR war goods shipments in the early years. Soviet Defense Minister Marshal Malinovsky in 1966 told an interviewer in Budapest that the USSR would have been able to give North Vietnam more aid if it had not been for the transport difficulties created by the Chinese.[35]

Soviet sea transport went either along the 7,500-mile route from Odessa in the Black Sea or from the eastern ports of Vladivostok, Nakhoda, and Khomsk. Upon arrival in Vietnam most shipments went into Haiphong, a 31-foot deep harbor about 18 miles up the Cua Cam and Dinh Vu Cut river system. Haiphong Port, until enlarged, could accommodate only six ocean-going vessels at a time (although several dozen more could moor in the river and discharge cargo into lighters). Other North Vietnamese ports, chiefly Hong Gay and Cam Pha, could accept coastal freighters but not the larger vessels from the USSR and East Europe. Some sea shipments were transferred to barges in China, at Chan-Kiang, and entered Vietnam via the coastal canal system. Much of the Chinese aid was shipped this route via barges.

Early on (around 1966) an average of 8 Soviet freighters arrived in North Vietnam monthly. In addition, an average of 5 East European vessels and 15 or so coastal freighters came from China, often carrying Soviet freight. Near the end of the war this traffic had risen to about 125 Soviet vessels plying the Odessa-Haiphong run and another 25 working out of Vladivostok. It was estimated that these 150 vessels accounted for about 75 percent of the total tonnage delivered from the USSR, the remainder coming overland from China.

Wartime seagoing activity was described by Moscow thus:

> Five years have elapsed since the establishment of the Friendship Bridge between Vladivostok and Haiphong. This navigation line was first opened by vessel Smirdrov in December 1966. Scores of Soviet vessels have sailed on the line since. Despite the U.S. planes' savage bombing of the vessels of the Soviet Far East Maritime Bureau, the imperialists could not obstruct the Soviet seamen from fulfilling their internationalist duty. Neither U.S. air pirates nor typhoons could hinder the Soviet vessels from sailing to the DRV. . . . We can positively state that the Soviet seamen contributed to the downing of about 3,500 U.S. planes over the DRV. The Soviet seamen have shipped to Vietnam modern military airplanes, antiaircraft artillery, and other weapons made by the Soviet workers.[36]

Later on, Hanoi also paid full tribute to the Soviet maritime effort. Said General Dong Si Nguyen:

The shipping line between the two countries was firmly maintained during the fierce war years. At various seaports in our country at that time, not a single day passed without seeing Soviet flag-carrying ships. Following the "dictates of their hearts and mind," Soviet cadres and sailors, with a high sense of international obligation, braved all sacrifices and hardships in making frequent visits to Vietnamese ports in order to ensure regular shipments of goods to our people.

We will never forget the good example set by senior sailor Yuri Shotov aboard the ship, Grisa Acopian, who sacrificed his life bravely under U.S. gunfire while performing his international duties in the area of Hon Gai and Cam Pha in May 1972. We will always remember Galina Camgneva, a female service worker—the mother of a daughter—aboard the ship (Pevev) who was injured by U.S. bomb fragments and bullets while stopping over at the Haiphong port. . . .

During the war years, many of our Vietnamese people might have seen "Soviet-made" trucks of all sizes everywhere— from the lowlands to the mountain region and from urban areas to the war-torn Truong Son [Ho Chi Minh Trail] road network. These trucks were among the tens of thousands of transportation means of all sorts which the Soviet Union donated to our people. . . . The Soviet Union has also provided the young merchant marine of Vietnam with dredgers, rescue ships, container ships and big oil tankers.[37]

Soviet military assistance came to full fruition with PAVN's 1972 Easter Offensive. By now General Giap had arrived at the kind of strategy he had wanted to pursue since 1965: a high-technology, big-unit war in which the enemy is outgunned. This required the best weapons the Communist world's armament factories could produce, and they met the challenge. The North Vietnamese armies in the 1972 offensive had more tanks (410) than the South Vietnamese (296) and more long-range artillery (130mm and 152mm guns). One observer at the time produced a list of Soviet-made military equipment and weapons used in the offensive, which ran to nearly four pages single spaced— in all, about 185 separate weapons or machines of war, which the USSR had shipped to North Vietnam for the campaign.[38] The offensive was defeated, but not for lack of logistic support by the USSR.

After the Paris Agreements were signed and during the so-called cease-fire period (1973–1975), the USSR helped rebuild the PAVN equipment and logistic system. Estimates on the cost of this effort vary but may have been as high as $2.5 billion. During the same period the USSR supplied the DRV with increased amounts of commodity aid such as food, petroleum, cement, fertilizer, and construction equipment. It also launched an intensive effort to restore and develop electrical production and expand the textile industry. Then, as a final gesture of open-handedness, the USSR wrote off all the debts incurred by North Vietnam before and during the war: "Following the signing of the Paris Agreements in 1973 . . . the Soviet Communist Party and government declared the cancellation of all past debts, even while continuing to give us economic and technical aid."[39]

Despite the extensiveness of Soviet military assistance, the dominant attitude held by many Vietnamese Communists was that inadequate assistance had been provided. The author had a long conversation in 1969 with a PAVN POW colonel whose branch was artillery. He complained at length about the USSR's failure to deliver surface-to-surface missiles to North Vietnam for use against Dixie Station and Yankee Station, the two U.S. Navy flotillas off Vietnam; he said he found it "incomprehensible that Moscow gives these to Ben Bella and Nassar but not to Ho Chi Minh." He, and the other North Vietnamese interrogated, also deprecated the Soviets' motives with respect to arms shipments, saying that Moscow's generosity was merely the result of the Sino-Soviet dispute.

The Kremlin today regards its aid to the DRV as having been a decisive factor in the final victory (which it was), and it is stung by what it considers a lack of gratitude on the part of the Vietnamese. Nikita Khrushchev expressed this sentiment of Soviet officials in his memoirs:

> In the Last Will and Testament of Ho Chi Minh nothing is said about the enormous, unselfish help which the Soviet Union is giving Vietnam. Our assistance has been decisive because without material aid from the Soviet Union it would have been impossible for Vietnam to survive under the conditions of modern warfare. . . . Vietnam has no choices but to rely on the Soviet Union. In order to achieve victory they must have the appropriate arms and these arms they can obtain only from the Soviet Union. China can't give Vietnam what it needs today. . . . Vietnam wouldn't be able to conduct its military resistance against American aggression if it weren't for the economic and material aid provided by the Soviet Union. For example, take an announcement that the North Vietnamese army of liberation has launched a rocket attack on a U.S. air base. Naturally these rockets weren't manufactured in the jungles of Vietnam. They came from the factories of the Soviet Union.[40]

Hanoi officials to this day seem unwilling to express enthusiastic public gratitude for Soviet wartime support and only grudgingly acknowledge the assistance received. This statement by Council of Ministers Vice-Chairman Tran Quynh is typical and is as close as Hanoi has ever come to saying thank you:

> During the anti-U.S. war of resistance for national salvation the Soviet-provided equipment and commodities as well as weapons, military hardware, missiles, anti-aircraft guns and aircraft enabled our intelligent and talented people to develop their military efficiency to the fullest. . . . Economic and military assistance [from the USSR] was one of the decisive factors leading to the total victory of our people.[41]

POSTWAR ECONOMIC RELATIONS

The Vietnam War ended suddenly and in a manner that no one in the Hanoi leadership had anticipated. The resultant pell-mell rush into the postwar world was nowhere more chaotic than in the economic sector.

North Vietnam's economy at war's end was agrarian—85 percent of its labor force was engaged in food production or food distribution; there was virtually no heavy industry in the full meaning of that term. The DRV agricultural plant had become antiquated by 1975 because there had been virtually no capital investment in agriculture since the early 1960s. Other sectors of the economy, particularly transportation, were in equally poor shape because of neglect or destruction by bombing. In the South the economy was more advanced, having been force-fed by an infusion of US$12 billion and was fairly close to economic takeoff by 1975. However, its economy, typical of wartime economies, was distorted by a poor service-production ratio and a host of fiscal problems.

Initially the victorious Politburo in Hanoi decided to retain the separate economic arrangement for perhaps five years, then to gradually merge the two. The second Five-Year Plan (1976–1980), in its draft stage at the time of victory (and, of course, applicable only to North Vietnam), went forward as originally written, with a separate economic plan for the South to be devised later. That policy, made in the first week of May 1975, lasted only a few months. At the Twenty-fourth Plenum in Dalat in August 1975, the slower merger decision was canceled, apparently on security grounds, and orders were issued to jam the two economic systems together as rapidly as possible. The confused economic scene deteriorated and within months the economies of both North and South Vietnam were nearly in a shambles. Mistakes and bad policy judgments made by the Hanoi leadership made matters worse. The economic malaise increased, stagnation deepened, and Vientamese dependence on the

USSR grew apace. By the late 1970s, 20 to 30 percent of the rice eaten in Vietnam was being supplied by the USSR. Vietnam was also completely dependent on the USSR for other vital commodities such as petroleum, chemical fertilizer, and spare parts for its transportation system.

Dependence on the USSR deepened with the breach of Sino-Vietnamese relations. China, in September 1975, had promised Hanoi some $3 billion for its 1976–1980 Five-Year Plan; about $1 billion of this had been delivered before Beijing ordered the aid cut off in mid-1978. This development presented the USSR with an irresistible opportunity and it moved quickly into the vacuum.

In the first twelve months after the war's end, under what was called an "urgent free assistance agreement" (i.e., emergency aid) signed June 9, 1975, the USSR pumped in an estimated $1.2 billion in food, petroleum, chemical fertilizer, and other commodity aid; pharmaceuticals; and rolling stock, vehicles, and spare parts for the transportation system.[42] This aid was supervised in Moscow by N. V. Talyzin, the minister of commerce, who over the next few years became Hanoi's chief economic contact in Moscow. Teams of economic advisers and specialists billed as experts on postwar construction arrived, along with high-level economic planners, to help prepare the new Five-Year Plan and to urge Vietnam to adopt the Soviet model for economic development. A special construction team from Moscow built Ho Chi Minh's mausoleum, which is larger than Lenin's. This initial outpouring of largesse by Moscow may have been one of the reasons why Vietnam inadvertently slipped so easily into economic dependence on the USSR.

Le Duan led a team of foreign aid experts on a trip to the USSR and seven other Communist countries (September through December 1975) in what was billed as a "tour of triumph." Its purpose was to thank Hanoi's socialist allies for their wartime assistance and to negotiate generous postwar economic aid agreements. The team was successful in the USSR and six East Europe countries, but not in China.

In Moscow Le Duan signed two agreements, one (on October 30, 1975) for long-term loans and the other (December 18, 1975) for economic aid and technical assistance. Both followed the framework of the SRV's second Five-Year Plan (1976–1980), which, it was being estimated at the time, would cost $3–4 billion. The USSR agreed to fund 60 percent of the Plan, at a cost estimated at $1.92 billion, and to make an additional $700 million in commodity aid available during the same period. The long-term (i.e., ten-year) loan agreement provided Vietnam with credit under highly favorable terms, to be used to rationalize and modernize the agricultural sector; to develop key industrial sectors, primarily electric power, mining, metallurgy, chemistry, and tool manufacture; and to supply oil, grain, raw cotton, and other commodities. The December agreements covered some forty major projects involving electric power, light industry, food industry, chemicals, machine manufacture, production of building materials, technical assistance in agriculture, and geological surveys. The biggest and showiest of these projects (described below) was the Hoa Binh (Peace) hydroelectric dam and water conservancy project, billed by the Hanoi press as the "project of the century."

In the first half-decade following the end of the war, economic aid for Vietnam increasingly meant commodity aid. Between 1976 and 1980 the USSR provided Vietnam with the following (either gratuitous or loan-funded): 5 million metric tons of petroleum products; 4.5 million mt of grain, mostly wheat; 1.5 million mt of chemical fertilizer; 400,000 mt of steel and iron; 1.6 million mt of cotton, and 100 million meters of cloth.[43] Food shipments, including grain, totaled 1.4 million tons in 1978, 2.1 million tons in 1979, and 1.9 million tons in 1980, at a three-year cost of about $900 million. Petroleum imports during the same time averaged about $120 million per year. Dependence on the USSR deepened with the Hanoi leadership's continuing inability to solve the country's basic economic problems and its 1979 two-front war. By this time the USSR through the Council for Mutual Economic Assistance (CMEA) mechanism (discussed below) was providing Vietnam with 70 percent of all its imports (which totaled about $12 billion worth in 1979)—that is, 94 percent of its raw cotton, 90 percent of its oil, steel, and fertilizer, and 70 percent of its imported grain (3 million tons). The total cost of this commodity aid and the second Five-Year Plan costs from 1975 to 1980 are conservatively estimated at $3.18 billion and probably come closer to $5 billion.

The second Five-Year Plan staggered through its allotted years to an end if not completion, beset by natural and manmade problems, stifled by Hanoi's overwhelming bureaucracy, savaged by the factional infighting between Politburo-level ideologues and pragmatists, and drained by emergency military needs occasioned by the invasion of Kampuchea and the border war with China.

COMECON

In the late 1970s the initial postwar economic relationship between Vietnam and the USSR, which was established in the turmoil of the war's end, began to change in subtle but basic ways. The change was a product of events: Vietnam's wars, its regional isolation, the Hanoi leadership's continuing inability to get the country's economic machine moving, and the growing impatience of the Soviets with the lack of economic progress. Gradually the relationship—not only in economic terms but the entire association—took on new characteristics. These are discussed in detail in the next chapter; suffice here to note that the economic sector moved toward greater Soviet-Vietnamese economic integration, more institutional structure and authority for Soviet advisers, intensive efforts to redress the horrendous trade imbalance, and, generally, more rational economic relations.

The year 1978 marked the beginning of this changed relationship. In that year Vietnam signed more than a dozen economic and other agreements with the USSR, six of them at one time. On June 29, 1978, Vietnam was admitted as the tenth member of the Communist common market system called Comecon, at the prime ministers' meeting of the Council for Mutual Economic Assistance in Bucharest.[44] Its admission came as something of a surprise to outside observers who interpreted it as a Moscow victory over China (which had made last-minute efforts to dissuade Vietnam from joining). Later it was learned that Romania and Poland objected to Vietnam's admission on the grounds that Vietnam was already an economic burden and now would become more so. Vietnam signed the CMEA Agreement on July 5, 1978. Actually it had been receiving CMEA assistance for several years; for instance, a CMEA geological team had surveyed Vietnam's oil and mineral deposits in August 1975.[45]

In November 1978, Le Duan and a large delegation of top Hanoi officials were in Moscow to sign a series of agreements pertaining to security, economic and military aid, trade, and science and technology. Specifically these were as follows: The USSR-Vietnam Friendship and Cooperation Treaty (discussed below); an agreement on economic, scientific, and technical cooperation; an agreement for the USSR to provide Vietnam with technological assistance to complete the Thang Long bridge over the Red River, rebuild the Hanoi railway terminal, and extend the track of the main railway line; an agreement to build a ground station in Vietnam for the Intersputnik space communications system and develop reliable rail service between Hanoi and Ho Chi Minh City; an agreement to establish a state-run farm for the cultivation of medicinal herbs and a plant to manufacture morphine and codeine; and an agreement to train and retrain Vietnamese specialists and technicians. In addition, both sides said they agreed on the importance of establishing more fundamental, long-term economic, scientific, and technological programs.

The philosophic basis of Comecon, of course, is the idea of a planned and integrated transportation, economic, and trade system. Probably the officials in Hanoi neither fully understood this concept nor realized what would be expected of them. Integration means restriction, which goes against the grain of the independent-minded members of the Hanoi Politburo. Their first public discussions of Comecon made no reference to any Vietnamese obligation. Rather, they spoke only of the benefits to accrue to Vietnam. Then, and even today, Hanoi leaders tend to regard Comecon as primariy an aid-generating mechanism. This commentary is typical:

> Ninety-two countries in Asia, Africa and Latin America have received economic and scientific-technical assistance from CMEA. Of the 4,600 industrial and other enterprises built in these countries with this assistance, 3,100 have been commissioned. Thanks to the funds earmarked by CMEA for this purpose in 1973, 4,000 students from 57 developing countries have been granted scholarships to continue their studies in various higher schools in socialist countries. . . . CMEA pays keen attention to the cases of its members with lagging economies: Mongolia, Cuba and Vietnam. Vietnam in particular, long before joining this organization, has received from the socialist community huge material and scientific-technical assistance. The Soviet Union alone has helped the community build 200 industrial and public-interest projects. . . . Brother countries have trained a huge contingent of scientists and technicians of higher and secondary levels numbering about 100,000, i.e., one-third of her total scientific and technical personnel. Bilateral and multilateral agreements have been signed within the framework of CMEA to help her catch up with the general level within the shortest time.[46]

Joining CMEA did provide Vietnam with new economic advantages, such as a preferential exchange rate in intrabloc trading. And, chiefly as a political gesture, CMEA quickly took over some of the aid projects abandoned by China:

> The restoration of the Thong Nhat railroad was a symbol of the solidarity of the fraternal socialist countries. The USSR supplied more than 300 kilometers of rail, 5,000 tons of chemicals to treat ties and thousands of tons of iron and steel to make bridges. Hungary supplied 700 tons of equipment for telegraph lines. Bulgaria supplied cement mixers. The GDR supplied compressors and truck-mounted cranes. Poland supplied rails, 10 diesel generating stations and so forth.[47]

By the mid-1980s Vietnamese officials appeared to have accepted the idea of integration into the socialist world's economic bloc. In January 1986 Vietnam was host to the thirty-seventh CMEA Cooperation in Planning Committee meeting, at which representatives from nine socialist countries sought to coordinate joint economic planning. (The conference slogan was "Progress to the Year 2000.") The chairman, Soviet Politburo member N. V. Talyzin, also met separately with SRV Planning Commission Chairman Vo Van Kiet, an important figure on the Hanoi economic scene. If nothing else these meetings demonstrated the steady and continuing integration of the Vietnamese economy.[48]

Vietnam is a member of the CMEA Permanent Commission on Foreign Trade, the CMEA Organization of Cooperation of Railroads, the CMEA Organization of Postal, Telephone, and Telegraph Communication, the CMEA United Institute of Nuclear Research, the CMEA International Center of Scientific and Technical Information, and the Conference of Representatives of the Academies of Sciences in Socialist Countries, which has CMEA affiliation. The organization provides services to Vietnam's civil aviation and governmental statistics-gathering institutions. It has sent in geologists to hunt for bauxite, tin, gold, and new coal deposits. Its experts have established a Vietnam patent office and biotechnology research facilities, and they act as advisers at the Dalat nuclear reactor.

CMEA membership involves participation in what is called the transferable ruble process, which imposes controls on international exchange. Apparently this is regarded with suspicion by some Hanoi ideologues. Explanations by Soviet economists are published in Hanoi journals to reassure; the following is typical:

> The transferable ruble is the most important element of the monetary financial system of the CMEA member countries. . . . In the international arena it is a totally new style of currency, unprecedented in world monetary practice. . . . All countries and organizations that have and use the transferable ruble have equality and similar rights. This is clearly the opposite of the measure and style of operation of the capitalist world, which reflects dominance and [a] tendency toward aggression.[49]

CMEA aid is bilateral; that is, its Executive Committee approves projects, but actual implementation is left to the individual country. Hanoi interprets this as meaning parity in arrangements among socialist countries. For instance, Nguyen Lam, writing on oil exploration by CMEA in Vietnam, described it as "cooperating (with us) in exploiting Vietnam's natural and abundant riches for building socialism."[50] Lam's usage is indicative of the changing public rhetoric in Hanoi with respect to Comecon; of particular interest is the substitution of the idea of *equity* for *assistance* and extensive use in the press of the phrase *all-around cooperation*. This "exploiting" of Vietnam's natural resources in joint ventures has drawn outsider charges of Comecon neocolonialism. These charges have stung the USSR and it has struck back in its media.[51]

Some observers predicted when Vietnam joined Comecon that the relationship would grow increasingly strained, but this has not proved to be the case to date. The highest-level officials are dispatched to Council meetings: Pham Van Dong attended the thirty-fourth conference in Prague in June 1980, and General Vo Nguyen Giap, the thirty-fifth conference in Sophia in November 1981. Normally the Council meets at the prime minister level. The session held June 12–14, 1984, for the first time in thirteen years met at the chief of state or "summit" level in Moscow; Le Duan and Pham Van Dong attended as joint chairmen of the SRV delegation. SRV Council of Ministers Deputy Chairman and Politburo member Vo Chi Cong in mid-1986 became the ranking Hanoi official to head the SRV delegation at the more important meetings, replacing the demoted To Huu. Routine meetings are led by Nguyen Lam, Central Committee member, Secretariat member, and chief of the Party's Central Committee Industry Department. Other Vietnamese who figure prominently in CMEA and in the USSR economic intercourse are Vice-Chairman of the Council of Ministers Tran Quynh (who is also chairman of the Vietnam-USSR Intergovernmental Commission for Economic Scientific and Technical Cooperation); Dau Ngoc Xuan, vice-chairman of the SRV State Planning Commission; and Hoang Trong Dai, SRV vice-minister of trade.

TRADE RELATIONS

Since 1975 Vietnam has had one of the worst trade deficits of any country on earth. In joining Comecon it hoped to ease this problem. It has not succeeded to date. Given the heavy burden that Vietnam has represented for a decade, the USSR has mainted steady pressure, in and out of CMEA, to improve bilateral trade relations—specifically, to increase Vietnamese exports to the USSR. Its buying agents scour Vietnam for exportable goods, but to a large extent the matter is one of trying to get blood out of a stone. The USSR remains Vietnam's biggest trade customer by far.

Vietnam is an impoverished country, barely able to feed itself, with little heavy industry and only limited light industry to produce trade goods. In modest amounts it can and does supply the USSR with five types of export: food, chiefly fruit, vegetables, tea, coffee, peanuts, fish, seafood, and spices; industrial agricultural products such as textiles, silk, rubber, jute, ramie, kenaf, lacquer, oil, and medicinal herbs; minerals such as coal and small amounts of tin, gold, and bauxite (eventually, perhaps, petroleum); handicraft such as carpeting, wickerware, sandals, and clothing; and fine art such as porcelain and lacquerware.

Soviet exports to Vietnam have risen steadily in the past two decades. It supplied first North Vietnam and now all of Vietnam in any one year with as much as 90 percent of all its petroleum, 77 percent of its food imports, 90 percent of its steel and chemical fertilizer imports, and 95 percent of its cotton.

The first major DRV-USSR postwar trade agreement, the five-year Commodities Exchange and Payment Protocol (signed in Moscow on October 31, 1975), called for an increase of trade by 1.5 times in the next five years. Soviet imports did increase by about 10 percent in the following year. Each year thereafter the pattern repeated itself, with an annual trade agreement that set norms that were not met. Hanoi spokesmen would cloud the trade reports by expressing trade in percentage increases over long periods of time, or by avoiding statistics entirely. Former Council of Ministers Vice-Chairman To Huu's comment is typical:

> Vietnamese imports from the USSR increased 205 times from
> 1955 to 1979 and exports to the USSR increased 134 times. . . .
> (We) import raw materials such as ferrous and non-ferrous
> metals, chemicals, fuels, chemical fertilizers and petroleum
> products; building materials; technical equipment; grain; cotton,
> cloth, fibers; and essential consumer goods. Sympathizing with
> our country's difficulties the USSR has granted us preferential
> terms [and] . . . has kept imports at their 1957 price level while
> the price within CMEA of course is much higher and the price of
> the world market has risen to unprecedented levels.[52]

An SRV-USSR Commodities Exchange and Payment agreement signed in Moscow on July 30, 1981, called for a 90 percent increase in Vietnamese exports to the USSR. Vietnam was to begin or increase shipments of rubber, lumber, coffee, spices, and handicrafts. The USSR would treble the amount of chemical fertilizer sent, double steel shipments, and increase shipments of construction equipment. Later Hanoi said:

> In the 1975–85 period the value of goods exchanged between the
> two countries increased almost tenfold, with Vietnamese exports
> to the Soviet Union going up 440 percent. In the 1975–84 period
> the value of Soviet exports to Vietnam increased 450 percent
> while the value of Vietnamese exports to the Soviet Union
> quintupled. In the 1981–84 period in particular, fine results were
> obtained. . . . In 1984 Vietnam's exports to the Soviet Union
> were up 165 percent compared to 1980. The Soviet Union
> accounts for 80 percent of the value of Vietnam's trade with

TABLE 6.2
The Vietnam-USSR trade balance (in US$ millions)

Year	Import	Export	Balance
1976	308.4	84.4	-224.0
1977	372.0	176.1	-195.9
1978	446.4	222.5	-223.9
1979	680.3	225.0	-455.3
1980	700.1	242.4	-457.7
1981	1,006.4	232.2	-774.2
1982	1,322.0	339.5	-982.5
1983	1,180.3	306.5	-873.8
1984	1,178.4	302.7	-875.7
1985	1,296.2	337.7	-958.5
1986 (est.)	1,300	340	-960

Source: Drawn from an unpublished manuscript on
Vietnamese trade by Tetsusaburo Kimura (Tokyo: Institute
of Developing Economies, 1986).

> CEMA member countries and 60 percent of the total value of its
> trade with foreign nations. To Vietnam, the Soviet Union is the
> main, steady,, and ever-expanding market that accounts for more
> than 65 percent of Vietnam's import value. The Soviet Union
> ensures the satisfaction of 80–100 percent of Vietnam's demands
> for petroleum, cast iron, nitrate fertilizer, iron, steel, cotton, and
> nonferrous metals.[53]

The bottom line, however, is that the SRV's annual trade deficit
with the USSR is about $850 million.[54] In January 1986 meetings were
held in Hanoi between the chairman of the USSR State Planning
Commission and his Vietnamese counterpart, Vo Van Kiet, at which it
was announced that trade between the two countries was expected to
increase 1.7 times during the current Five-Year Plan (1986–1990).[55] By
1986 it was estimated that the SRV's trade debt to the USSR amounted
to about $5 billion, interest on which ran to about $360 million a year.
How much of this was merely the result of a bookkeeping formality
was impossible to determine. In any event such an obligation is beyond
Vietnam's financial capacity. Hanoi officials apparently believe that
eventually, as it had in the past, the USSR will write off the debt.
    Soviet trade with Vietnam has increased at a faster rate than trade
with other Comecon countries (see Table 6.2). From 1976 to 1981 it
increased by 4.9 times, whereas it doubled with other USSR-CMEA
countries. The more trade, the more subsidy, of course. By comparison,

Soviet trade subsidies to East Europe rose from an average annual rate of $5.6 billion in the 1974–1978 period, to $10.4 billion in 1979, to an estimated $21.7–$24 billion in 1980.[56]

Soviet trading with Vietnam is no easy matter, as illustrated by the story about a shipload of empty beer bottles told by a Vietnamese refugee who had worked at the La Rue Brewery on Hai Ba Truong Street in Saigon. His beer plant was nationalized in 1976 and for a time managed by longtime employees. In 1978 a northern cadre with no experience in beer-making arrived as the new director. During his initial inspection of the plant the new director noted that the metal beer caps used in the plant were lined with cork. Where did the cork come from, he asked? From Algeria, he was told. It must be expensive, he replied. Yes, said the brew-master, but necessary. Start using cardboard instead, said the new director. The beer-maker explained that cardboard did not have the properties required, but the director would hear no argument. So an order went out to a local paper company, and eventually several million rounds of cardboard were delivered to the brewery and substituted for the cork in the beer caps. About this time, a Soviet trade delegation arrived on the scene in search of exportable goods. Discovering the La Rue Brewery, the visitors placed an order for an entire shipload of beer. In due time several tens of thousands of cases of beer were delivered to Saigon River dockside and loaded aboard a Soviet freighter that set sail, in the heat of summer, on a 6,500-mile journey around India, through the Suez Canal, into the Black Sea to Odessa. All the while, because the cardboard rounds in the beer caps had shrunk, breaking the seal, the beer in each bottle slowly evaporated. When the hatches were opened in Odessa, stevedores found as cargo a shipload of empty beer bottles, still capped.

Vietnam is short on exports but has one commodity to offer that is both plentiful and highly marketable, that is, hard-working, disciplined, semiskilled labor. Vietnam exports such labor under what is called its "creative labor cooperation program" (in the USSR and Europe it is commonly called "guest worker" program). Vietnam has formal agreements to supply labor to the USSR (as well as agreements with Czechoslovakia, Bulgaria, and East Germany). The basic purpose of these agreements is to help ease the USSR's labor shortage, fixed in 1985 at about 2 million job vacancies.

Export of Vietnamese labor to the USSR began on an experimental basis following negotiations in Hanoi in November 1981 between a Soviet delegation headed by L. A. Kostin, chairman of the State Committee for Labor and Social Questions, and Vice-Premier Nguyen Lam for the Vietnamese.[57] The next year (April 2, 1981), following an eight-day conference in Moscow, the SRV-USSR Labor Cooperation Agreement was signed by M. Lomonsov, chairman of the USSR State Committee for Labor and Social Problems, and SRV Minister of Labor Dao Thien Thi, who was put in charge of the program, which is administered by his ministry's International Labor Cooperation Department. Under the agreement Vietnamese workers go the USSR for three-year (in a few cases seven-year) tours. These "guest workers" are paid Soviet wage scales, but 30 percent of their salaries are remitted to the SRV treasury (possibly assigned to reduce the interest on the SRV debt). The program has been denounced by Vietnamese refugee groups in the United States as "Siberian slave labor" because some Vietnamese are reportedly in Siberia working on the natural gas pipeline being constructed from the Urengoy gas fields in Siberia, 2,800 miles across the USSR to Waidhaus, West Germany. How many Vietnamese are involved in this USSR work program is difficult to determine. A March 1986 Hanoi announcement indicated that in the previous five years a total of 73,000 guest workers had gone to the USSR, Bulgaria, Czechoslovakia, and East Germany, but no breakdown by country was given. The report also indicated that a total of 9,000 workers would leave for the USSR during 1986.[58]

A second means by which the USSR taps the Vietnamese Labor market is through local contract. This system was established as part of the SRV-USSR Goods and Exchange and Payment Agreement of July 31, 1981. Shortly after it was signed, the USSR began sending components of radios, calculators, and other small electronic and mechanical items to Vietnam for assembly and return to the USSR. Later this system was expanded to include other sectors, such as wool to be manufactured into rugs and carpets and medicines to be hand-packed. Under the agreement Vietnam retains 10 percent of the goods manufactured and ships the remaining 90 percent to the USSR.

LONG-TERM PLANS

The "new-type" Vietnam-USSR economic relationship—foreshadowed in the first CMEA program and in the Vietnamese and USSR statements of 1978—by the 1980s had taken on form and substance. This overhaul of the economic bondage that had begun so inadvertently at war's end was a consummation very much desired by both sides. Hanoi wanted it as a means of deepening and entrenching Soviet commitment. Moscow wanted it as a means of further melding the Vietnamese economy into the world Marxist system and, it hoped, as a less expensive way to aid Vietnam. Both sides wanted it as a means of rationalizing and generally making more cost-effective the entire economic association.

The changes are essentially institutional ones. The instrument employed is the planning mechanism. Since neither society ever makes a move without a plan—and both have major and minor plans as well as short- and long-range plans—what is required is collective planning, particularly joint, long-range, integrated planning.

The parameters and general guidelines of the planning function of the new relationship were hammered out at the June-July 1980 "summit" meeting in Moscow (Le Duan, Pham Van Dong, and Nguyen Lam were the chief Vietnamese representatives). The specific purpose of the gathering was to discuss the draft of Vietnam's next development plan, the SRV 1981–1985 Five-Year Plan. The two sides also negotiated a new oil exploration and exploitation treaty. But the significance of the meeting later proved to be the agreement in principle that economic relations would be institutionalized—that is, made more structured and longer ranged. The first victim of this decision was the annual economic aid agreement, which had been negotiated and signed each December since 1955. It was replaced by what was called "the state plan coordination system," defined in terms of permanent continuous rather than annual economic planning.

It appears that this arrangement was easily reached, although the ever-watchful Chinese asserted later that the central event at the summit meeting was Moscow's demand for greater authority in day-to-day administration of Soviet-funded economic programs in Vietnam—demands that it said Le Duan accepted with great reluctance, as discussed below. The SRV's third Five-Year Plan (1981–1985) clearly reflects the "new-type" economic thinking. Many of the current Soviet aid projects, perhaps a majority of them, involve advisory and specialist assistance and technology transfer rather than simply capital construction or commodity aid. Most of the projects are defined as joint ventures. Some seventy-three involve Soviet assistance in research and development in the fields of geology, agriculture, water conservancy, biology, marine resources, botany, ecology, metallurgy, communications, and public health.

Soviet project statistics are supplied by the Hanoi press (see Table 6.3). The difficulty in dealing with them is that the Hanoi media report USSR aid cumulatively, from year to year, each year giving totals that include new projects, ongoing projects from previous years, and sometimes even projects that have been completed. This statistical treatment tends to be contradictory. The following is a cumulative list of USSR aid projects over the years as reported in the Hanoi media:

- The 1950s: 31 industrial projects
- The first Five-Year Plan (1961–1965): 121 projects

TABLE 6.3
USSR assistance to DRV/SRV[a]

Year	Economic Aid	Military Aid
1955	$200 million	$10-15 million
1956	$100-120 m.	$15-25 m.
1957	$100-125 m.	$15-25 m.
1958	$110-135 m.	$15-25 m.
1959	$115-150 m.	$20-30 m.
1960	$100 m.	$20-30 m.
1961	$100 m.	$20-35 m.
1962	$100 m.	$20-35 m.
1963	$100 m.	$30-40 m.
1964	$100 m.	$35-50 m.
1965	$278 m.	$210-270 m.
1966	$150-165 m.	$360-455 m.
1967	$200-240 m.	$505-650 m.
1968	$290-305 m.	$390-440 m.
1969	$290-385 m.	$175-195 m.
1970	$320-345 m.	$110-205 m.
1971	$310-370 m.	$115-165 m.
1972	$300-330 m.	$300-375 m.
1973	$350-390 m.	$150-180 m.
1974	$400-450 m.	$170-245 m.
1975[b]	$450-500 m.	$123-150 m.
1976	$560-750 m.	$44-50 m.
1977	$570-1 b.	$75-125 m.
1978	$700-1 b.	$600-850 m.
1979	$800 m.-1.1 b.	$890-1.4 b.
1980	$2.9-3.2 b.	$790-905 m.
1981	$.9 b.	$.9 b.-1 b.
1982	$1.18 b.	$.95 b.
1983	$1.3 b.	$1.2 b.
1984	$1.4 b.	$1.3 b.
1985	$1.6 b.	$1.7 b.
1986 (est.)	$1.8 b.	$1.5 b.

[a]This chart was assembled over the years from a wide
number of sources including U.S. government agencies,
Japanese institutes, and government and private sources
in London, Paris, and Moscow. For most of these years
the sources supplied differing statistics. Hence what is
offered here is a high-low range of estimates. Though
not perfect, it is the best tabulation that can be offered
on Soviet assistance to Vietnam. The values are expressed
in U.S. dollars as of the dates given.

[b]After April 1975, statistics apply for all of Vietnam.

- The wartime years (1965–1975): No project breakdown but assistance to keep the war going
- The second Five-Year Plan (1975–1980): 162 projects
- The third Five-Year Plan (1981–1985): 300 projects
- The fourth Five-Year Plan (1986–1990): 550 projects

Thus, as the Hanoi press points out, the number of projects in the second Five-Year plan was greater than the total of the previous twenty years, and the number of projects in the third Five-Year Plan was double that of the second Five-Year Plan.[59]

By the mid-1980s USSR aid projects represented a significant portion of Vietnam's total economic infrastructure. These "lighthouses of Soviet-Vietnamese fraternal love," as they have been described, account for 23 percent of the coffee produced, 25 percent of the tea grown, 33 percent of the tin mined, 35 percent of the electricity generated, 35 percent of the cement manufactured, 71 percent of the machine tools manufactured, 89 percent of the coal mined, 90 percent of the sulphuric acid produced, and 100 percent of the superphosphate fertilizer manufactured, apatite mined, and die-cutting tools manufactured.[60]

In terms of cost to the USSR, the third Five-Year Plan was about 350 percent greater than the second Five-Year Plan and is estimated by outsiders at about $1 billion per year, or $5 billion for all nonmilitary aid during the entire plan.[61] This includes the twenty-three major and fifty smaller projects of the third Five-Year Plan; additional funding for the second Five-Year Plan projects that encountered cost overruns; commodity aid; and the cost to the USSR of salaries plus other expenses of some 7,000 Soviet advisers serving in Vietnam. The fourth SRV Five-Year Plan (1986–1990), according to *Nhan Dan* (July 18, 1985), will see a 100 percent increase in Soviet contributions over the third Five-Year Plan. Presumably this increase will mean a total cost to the USSR of $10 billion.

Another dimension of long-range planning between the two countries is research and development, which began in earnest at the sixth session of the Vietnam-USSR Joint Committee on Economic, Scientific, and Technical Cooperation (Moscow, June 16–20, 1980). The SRV delegation was headed by General Vo Nguyen Giap, who a few years earlier had left his military duties to take on the assignment of czar of Vietnam's science and technology program—essentially a training program to develop quickly large numbers of Vietnamese science and technology cadres. As stated in the joint statement at the end of the meeting:

The Committee discussed the development of scientific and technological cooperation between the two countries; using the results of joint scientific research for commercial purposes; training Vietnamese economic management specialists; and establishing policy for a Vietnamese scientific and technological development program. The committee studied the findings of the conference held by institutions of both countries on the 1981 to 1985 5-year plan. A joint protocol reflecting complete agreement by both sides on the issues discussed was signed.[62]

Throughout 1981 the "transformation" of Moscow-Hanoi economic planning relations continued at an ever-quickening pace. Le Duan led a party delegation to Moscow (February-March) for the twenty-sixth CPSU Congress, during which he and To Huu discussed new trade and aid arrangements with the Soviets; then the two returned early in September for additional meetings on aid and trade. In the summer of 1981 the two sides signed a series of economic and trade agreements: one on oil exploration-exploitation (noted above), which also established the Viet-Sov Petro organization (June 19); the Agreement to Coordinate National Economic Planning (July 9), which officially ended the practice of signing annual economic aid agreements; the SRV-USSR Economic, Scientific, Technical Cooperation Agreement (July 24), which facilitated schooling for Vietnamese students in the USSR; and the SRV-USSR 1981–1985 Commodity Exchange and Payments Agreement (July 30).

The July 9th agreement to coordinate the national economic planning of the SRV and the USSR covered the period 1981–1985, and the protocol signed stressed that there should be "long-term cooperation" in several areas and on the main programs of the SRV's third Five-Year Plan. The July 24th agreement on economic and technological cooperation set forth the institutional format; it also itemized some forty specific aid projects.

The drive to devise a mechanism for better long-range economic planning came into full bloom on October 31, 1983, with the signing in Hanoi of the USSR-Vietnam Long-Term Plan for Economic, Scientific, and Technical Cooperation and Development during the visit by a Soviet delegation headed by First Deputy Premier Geydar Aliyev; Le Duan signed for the SRV.

The thrust, in institutionalizing this long-range planning, was to establish what were called "priority areas." The principal priority areas were defined as development (and mechanization) of Vietnamese agriculture; fostering industrial support of agriculture (with increased steel production and machine tool manufacture capacity); increased energy and fuel production; expansion of transportation and communication sectors (more rolling stock, and improved maintenance); increased production of chemical fertilizer; and increased exports, primarily to the USSR (based more on "mutually beneficial compensation for the USSR"—that is, on meeting Soviet needs more closely).

At the end of the meeting, Aliyev explained the new arrangement at a press conference:

> During our talks it was agreed that we, the Soviet and
> Vietnamese peoples, must better use our latent powers in the
> area of economics and use them more effectively to build
> communism and socialism. We have sufficient reason to believe
> that the first long-term plan concerned with expanding economic,
> scientific, and technological cooperation in the history of Soviet-
> Vietnamese relations which was signed today will magnificently
> serve this purpose. This plan is something that effectuates—more
> correctly—gives concrete shape to the USSR-Vietnam Friendship
> and Cooperation Treaty in accordance with the conditions and
> capabilities of cooperation that exist today in the areas of
> economics. This plan gives us a realistic target for cooperation.[63]

One of the central characteristics of the new system was a shift to greater USSR aid in the form of more Soviet advisers and technology transfers, and more training programs for Vietnamese in the USSR. A *Pravda* article (November 11, 1983), in noting that Soviet aid to Vietnam in the following five-year period would be three times that of the present five-year plan, said much of the increase would be spent on personnel. Under various recent agreements, many projects have now become personnel oriented. Typically, they call for Soviet geologists to do survey work in oil and mineral fields; for engineers and architects to train Vietnamese teachers of these subjects; for specialists in education, medicine, and culture; for joint research projects in agriculture; for technical transfers in the form of technical documents and scientific studies; and for Soviet advisers to consult on ways for Vietnam to increase its exports and hard-currency earnings. Many of the projects remain "hard," but a clear shift has occurred toward coaching the Vietnamese in economic problem solving rather than simply shipping in machinery and goods. The years 1984 and 1985 saw a series of "specialist conferences" in which some 165 different technical topics were discussed. Some of this technical assistance is what might be called classified aid. References to it in the Hanoi press is guarded. For instance, a Hanoi press report indicated that the USSR was involved in a communications and liaison project for the Committee for State Security of the Ministry of the Interior, the purpose of which was "to safeguard national security." The nature of the project was not specified, but it appeared to have been a large undertaking, whatever it was.[64] It seems clear that the USSR in the future will seek to use research and development and advisory consultation in Vietnam as a partial substitute for the older forms of economic aid.

As the second half of the 1980s began, Vietnamese dependence on USSR largesse appeared to be easing.[65] Food production had started to rise and was at last above the subsistence level. Some of the worst malaise in agriculture and stagnation in domestic trade appeared to be ending. Oil production, though limited, finally was under way. Indeed, once the oil refinery being built by the USSR is completed, Vietnam may no longer be dependent on the USSR for its petroleum needs. Nevertheless, as of this writing, Vietnam continues to be a heavy burden for the USSR.

Future economic relations remain clouded. They depend, of course, on the success of the newly devised policies. Being tested now is a new approach to old SRV-USSR economic problems. The prospects for and the meaning of this changed approach can be identified in the larger framework of change in the overall relationship, which is the subject of the next chapter.

APPENDIX

USSR FOREIGN AID PROJECT LIST

This appendix contains a list and a discussion of USSR project aid to Vietnam since 1975. As noted in the text, the Hanoi press lists its aid projects cumulatively, lumping together the old and the new, the completed, the incomplete, and those still only on paper. As of January 1985 a total of about 950 projects (about 300 of them major) had been launched in thirty years, the majority of them since 1975. Of these, as of that date, about 200 major projects had been "put into operation" (to use the Hanoi press terminology), meaning they had been finished or were partially operational. Many projects during the first ten years were subjected to great delays because of poor Vietnamese Politburo planning; destruction by the Chinese during the 1979 border war; loss of key Vietnamese and ethnic Chinese personnel as "boat people"; inept management; corruption; and economic confusion generally. The result has been confusion in reporting aid projects by Hanoi. Projects are carried over from one aid agreement to the next; sometimes a project long under way will be listed as a new one; and there is much overlap and duplication in reporting. What appears below is a list, by sector, of the major economic aid projects funded by the USSR in the post–Vietnam War period.

ELECTRIC PRODUCTION

Soviet-built electric power plants now produce about 60 percent of all the electricity generated in what formerly was North Vietnam.[66] The USSR places great emphasis on electric power projects and over the years has gained considerable experience and capacity for such work. Moscow began its assistance to North Vietnam in this field with power plants as Vinh (thermal plant, 8,000 kw, 1955); Thanh Hoa (thermal, 500 kw, 1957); Phu Tho (thermal, 500 kw, 1957). It also rebuilt French hydroelectric plants at Ta Sa, Na Ngan, Dat Sa Na Pu Kong, and Cac Ba (1957); the Lao Cai and Dong Anh thermal plants (1959); the Ban Thach Hydroelectric Plant (1,000 kw) in 1962; and the Thac Ba Hydroelectric Plant (100 kw) in 1964.

Current electric power plant projects include the following:

1. The Hoa Binh (Peace) Hydroelectic Complex on the Da (Black) River[67] in Hoa Son Binh Province about 70 km west of Hanoi was begun in November 1979. This $2 billion venture, billed as the "project of the century" by the Hanoi press, has become the premier showcase of Soviet foreign aid in Vietnam. It is the largest electrical energy installation in Southeast Asia. Its original planned output (according to its 1975 design) was 1.9 megawatts (reduced to 1.7 megawatts), with a completion date of 1987; it has since been replanned with a 1.92 megawatt capacity (eight 240,000 kw turbines) and a completion date of 1990.[68] These revisions were due to changed planning for downstream use of the power. Final rated output is to be 8.16 billion kwh. Some 400 Soviet engineers and technicians have been on site since the early days; they have total design and construction authority over about 5,000 Vietnamese workers.

2. The Pha Lai Thermoelectric Power Plant, along the Pha Lai River near Thai Nguyen, in Hai Hung province, 60 km north of Hanoi, was begun in May 1980 and will be Vietnam's second largest electric energy producer. It is a thermal coal power plant with a planned initial capacity of 640,000 kw, and eventually, 1.3 million kw. One generator went on line in 1984; the next five are due to start during the rest of the decade. Some 4,200 Vietnamese workers are constructing it under the supervision of Soviet engineers.[69]

3. Uong Bi Thermal Coal Power Plant, built originally by the USSR in 1961, is now being renovated and enlarged by a team of fifty-five Soviet engineers and technicians. Its new rated capacity is to be 500,000 kw.

4. The Dong Hoi oil-fueled power plant (400,000 kw) was constructed in the early 1960s.

5. The Tri An Hydroelectric Power Plant in South Vietnam, on the Dong Ngai River in Dong Ngai province, some 70 km northeast of Ho Chi Minh City, was begun in March 1982 and as of early 1985 was still in its preliminary stage. It is to be completed at a cost of 6 billion dong, and its rated capacity of 400,000 kw makes it larger than any existing power plants in what was once South Vietnam. A November 1983 report indicated that a 1,500-person Soviet-Vietnamese labor force was on the scene doing site work. The estimate at the time was that the plant would go on line sometime in late 1987.[70]

6. The Thac Ba Electric Power Plant has a capacity of 220,000 kw.

7. The Ban Thach Hydroelectric Power Plant on the Ma River in Thanh Hoa province is of an unknown capacity.

8. Power plants at Ta Sa, Na Ngan and Lo Gam are being renovated.

9. Transmission lines with about 2,500 km of electric power are being installed, and the Hanoi electric power system is being modernized.

MINING

The USSR provided early assistance to the DRV coal mining industry, sending a team of engineers to the Quang Ninh mine in April 1955 to help open it and to other mines in the Hon Gai–Cam Pha area that had been abandoned during the Viet Minh War, when most of the French mining engineers and technicians departed. The team also helped open a new mine at Ha Lam. In the DRV's first Five-Year Plan (1961–1965), the USSR helped open or develop the Ha Ty, Deo Nai, Coc Sau, Vang Danh, and Moang Duong mines, thereby increasing the DRV's coal production from 600,000 mt in 1961 to 900,000 mt in 1965. In October 1971 the USSR and the DRV signed an ambitious agreement to expand coal production in North Vietnam. The major project here was the Cao Son open pit mine, which eventually became North Vietnam's largest coal mine, producing some 2 million mt of coal annually.

Vietnam today has twelve major coal mines in operation; six of these were built by the USSR and three others benefit substantially from Soviet aid. The six built by the USSR account for 80 percent of all current coal production in Vietnam. By late 1983 the USSR was involved in twenty major coal projects in Vietnam, including seven strip mines and five deep mines; road and railroad construction serving the mines; and the training of an estimated 2,000 Vietnamese coal engineers and technicians.[71]

Coal production in 1985 was estimated at about 4 million mt; the state plan goal for 1985 was 4.2 million mt. These figures pertain mostly to anthracite and bituminous coal; lignite is virtually unexplored. Vietnam is believed to have some 20 billion tons of coal deposits.[72] The following projects are now completed or under way:

1. Enlargement of the Cao Son strip mine in Quang Ninh province, north of Hanoi—Vietnam's largest coal mine (Soviet engineers in July 1980 began work to raise its annual production rate from 2 to 3 million mt).

2. Expansion of the Mao Khe coal mine from 500,000 to 2.1 million mt and construction of a coal-screening plant to serve the Pha Lai thermoelectric plant.

3. Expansion of the He Nui Hong coal mine from 100,000 to 500,000 mt p/a (Soviet trucks now deliver the coal from the mine to the An Hoa ferry terminal, and Soviet railroad builders have extended the rail service from the mine to Quan Trieu).

4. Expansion of the new (1983) Na Duong coal mine from 200,000 to 600,000 mt p/a to serve the coal-burning factories in Haiphong and Thanh Hoa (this project also involves construction of railroad lines from the mine to Lang Son).

5. Expansion of the Mong Duong mine to double its present annual output of 450,000 mt p/a.

6. Opening of new mines at Nue Beo, Khe Tam and Duong Huy.

7. Construction of coal-sorting plants for the mines at Khe Tam and Duong Huy.

8. Construction of a coal mine equipment factory at Cam Pha.

9. General assistance to the coal mine industry, including technical advisers, replacement of mining equipment, vehicles to transport coal from mine to port and a maintenance facility for these vehicles (at Cam Pha), installation of mine rescue facilities for underground mines, training of engineers and technicians at coal enterprises in the USSR, and general trouble shooting and problem solving for coal mining in Vietnam.[73]

Elsewhere in the mining sector, USSR assistance currently includes the following:

1. Enlargement of the Lao Cai apatite mine, which the USSR has supported since 1956 (it produces annually about 300,000 tons of concentrate, used in fertilizer manufacture, with a target at the end of the current Five-Year Plan of 1.5 million mt).

2. Renovation of the Tin Tuc tin mine in Cao Bang province near the Chinese border (production unknown).

3. Exploitation of an estimated 1.5 billion tons of bauxite in Vietnam, much of it in the Bao Loc region in southern Vietnam.

4. Exploration of other mineral deposits in Vietnam, including antimony, cassiterite, gold, iron, chromite, manganese, silica, and silver.

OIL AND GAS

What the Hanoi press terms Vietnam's "big hope for the future," one apparently shared by Moscow, is that its oil and natural gas reserves will prove sizable and their exploitation profitable.

Soviet exploration work on North Vietnam's oil reserves began in 1959, when S. K. Kitovani of the USSR's Ministry of Geology arrived in Hanoi to make a two-year oil geology survey. The first test well was drilled in Thai Binh province in 1960, and the first production drilling, Oil Rig One, went down near Thien Hai in Thai Binh province in September 1970 but was unsuccessful.[74] Commercially feasible deposits of natural gas were found in January 1975 in Thai Binh province. In the next ten years Soviet technicians drilled some sixty test wells in northern Vietnam, chiefly in Thai Binh and Ha Nam Ninh provinces. Work was halted during the war and resumed in 1976. Since mid-1979, Soviet petroleum specialists have been stationed in Vietnam, rather than making brief periodic visits as in the past. At least one hundred Soviet geophysicists, geologists, and oil technicians are now based at Vung Tau. Exploration work in the North has proved disappointing. Currently the chief hopes lie in oil and gas deposits on the continental shelf off the southern coast. In March 1980 a high-level team of Soviet officials and oil specialists began a new overall survey of Vietnam's petroleum potential. Their findings form the basis of a new master plan agreement between the two countries. A Continental Shelf Oil and Gas Survey and Exploitation agreement was signed in Moscow on July 3, 1980, by USSR State Planning Commission Chairman N. K. Baybakov and SRV State Planning Commission Chairman Nguyen Lam, with Pham Van Dong and Defense Minister Van Tien Dung looking on. In a speech the same day Brezhnev said of the new agreement: "Now we have taken on much more extensive tasks than previously. Suffice to say we are able to undertake such a large scale project as locating and obtaining rich petroleum and gas deposits on the South Vietnamese shelf." On June 19, 1981, oil exploitation was advanced with the signing of the Joint SRV-USSR Continental Shelf Oil-Gas Exploitation Enterprise Agreement by SRV Vice-Premier Tran Quynh and Soviet vice-chairman of the Council of Ministers, Konstantin Katushev. This "mixed enterprise" agreement, as it is commonly called, established the bureaucratic mechanism to explore and exploit the oil fields. It formed a new organization called Viet-Sov Petro, co-chaired by Nguyen Hoa, director of the Vietnam General Department for Oil and Natural Gas, and by Y. V. Zaisev, deputy minister of the USSR Gas and Offshore Oil Industry. The governing Council of Viet-Sov Petro, at its organizing meeting in Hanoi on November 23, 1981, blocked out a five-year program with a budget for joint work including offshore drilling near Vung Tau in the south; it also made arrangements for the dispatch of Vietnamese to universities and technical schools in Moscow and Baku to study oil technology.[75] In June 1986 a new Five-Year Plan (for 1986–1990) was signed in Vung Tau under which three offshore rigs will drill for oil; a 700-meter wharf and landing pier will be constructed capable of taking 10,000 ton ships; and the total Soviet investment in Vietnam's oil industry will be quadrupled over the 1980–1985 period.

Viet-Sov Petro's prospecting in the Red River delta and on the southern continental shelf seeks to answer four questions: What is the general history and geological structure of sedimentary deposits in the two areas? What is their geological composition? Where are the known deposits? and What special techniques and methods will be required for deep drilling?[76]

Viet-Sov Petro has already invested considerable resources in survey, exploration, and exploitation work. Expensive drilling rigs and geophysical research equipment have been sent to Vietnam. The 1600-ton derrick vessel, *Hero*, was moved from the Black Sea to Vung Tau to service the offshore drilling stations constructed by Vietnam. Work has continued exploiting the commercially feasible deposits found by Shell Oil and others for the South Vietnamese government in the early 1970s. Additional deposits were found in the 1980s.

Vung Tau, the popular beach resort town on the southern Vietnamese coast, has become the headquarters for Viet-Sov Petro and the fledgling Vietnamese oil industry. The Vung Tau–Con Dai Special Economic Zone, only one of its kind in Vietnam, was created apparently on the model of the Chinese special economic zone. A vast oil-gas industrial complex, including oil refineries, was laid out at Vung Tao, and ground was broken on the project in November 1981. Three offshore rigs were in operation by mid-1980s, and on March 10, 1986, Hanoi officials announced their first new oil strike, made in what was called the Bach Ho block. The other two rigs were drilling in what was called the White Tiger block. The size of the Bach Ho strike was not revealed. At the same time, Viet-Sov Petro officials announced that oil and gas exploration investment in the next Five-Year Plan (1986–1990) would be four times the current (i.e., 1985) level.[77]

Much of this work is being done by Soviet technicians from the Caspian petroleum and gas fields. To accommodate them and their families at Vung Tau, Viet-Sov Petro in June 1984 contracted with various SRV ministries to construct or renovate fifty-seven private villas for the top officials and thirty-seven hotel-apartments for the staff. Also under construction in the complex are schools, hospitals, clubs, theaters, soccer fields, and a shopping center—seventy-two "projects" in all—to serve an estimated 2,000 Soviet oil technicians and their families.[78]

MANUFACTURING AND INDUSTRIAL PROJECTS

Vietnam has a relatively small industrial sector,[79] and most Soviet-sponsored projects are designed either as industrial support for agriculture or to serve the construction sector. These projects include the following:

1. The Bim Son Cement Plant in Thanh Hoa province (140 km south of Hanoi), billed as the largest industrial venture of the USSR in Vietnam, was begun in February 1978. Inaugurated on January 3, 1985, it employs the services of 700 Soviet engineers and technicians. Its output for 1985 was estimated at 550,000 tons. When fully operational it is expected to produce 1.2 million tons of cement annually (total SRV cement production in 1984 was estimated at about 1.6 million mt). A second Soviet-aided cement plant (designed to produce 100,000 cubic meters of cement annually) is under construction at Xuan Mai; it will specialize in ferro-concrete slabs for use in prefabricated housing. In addition, the USSR has assisted in the construction of the Dai Thanh Concrete Plant in Hanoi, the Thuong Ly Concrete Plant in Haiphong, and the Phao Son Ceramic Plant in Hai Hung.

2. The Lam Thao Superphosphate Plant (Vinh Phu province) constructed by the USSR in 1962 was renovated in the 1980s and enlarged to an eventual capacity of 300,000 mt p/a of fertilizer (currently about 200,000 mt p/a). Nitrogen fertilizer plants have been constructed at Bao Loc[80] in the South, near Ha Bac, with a rated output of 200,000 mt per annum each; there is also a plant at Lao Cai in Hoang Lien Son province. In addition, Soviet engineers have designed a caustic soda plant to be built near Hanoi, with a scheduled production of 66,000 tons per year.

3. The Hanoi Machine Tool Plant Number One, the original Soviet-built engineering plant and Vietnam's largest machine works, is currently being renovated and enlarged. The USSR has also built diesel engine assembly plants at Song Cong and Go Cam; tractor-repair plants at Lam Dong and Thuan Hai; a truck-rebuilding plant at Cua Pha; and tool and die plants at Hanoi, Uong Bi, and Cam Pha. About 80 percent of all die and tool cutting equipment used in Vietnam is Soviet made. The Cong River (a diesel engine factory in Bac Thai province) is the largest industrial plant of its kind in Vietnam. The factory is 55,000 square meters in size, and the entire plant covers 15 hectares. It includes forging and casting facilities and is capable of producing per year about 2,000 diesel engines (each with a power rating of 55 hp, to be used mainly for tractors and to power water pumps).

4. Light industry plants include a textile plant near Hanoi that produces 20,000 tons of viscose fibers per year, several cotton mills, a tapestry-manufacturing plant, several pharmaceutical plants, and the Cam Pha Oil Recycling Plant at Hong Ai.

5. The Dap Cau Glass Factory outside Hanoi, built by the USSR, was opened in December 1984 and can produce 2.3 million square meters of sheet glass per year.

6. The Lao Cai apatite processing plant and fertilizer factory serving the mine at Lao Cai was rebuilt in 1980 with USSR assistance after it had been destroyed by Chinese troops in 1979 during the border war.

7. The agreement to construct a pharmaceutical plant to make antibiotics was signed in July 1984.

8. Several Minsk 32 computers were installed in 1981 for use by the Vietnam General Statistics Department in Hanoi.

9. Commodity aid in the form of industrial raw material, metals, chemicals, petroleum products, nitrate fertilizer, and pharmaceuticals was provided in the early 1980s.

OTHER INDUSTRIAL PROJECTS

1. The Hanoi housing project is included in the third Five-Year Plan (1981–1985). The USSR agreed to construct sixty five-story apartment buildings and will supply all materials except lumber and cement. It is also constructing housing at Xuan Mai and Hoa Binh, apparently chiefly for use by its own personnel stationed there.

2. Construction is planned for a plant to recycle scrap iron and steel, with a capacity of 5,000 mt per year.

3. Construction is also planned for four major vehicle repair and overhaul plants, fifteen vehicle maintenance shops, and two tank-repair stations—one at Kien An near Haiphong and the other at Gia Bat outside of Ho Chi Minh City.

4. Modern meteorology research facilities at Nha Trang and outside of Haiphong were installed in 1985.

TRANSPORTATION AND COMMUNICATION

The following Soviet projects concentrate on railroad, bridgework, and advanced communications:

1. Installation of a Soviet-run coastal freighter and barge system between Haiphong and Soviet Far Eastern ports, billed as "the most modern means of transportation in the world"[81] and apparently designed to be an assured method of military hardware delivery in that it would cause the Chinese maximum difficulty to disrupt it. Currently most

transoceanic shipments in and out of Vietnam are in USSR or Comecon bottoms, given that the SRV has only a small seagoing maritime fleet.

2. Renovation, extension, and modernization of the French-built Vietnam Railway system, including its conversion to wide-gauge track; and construction in Hanoi's Dong Anh district of a plant to manufacture railway switches and spare parts.

3. Expansion of port and harbor facilities chiefly in Haiphong. (This project involves construction of new piers and berths, installation of a dozen ten-ton mobile cranes, and construction of warehouses and container facilities; it also provides the port with boats and a modern navigational system. Vinh Port is being enlarged as well, and Soviet dredges have deepened the channel at Haiphong harbor and the Saigon River channel in Ho Chi Minh City.)

4. Road and bridge reconstruction work in northern Vietnam, including rebuilding of the famous 1688-meter (Vietnam's longest) Thang Long bridge over the Red River north of Hanoi, which was destroyed by U.S. bombers and then abandoned by Chinese engineers who had begun rebuilding work.[82]

5. Construction of the Bai Chay to Phu Ly oil pipeline as well as construction of an oil pipeline between Hanoi and Haiphong.

6. Expansion of Radio Hanoi facilities (officially the Voice of Vietnam), including two 1,000-kw medium-wave transmitter stations that went on the air in May 1981.

7. Expansion and modernization of Vietnam's long-distance coaxial cable system between Hanoi and Quang Ninh and between Hanoi and Vinh, and microwave communication between Hanoi and Ho Chi Minh City.

8. USSR support (planes, personnel, and spare parts) for Vietnam's civil aviation sector, under the DRV-USSR Civil Aviation Cooperation Agreement signed July 20, 1969, and renewed annually. (Moscow-Hanoi commercial air service was inaugurated by Aeroflot in March 1983.)

9. Construction of the Lotus (Hoa Sen) One Satellite Communication Station in Ha Ninh province, 100 km south of Hanoi, which made the SRV part of the Soviet Intersputnik Communication Satellite Organization. (The project was begun in January 1979 and inaugurated in July 1980 in time to bring the Moscow Olympics in color television to Vietnam. Lotus Two, a second station, was opened near Ho Chi Minh City in April 1985 and carried broadcasts of the ceremonies marking the tenth anniversary of the end of the Vietnam War. The system permits direct circuit Moscow-Hanoi-Ho Chi Minh City links. It also has military uses and is similar to the system operated by the USSR in Cuba. The stations in Vietnam are reportedly manned entirely by Soviet personnel.)

AGRICULTURE

USSR assistance to Vietnamese agriculture is not broken down by project so much as dispensed through ongoing programs, some of them begun early[83] and continued over the years. In general, these programs are designed to increase and extend the variety in Vietnamese agricultural production. This aid was described by SRV Minister of Agriculture Nguyen Ngoc Triu in 1983 thus:

> The Soviet Union has supplied Vietnam with a sizeable number of agricultural machines, equipment and materials. Nearly 20,000 Soviet-made tractors, bulldozers, combine harvesters, sowing machines and other heavy-duty machines are operating in all parts of the country. Agricultural machine stations or units have been set up in 200 districts and can handle 30 and more percent of the tilling of all arable lands. The Soviet Union helped Vietnam form a fairly comprehensive network of agricultural engineering workshops of nine tractor-repair shops each capable of repairing some 250 to 300 tractors a year. Vietnam with Soviet assistance has built 120 stations for minor repairs of tractors, 45 maintenance workshops. . . . The farm engineering service is staffed by nearly 800 engineers and 30 associated doctors, most of them having graduated in the Soviet Union.[84]

Earlier, Triu had said, "thanks to increasing cooperation with the Soviet Union and its assistance . . . we have reclaimed 500,000 hectares of fallow land, cleared and put under crop cultivation almost 500,000 hectares of virgin land, and begun double cropping on 790,000 hectares. Therefore we have expanded the cultivated area from 6.3 million hectares in 1975 to 8.09 million hectares in 1980 [and] . . . we have built irrigation projects for 1.2 million hectares."[85]

Soviet agricultural projects in Vietnam include the following:

1. Enlargement of the Phu Rieng Rubber Plantation in Song Be Province (an additional 50,000 hectares), and the Dau Tieng Plantation (adding 20,000 hectares).

2. Cotton research at the Bao Loc Technical School in Lam Dong province that includes training Vietnamese specialists in the USSR, with a view to beginning extensive cotton production in Thuan Hai, Phu Khanh, and Lam Dong provinces. A fourteen-man Soviet team of cotton-growing specialists has been at work in the region since late mid-1980.

3. Construction of nine tea-processing plants, mostly in the highland region of southern Vietnam near Bao Loc, with a combined processing capacity of about 180 tons of tea a day.

4. Conducting pilot programs to develop silk production, increase coffee production, and enlarge fruit orchards.

5. Expansion of Vietnamese industrial crops such as rubber, ramie, kenaf, lacquer, and hemp.

6. Expansion of the Vietnamese fishing industry. Eight Soviet fishing advisers have been working in Vietnam since early 1980. The USSR built the Haiphong Fish Processing Plant, which can quick-freeze some 5,000 tons of fish and seafood a year, supplied by the Ha Long Fishing Commune at Haiphong, which is equipped with eleven Soviet-supplied fishing trawlers. Moreover, Soviet technicians from the USSR Institute of Pacific Fish and Oceanography are involved in a five-year program to survey the Vietnam coastal sea bottom, sea currents, and fish life, with a view to developing the Vietnam fish and seafood industry.

Of the 300 state farms in Vietnam (the state farm being the largest communal form of agriculture), 42 were built by the USSR; in addition, there are Soviet technicians and projects at ten others. Of the present 600 farm machinery repair and maintenance stations in Vietnam, about 200 are staffed with Soviet technicians. The Vietnam Institute of Agricultural Science and Technology, the leading institute for support of agriculture, said in 1985 that it and the USSR were involved in 40 agricultural research projects, 16 on rice, 12 on subsidiary food crops, and the rest on industrial agricultural crops. This work was being done at some 50 institute stations throughout the country.[86]

The USSR's motive in providing this assistance is in part to increase production of food that can then be shipped to eastern USSR. A visiting Soviet-Asia trade team in Ho Chi Minh City in June 1984 listed the products it hoped to encourage Vietnam to produce for export to Vladivostok: "Pineapples; bananas; segmental fruit such as oranges, lemons, tangerines, grapefruit; watermelons; mangoes; rambutans; mangosteens; custard apples; guava; cabbage; carrots; kohlrabi; potatoes; violet eggplants; French beans; cauliflower; cucumbers; tomatoes; onions; pepper; garlic; cayenne; ginger; galingale and saffron."[87]

EDUCATION AND TECHNICAL ASSISTANCE

A major form of Soviet aid to Hanoi over the past thirty years— perhaps the key form, in Moscow's estimate—has been support of Vietnamese education. The Soviet presence in the educational process, properly handled, can effect subtle and persuasive influences that will yield far greater returns than any amount of commodity aid or construction work. Educational assistance began early on and may have been the very first assistance ever provided Vietnam by the USSR. Since 1978, there has been an intensive effort by Moscow to insinuate itself into the Vietnamese educational system. The USSR now is the major, and in some instances only, source of advanced and specialized training for Vietnamese students. Increasingly, educational institutions in Vietnam rely on Soviet sources for everything from textbooks to school buildings.

The first North Vietnamese group to go to the USSR to study consisted of twenty-one students, who in the summer of 1951 were enrolled in six professional schools or institutes to study medicine, mechanical engineering, governmental finance, chemical engineering, machine tool manufacture, and steel and metal alloy technology.[88]

Formal assistance began with the signing of the DRV-USSR Treaty on Scientific and Technical Cooperation on March 7, 1959, which was renewed annually at first and then at five-year intervals. This treaty provides the framework whereby Vietnamese can study in the USSR and Soviet advisers can assist in educational development in Vietnam. In the early years, most of the work here was done in agricultural science, water conservancy engineering, and public health. Gradually the field was broadened, although it remains overwhelmingly concentrated on technology rather than liberal arts and exists at the vocational training level rather than at the level of basic or advanced research.

During the Vietnam War the USSR established and administered special three-year training courses in the USSR. These courses were apparently war related.[89] At the end of the war, as part of the DRV's 1976–1980 Five-Year Plan, the USSR undertook the training of 2,000 technicians and 400 vocational education teachers per year. In November 1978 a ten-year agreement was signed as part of the broader economic assistance agreement that vastly increased Soviet participation in Vietnamese education. The wartime three-year courses in the USSR were converted to coursework for economic management cadres, educational administrators, and apparently certain specialists in the armed forces. Other coursework today includes engineering and technological training in electricity, radio, television, die casting, metallurgy, chemistry, geology, mining, petroleum geology, motion pictures, public health, topography, construction, communications, transportation, agriculture, forestry, and fishery.

By 1985 more than one hundred Vietnamese educational institutions and state research institutes were involved in systematic educational programs with the USSR. Typical programs involve chemical fertilizer technicians trained in Siberia; textile workers in plants in the Altai Oblast industrial zone; cinematographers in the Black Sea region; and petroleum and natural gas technicians at Baku and Grozny. Most of these programs involve either work-study or on-the-job training. In many instances a student will spend half of his or her time in school and the other half in a Soviet factory or facility. From 1950 to 1980 some 60,000 students from Vietnam did extended coursework in the USSR. Of these about 17,700 studied at the university level and about 41,000 attended trade schools or their equivalents.[90] In the 1980s these numbers began to climb sharply. During the 1980–1985 Five-Year Plan period the number of Vietnamese full-time students in the USSR at any one time was about 30,000; the durations of their coursework ranged from six months to five years, and some fifty schools in eleven USSR republics were involved. The students were studying seventy different subjects, although they appeared to be concentrating on mining, construction, oil technology, and agriculture.

An extensive Moscow report on Soviet assistance to Vietnamese education, published in 1985, provided these statistics:[91] The total number of Vietnamese with an education above the high school level was given as 300,000, of whom 20,000 had the equivalent of a B.A. degree; 2,000 had the equivalent of an M.A. degree and 70 the equivalent of a Ph.D., and the remainder had advanced training but received no degrees. Some 5,000 of the 20,000 had studied in the USSR. At the two major Vietnamese institutions of higher education, the Hanoi University and Hanoi Polytechnic, 30 percent of the entire teaching staff had studied in the USSR as of 1984, and half the faculty with advanced degrees had studied there. In all, at least 70,000 Vietnamese had received some educational training in the USSR, ranging from two-week refresher courses to full Ph.D. programs. About half of these studied in advanced technical institutes, which fall somewhere between the level of advanced trade schools and that of the university. The other half, perhaps 60,000, studied at the university level, and about half of these were awarded degrees or some sort of certificate.[92]

The difficulty in evaluating these statistics is that Hanoi reporting tends to lump together long-term study, short courses, science education, and nonscience studies. Another way of describing the educational relationship has been offered by Moscow: As of early 1986 Vietnam had a total science-technical cadre corps of about 1 million, broken down as 650,000 with vocational/middle school education and about 350,000 having done academic work after high school or university; of these, about 2,500 received degrees, and half of these degrees were earned in the USSR.[93]

In the 1980s the bulk of Soviet educational assistance began to shift away from educating Vietnamese in the USSR and toward educational efforts by the USSR in Vietnam. Soviet teachers and specialists with on-the-job training responsibilities had long been fixtures in Vietnam; some 1,400 of them had short- or long-term assignments there in the period 1955–1960. This activity dropped off during the war years. It was resumed in 1975 but did not pick up speed until the 1980s. On

January 23, 1981, the SRV and USSR signed an agreement under which the USSR would establish and staff an advanced training center for Vietnamese economic cadres and economic managers offering 18-month courses for some 400 students at a time. The agreement also arranged for increased teaching of Russian to Vietnamese students and for the training of Vietnamese students a Russian-language teachers. On July 21, 1981, the two countries signed a new technical cooperation agreement involving some 200 separate educational projects to be administered by a special 70-person staff assigned to the Soviet Embassy in Hanoi.[94] By 1982 it was estimated that some 2,000 USSR educators and educational advisers were working in Vietnam. One perceptible shift in emphasis by the USSR in the educational aid field was toward educating higher-level Vietnamese officials, including those at cabinet level. In February 1986 an intergovernmental treaty was signed in Moscow under which the USSR would provide training and enhancement of professional skills for "leading cadres" and "high-ranking specialists" during the 1986–1990 Five-Year Plan period. Earlier, during the 1980–1985 period, some 1,356 such officials—including 113 at the ministerial level—received some form of training in the USSR.[95]

Soviet aid to Vietnam education includes school construction. Since the end of the Vietnam War the USSR has constructed eight vocational training schools and three industrial teachers colleges, and it has equipped three more. It also designed, built, and equipped the Hanoi Polytechnical College.

A new institution begun in 1981 involves the "adoption" of an educational establishment or single school by an equivalent in the USSR, which then provides assistance on a direct basis and engages in individual exchanges of students, teachers, and administrators.

NOTES

1. Senior General Hoang Van Thai, "The Military Art in the 1953–54 Winter Spring Offensive and Dien Bien Phu Campaign," *Tap Chi Cong San*, No. 3 (March 1984).

2. *Pravda* (May 9, 1953), reporting the UN debate on the subject. For discussion see Robert Owens, *The French Socialist Party and Its Indochina Policy 1941–51*, Publication No. 12318 (Ann Arbor, Mich.: University Microfilms, 1955).

3. French forces in Indochina captured large numbers of U.S. M-1 carbines that proved to be copies. Later it was established that in 1950 the USSR had built a factory near Vladivostok to manufacture these weapons, for North Korean and Chinese use in the Korean War.

4. Albert Perry, "Soviet Aid to Vietnam," *Reporter Magazine* (January 12, 1972).

5. See D. Stefanovskiy, "SRV: Confident Strides," *Selskaya Zhizn* (Moscow) (August 18, 1985), quoted in FBIS *Daily Report* for the USSR (August 21, 1985). See also M. Ilinskiy, "Combat Tradition of Solidarity," *Izvestiya* (September 17, 1971); and *Pravda* (September 2, 1971).

6. *Nhan Dan* (October 25, 1983).

7. See the article by I. Arkhipov (deputy chairman of USSR Council of Ministers, Foreign Economic Relations Committee) entitled "Together with the Heroes of Vietnam," *Pravda* (September 2, 1971).

8. *Nhan Dan* (July 21, 1980).

9. Ibid.

10. VNA and *Nhan Dan* (May 14, 1956). For a description of the signing of the 1958 Trade and Navigation Agreement, see *Nhan Dan* (March 15, 1983).

11. *Washington Post* (May 4, 1966).

12. Radio Hanoi (January 18, 1964) lists and describes the projects of the first five-year plan. The list contains some carryovers from earlier aid agreements.

13. Assembled from official sources and reported in *USSR in World Affairs,* No. 49 (1971).

14. Radio Hanoi (November 6, 1957).

15. The official exchange rate at the time was 1 ruble = US$1.10. Soviet military assistance pre-dated the U.S. decision to intervene fully in the Vietnam War. That decision was made in mid-February 1965; Soviet-made 37mm radar-controlled anti-aircraft weapons began appearing in North Vietnam in December 1964.

16. VNA (February 16, 1965).

17. Radio Moscow (September 17, 1965).

18. *Red Star* (December 29, 1965).

19. *Pravda* (December 24, 1965).

20. Radio Moscow (January 10, 1966).

21. Radio Moscow (July 27, 1966).

22. Quoted in *Die Welt* (West Germany) (March 21, 1966).

23. *Hoc Tap*, No. 11 (November 1967).

24. TASS (August 9, 1971).

25. Radio Moscow (May 2, 1986); FBIS *Daily Report* for the USSR (March 4, 1986).

26. About 75 percent of these aircraft were stationed in the Hanoi/ Haiphong area; the remainder flew out of Chinese sanctuary. The major military airfields in North Vietnam were Phuc Yen (the biggest near Hanoi); Kien An, outside of Haiphong; Kep, 37 miles northeast of Hanoi; and Yen Bai, 80 miles northwest of Hanoi.

27. See *Aviation Week* (October 3, 1966) for the photo story on Bataisk.

28. *New York Times* (November 14, 1966).

29. Cited in the author's *PAVN: People's Army of Vietnam* (Novato, Calif.: Presidio Press, 1986), p. 87.

30. Ibid.

31. For sixty years, government analysts, academics, and economists have wrestled with the problem of meaningfully converting cost/prices in a socialist

economy into capitalist currency figures. They have still not agreed on the best method. Various formulas can be employed, including (a) the official exchange rate method; (b) the income ratio method (based on comparing workers' incomes, teachers' salaries, etc., in the two systems); (c) the purchasing power ratio method (comparing payments based on manhours of labor required to produce a cross-section of goods or services, such as a pair of shoes, a quart of milk, a television set, surgical removal of an appendix, etc.); and (d) the absolute production cost method, favored by military analysts (in which the cost of an item, say a tank, is determined on the basis of what it would cost to produce that same tank in the United States). None of these methods is entirely satisfactory.

32. Shipments went by broad gauge track (5-foot rail gauge) across the USSR to the China border. China's railroads have a gauge of 4 feet, 8.5 inches, that necessitates a shift of cargo. Upon reaching the Vietnam border the railway cargo had to be transferred to Vietnamese boxcars, inasmuch as the North Vietnamese railroad was still another gauge.

33. A *People's Daily* editorial (December 22, 1965) noted that the USSR was sending "damaged weapons and obsolete equipment already discarded by the Soviet armed forces to North Vietnam."

34. Radio Moscow (October 18, 1968).

35. Radio Budapest (April 22, 1966).

36. Radio Moscow, broadcast in Mandarin to China (December 26, 1971).

37. *Nhan Dan* (October 17, 1983).

38. Nguyen Ngoc Bich, "The Soviet Role in North Vietnam's Offensive," *Vietnam Bulletin* (April 1972).

39. *Nhan Dan* (July 12, 1980).

40. Nikita Khrushchev, *Khrushchev Remembers* (Boston: Little, Brown, 1971), p. 260.

41. Tran Quynh, "The Victory of Vietnam-USSR Friendship and All-Around Cooperation," *Nhan Dan* (July 18, 1985).

42. VNA (June 9, 1985).

43. Radio Hanoi (January 29, 1985). In addition to the commodity aid, the report listed 16,000 vehicles and 5,000 tractors.

44. "Comecon" is the Russian acronym for Council for Mutual Economic Assistance. However, the Vietnamese prefer to use the abbreviation CMEA in English language translations; frequently the abbreviation CEMA is also used.

45. For a good detailed study of the overall activity of the Council, see "Inside Comecon: A Survey," *The Economist* (April 20, 1985).

46. Vu Can, "CMEA and the Developing Countries," *Vietnam Courier*, No. 7 (July 1984).

47. "CEMA: World Carpet Organization for Economic Cooperation," editorial in *Quan Doi Nhan Dan* (February 4, 1985).

48. See the FBIS *Daily Reports* for Asia and Pacific, and the USSR (January 9–18, 1986). The Asia and Pacific *Daily Report* for January 12 contains the communiqué of the CMEA committee meetings.

49. See "The Monetary System of the Socialist Economic Union," *Tap Chi Cong San* (February 1981).

50. Nguyen Lam, as interviewed in VNA (June 5, 1981).

51. See the FBIS *Daily Report* for the USSR (February 1, 1985). For a discussion of the Soviet view of Vietnam's association with CMEA, see M. Trigubenko, "On the Participation of the Soviet Union's Far Eastern Areas in the USSR's Trade and Economic Cooperation with Vietnam," *Far Eastern Affairs*, No. 4 (Moscow, 1983). For a typical Moscow response to the "exploitation" charge, see *Sovetzkaya Rossiya* (January 23, 1985), which essentially argues that Vietnam gets more than it gives.

52. *Nhan Dan* (July 18, 1980).

53. Radio Hanoi (July 17, 1985).

54. See the SRV UN Mission press report dated January 11, 1986.

55. *Wall Street Journal* (April 3, 1983).

56. *Wall Street Journal* (January 15, 1982).

57. A related agreement—the Movement of Citizens Agreement—was signed a month later (July 15, 1981); it deals with visa arrangements and restrictions and is designed to facilitate easy movement of individuals between the two countries by simplifying travel regulations, ending travel restrictions, and providing for multiple-entry visas. The agreement also establishes legal jurisdiction for Vietnamese citizens in the USSR and for Soviet citizens in Vietnam.

58. See the transcript for Radio Hanoi (March 9 and March 30, 1986). See also VNA correspondent Le Manh Binh's "Five Years of Vietnam-USSR Labor Cooperation," VNA (April 2, 1986); and FBIS *Daily Report* for Asia (April 4, 1986). For further details on Vietnamese workers in the USSR, see the *Washington Post* (March 13, 1983); *Swiss Review of World Affairs* (April 1983), and *Sankei Shimbun* (Tokyo) (April 6, 1983); the last contains quotes from letters written by Vietnamese from Siberia circa early 1983.

59. *Tap Chi Quan Doi Nhan Dan* and VNA (October 30, 1983); see also Radio Hanoi (January 29, 1985) for an updated version of the same concept.

60. VNA (November 18, 1982).

61. *Times* (London) (January 23, 1984), quoting sources in Bangkok.

62. VNA (June 24, 1980).

63. VNA (November 1, 1983); FBIS *Daily Report* for Asia and Pacific (November 4, 1983). The text of the agreement was broadcast by VNA (November 4, 1983) and is found in FBIS *Daily Report* for Asia and Pacific (November 7, 1983). See also the TASS (October 31, 1983) commentary on the "cooperation document."

64. Radio Hanoi (November 7, 1985).

65. *New York Times* (January 23, 1983).

66. Electric power production in northern Vietnam in the first postwar decade increased from 120 million kilowatt hours to about 3.7 billion kwh (1984 estimate)—almost entirely as a result of USSR assistance. With production in southern Vietnam of over 400 million kwh, the total for the country is about 4 billion kwh. The long-range target is 14 billion kwh.

67. The Da River, one of four Red River tributaries (980km in length, which makes it the second longest in Vietnam), carries about 70 percent of the

Red River system water. Under the Le Duan–Brezhnev agreement signed in December 1975, the USSR is also constructing two smaller dams some 70km upstream, on the Ta Sa Na Ngan River and the Thac Ba River (one is to be 600 meters wide and 123 meters high and will require the moving of 10 million cubic feet of earth). Some 27 factories designed to use the power produced at Hoa Binh will be built as well. For details see Wolfgang Georgi, "A Piece of the Future Grows on the Song Da," *Berliner Zeitung* (East Berlin) (February 1, 1984).

68. A megawatt is 1 million watts (or 1,000 kilowatts). One kilowatt hour, the electricity produced in one hour, is usually expressed in annual terms (i.e., capacity multiplied by 24 [hours] or by 365 [days]).

69. The slow construction pace is apparently due in part to the fact that earth-moving at Pha Lai—involving some 7 million cubic meters—is done largely without machines.

70. VNA (November 6, 1983).

71. *Quan Doi Nhan Dan* (November 9, 1983).

72. Selected Vietnam coal production figures: 1955, less than 500,000 metric tons; 1965, 3.7 million metric tons; 1975, 5.6 million metric tons; 1980, 5.3 million metric tons; 1985, 6.2 million metric tons (est.). Target for 1990 is 13–14 million metric tons. Japan is the major buyer of Vietnamese coal (*Vietnam Ten Years After* [Hanoi: Foreign Language Publishing House, 1985]).

73. SRV Minister of Mines and Coal Nguyen Chan listed as the most pressing of these problems "the extraction of coal from thick and inclined seams; the mechanization of coal extraction in work faces and underground excavation to expand the output of these faces and increase underground haulage speed and labor productivity; the improvement of proficiency in the production and exploitation of coal under complicated geological conditions, such as strata overlying coal seams, underground water, sidewall dirt and rocks, and unstable pillars; the increase in the depth of open-pit mines; the handling of accidents caused by the fall of mine roofs and sides; the increase in the productivity of mining equipment, particularly trucks and augers; and the improvement of the methods of drilling with the use of explosives and performing open-pit mining operations under complicated geological and hydrological conditions." See *Nhan Dan* interview (October 19, 1983).

74. *Nhan Dan* (October 28, 1973).

75. VNA (November 23, 1981).

76. VNA (June 14, 1984).

77. See *Lao Dong* (Hanoi) (April 3, 1986), *Giai Phong* (January 8, 1986). See also "At the White Tiger Block," *Vietnam Courier* (April 1986), and "Young Oil Workers in Open Sea," *Tien Phong* (April 29, 1986), for descriptions of the joint Vietnamese-Soviet oil exploration work.

78. Radio Hanoi (June 29, 1984).

79. U.S. Air Force target planners making initial assessments of industrial targets in North Vietnam in early 1965 by means of World War II European military theater criteria found only six industrial targets in all of North Vietnam.

80. According to a *Nhan Dan* article (January 30, 1979), these plants were paid for in tea.

81. See the PAVN newspaper, *Quan Doi Nhan Dan* (October 25, 1983), which also reported that the first delivery of the new "super cargo" system was a launch carrier named the SS Aleksey Kosygin. It towed 82 barges and carried 30,000 tons of cargo that arrived at the Ha Long pier in Haiphong in February 1984. The launches are able to deliver direc'.ly to inland river ports, bypassing the road and rail systems.

82. These engineers made the work for their Soviet successors doubly difficult by taking with them back to China all of the bridge's blueprints and specification lists.

83. In 1956 a team of Soviet technicians did a general soil survey of North Vietnam; in the same year, the USSR equipped ten agricultural research laboratories with soil-testing equipment.

84. VNA (October 26, 1983).

85. *Nhan Dan* (November 7, 1981).

86. Radio Hanoi (February 19, 1985). The Hanoi press carries frequent interviews with Soviet agronomists and other agricultural experts who describe their research work. Some examples: They have discovered 84 kinds of fungus, 9 forms of virus, 19 bacteria, and 74 types of insect; they have experimented with developing brown pest-resistant rice strains; and they complain about the heat and humidity (one reported that it is three times as humid in Vietnam as in Kazakhstan).

87. See Soviet writer "M.T.," "Vietnam-USSR Long-Term Cooperation in Producing and Exporting Vegetables and Fruit," *Saigon Giai Phong* (June 28, 1984). For an informative discussion of USSR assistance to SRV agriculture in the past decade, see SRV Vice-Minister of Agriculture Nguyen Dang's article "Great Assistance," in JPRS-SEA 86-041 (March 6, 1986).

88. *Pravda* (July 28, 1981).

89. *Nhan Dan* (October 28, 1981).

90. *Ekonomicheskoye Sotrudnichestvo Stan-Chlenov* (Moscow), No. 1 (1980).

91. A. Yermolayev, "Soviet-Vietnamese Scientific and Technical Cooperation," *Far Eastern Affairs* (Moscow), No. 1 (1985).

92. Radio Hanoi (January 29, 1985).

93. Radio Moscow (March 31, 1986); FBIS *Daily Report* for the USSR (April 4, 1986).

94. *Pravda* (August 27, 1981).

95. Radio Moscow (February 18, 1986).

Seven

THE SUBLIMINAL DIMENSION

AN OLD VIETNAM hand—an American—returned to Saigon recently for a visit, and one afternoon, while browsing in a Tu Do street antique shop, found himself trailed closely by the ancient proprietor whose manner clearly communicated unfriendliness. There followed this conversation:

SHOP KEEPER: You are a Russian, aren't you?

AMERICAN: No, as a matter of fact I'm an American.

(Long pause)

AMERICAN: You don't think I'm an American?

SHOP KEEPER: What I think is that you Russians will lie about anything.

There is in the relationship of a Vietnamese with any foreigner an intuitive level that is elusive and totally intangible, but one the outsider ignores at his peril for it also is the ultimate reality of the association. In this chapter we shall examine the Soviet-Vietnamese association at the subliminal level by considering certain fundamental cultural differences and conflicting patterns of thought.

The focus of the examination is perception, the way the Vietnamese see the individual Russian and the USSR *en masse.* Years in Vietnam can convince a foreigner that it is necessary to rewrite the nineteenth-century aphorism on foreign relations—that there are no permanent alliances, only permanent interests—and write a new one appropriate for the last half of the twentieth century—that there are no permanent relations, only permanent perceptions. Again and again one is struck by the enormous durability of Vietnamese perceptions. Antipathies based on these perceptions surface after centuries of burial, as with Cambodia. Apparently changed perceptions eventually prove not to have changed at all, as with China. Far more than elsewhere, it seems, future developments involving Vietnam and Vietnamese dealings with outsiders to a large degree will be conditioned more by perceptional chemistry than by the application of power. Whether a perception is factually correct is irrelevant. What counts is how strongly it is held.

Perception in transcultural terms is both product and function of the two-way communication of ideas. The subliminal level of the process is largely determined by the kind of affective or emotive communication that takes place. Vietnamese and Soviet efforts to communicate at this empathetic level are subject to two major impediments, one of them peculiarly Vietnamese, the other more or less common to Asia and the West.

The first barrier is a product of various Vietnamese religious and secular influences: Buddhist modesty, self-effacement, other-worldliness, Confucian scholarly reserve, and the "island in the lake" mentality. It dictates that efforts to communicate affectively, to explain or plead one's case, to "reach out and touch someone" (to use the advertising slogan) is improper and beneath one's dignity. Intermixed with this is the singular Vietnamese heritage of the politics of clandestinism, which the Vietnamese have always used in their dealings with foreign occupiers—first the Chinese and then the French—in which, if possible, all straightforward communication is eschewed.

The second communicational barrier arises from the conflicting patterns of Soviet and Vietnamese thought. It is cognitive, involving the "mind" of Vietnam versus the "mind" of Russia, and of course it is traceable to differing conceptual or philosophic frameworks. The USSR may be both European and Asian in its geography, but it is western in its policymaking. The heritage of the USSR is Greek aesthetics, Roman engineering, Christian monotheism (transferred to the party), and Judaic judicial thought, and as such it is rational, geometric, and Kantian. The Vietnamese heritage is circuitous, amorphous, and multidimensional. The two systems have given rise to differing value concepts involving space, time, and causality, and permanent unbreachable walls have been formed between them.

Much of what appears in this chapter on the subliminal Vietnamese-Soviet relationship is drawn from the work I did in the summer of 1969. I spent that summer in South Vietnam POW and *Chieu Hoi* (returnee) camps conducting in-depth interviews with middle-ranking North Vietnamese cadres and field-grade military officers in their mid-30s. Some of the interviews went on for days and ranged over almost every subject, although my primary purpose was to learn more about the mindset and political outlook of North Vietnam's next generation of leaders. Although the findings of the study are beyond the scope of this book, I can briefly summarize my main impressions. First, the cadres demonstrated a uniformly high level of idealism. They made elaborately detailed moral judgments and maintained a highly ethical value system (strikingly singular when compared to the value system extant in South Vietnam at the time). Second, they tended to be credulous, even naive, about international relations and world politics in general. Both of these findings reflect the fact that the North Vietnam educational system at the time was highly insulated from the infusion of foreign ideas, even Marxist ideas, and that North Vietnam was indeed the "convent society" it had been termed. Third, there was virtually unanimous allegiance to the North Vietnamese sociopolitical system and commitment to Hanoi's enunciated goal in the war—that is, unification of Vietnam. More striking was the fact that it had hardly ever occurred to these cadres that they *might* question authority or the underlying philosophic basis of their society. Fourth, most of the cadres demonstrated considerable hostility, tinged with xenophobia, toward both the USSR and China (although for differing reasons) and to some extent toward the world in general. Even among party members, the call of proletarian internationalism seemed to exert little influence. The findings of the study as they relate to the USSR appear throughout this chapter.

CULTURE AND LOGIC

The first dimension of the Soviet-Vietnamese subliminal relationship has to do with racial perceptions that stem from vastly differing cultural heritages and are conditioned by entirely different mindsets.

There is a paradox here. If ever there were two vastly different cultures, they are the Vietnamese and the Russian. Yet the individual personality in each has the same dark side, born of equally conspiratorial and brutalizing histories. Both exhibit paranoid tendencies manifested by unremitting suspicion of strangers and a xenophobic inability to trust. Both display the phenomenon of the tortured soul, as abundantly illustrated in their respective literatures of martyrdom and despair. Both societies have also given rise to genius and creativity in art and music.[1]

The Vietnamese view foreigners through a special prism, one that both distances and stereotypes. What counts is the *quality* of the association, not what is inherent in it, such as mutuality, or its physical or material manifestations. As a result, in Hanoi, the individual Vietnamese perception of the Russians is almost entirely affective. It is idealized, officially and individually, and is almost always expressed in abstract terms. For instance, although the actual USSR-Vietnamese relationship over the past decades has been largely and importantly material—indeed, the Soviet ruble permitted Vietnamese communism to persevere and finally succeed in war—there is virtually no recognition of this fact in the Vietnamese consciousness. The attitude was captured by the Hanoi intellectual, Nguyen Van Kinh:

> The fraternal peoples of Viet Nam and the USSR have always been closely bound by relations of friendship and militant solidarity. Upholding their spirit of proletarian internationalism, the Soviet people have warmly supported and assisted the Vietnamese revolutionary movement right from its embryonic stage. The great victory of the USSR in World War II created favourable objective conditions for the Vietnamese people to successfully wage the August revolution and set up the Democratic Republic of Viet Nam. In Viet Nam's resistance to French colonialism in the past as well as in her present anti-U.S. struggle for national salvation and socialist building through many rich and lively forms such as meetings, demonstrations, etc., the Soviet people have always deeply sympathized with, and vigorously supported the Vietnamese people's just cause. Solidarity with Viet Nam has become a mass movement throughout the USSR. "Weeks" and "Months of solidarity" with Viet Nam have become a tradition for the Soviet people to support and assist the Vietnamese people against U.S. imperialist aggressors.[2]

Note the *affective* quality of this typical description of the relationship. It is entirely immaterial and intellectualized. Kinh writes of Soviet support, but not in terms of surface-to-air missiles, rice shipments, or fuel for PAVN's tanks. Instead, he speaks of militant solidarity, of rich and lively demonstrations of sympathy, later of blood donations. Moscow is seen not as a vital ally but as a supportive symbol. The Soviets are not fellow players in the revolutionary game but spiritual cheerleaders.

The reason for this is not what might be supposed; it is not a matter of selfish Vietnamese unwillingness to give credit where it is due or of ungrateful Vietnamese willfulness in refusing to acknowledge the fact of Soviet assistance. Rather, it is a product of the fundamental attitude Vietnamese hold regarding the proper relationship with a foreigner.

Most Vietnamese have a fairly strong emotive sense of the individual Russian. It is in no way as intricate or psychologically complex as their attitude toward the Chinese. The Russian in Vietnam is a strange foreigner from a distant country of alien customs. Culturally, most Vietnamese regard themselves as closer to the French, the Chinese, or even the Americans—partly because of education. Most of today's top leaders in Hanoi received French schooling, and no important figure was educated in the USSR. Until recently at least, the average Vietnamese school child learned little about the USSR. Those interviewed by the author during the war said their teachers' lectures dwelled on Peter the Great and Ivan the Terrible, with the result that the images of Russia that most quickly came to their minds were associated with strength, brutality, and barbarism. Vietnamese schools today teach Russian history extensively, but changing a cultural perception in society through education is a slow process.

Vietnamese returning home from stays in the USSR often bring with them tales of racial prejudice personally encountered, thus giving rise to the common belief that the Soviet citizen is more racist than the average French person or American. This belief is reinforced by the behavior of Soviet officials and tourists in Vietnam, as discussed below.[3]

With the onset of intimate official relations with Moscow in the post–Vietnam War era, Hanoi officials sought to change the perception of both the USSR and China held by party cadres and the general public. Official history now records that the USSR is and always has been a total and enthusiastic supporter of the Vietnamese Communist cause, while Chinese support was always minimal and half-hearted. This rewriting of history is not likely to change opinions; nor is it certain that Hanoi officials really want people to alter their view of the USSR.

Theoreticians and influential writers within the Vietnamese Communist party, where attitudes and perceptions are important, have for a long time privately stigmatized the USSR as a land of barbarians whose leaders are intellectually incapable of grasping the subtle Vietnamese world view and, as a defense mechanism, are cultural chauvinists. Party historians may laud the USSR for its revolutionary accomplishments but not for having understood Vietnam's revolution. At best, USSR history serves as a vague source of ideological inspiration. A 1970 official party history,[4] for instance, contains only five references to the USSR: (1) that the Russian Revolution took place; (2) that the USSR was "unable to help Vietnam fight the Japanese in World War II because it was too hard pressed"; (3) that the USSR defeated Germany; (4) that the USSR declared war on Japan on August 8, 1945, and that the war ended on August 15; and (5) that the USSR granted diplomatic recognition to the DRV in January 1950, immediately following Chinese recognition. Three of these five references (2,4,5) are slyly malicious when related in the original Vietnamese language. No note is taken of Viet Minh War economic assistance, and in the account of the 1954 Geneva Conference no mention is made of the USSR presence. The only Soviet leader's name to appear is that of Lenin, and that only once. In another work, the party's official biography of Ho Chi Minh, Ho's years-long association with the USSR is reduced to one sentence: "Ho stayed in the Soviet Union for awhile to study the Soviet system and the experience of developing a Party in accordance with Lenin's theories."[5] In Ho's entire book-length biography, the name *Soviet Union* appears only twice—in the citation above, and in the comment that in the early years "Ho taught Party cadres . . . to protect the Soviet Union, China and other fraternal socialist countries," which in Vietnamese reads as mockery.

This offhanded treatment of the USSR in the past was systematic. The historical role played by the USSR in Vietnamese affairs was consistently given slight treatment. At the Ho Chi Minh Party School outside of Hanoi, and earlier at the huge Xuan Mai Infiltration Camp, where cadres were prepared during the war for their assignments in the South, students were required to take a course titled "Contradictions of Socialism," using the texts *History of Bolshevism* and *History of Communism in China.*[6] Those who took the course say the tone of the lectures on the Sino-Soviet dispute was "plague-on-both-houses." Many cadres told the author that the belief they carried away from the course was that neither the USSR nor China supported the Vietnamese Revolution in the manner it deserved and, further, that such support as was provided was given for the wrong reason—that is, to "best" the other country in the Sino-Soviet dispute. Some lecturers held up the USSR-Finland relationship as a proper model for Vietnam, with Finland's posture interpreted as bristly independence modified by tacitly admitted restraint in certain actions. Some cadres left the Xuan Mai course with a strong sense of bitterness about the USSR. A personalized example of this attitude is found in the following transcript of the author's interview with one DRV cadre in June 1969.

Q: Did you take the course in "Contradictions in Socialism" at Xuan Mai?

A: Yes.

Q: What do you recall the cadre lecturer saying about the Sino-Soviet dispute?

A: Well, I don't remember very much. Just that the Russians were wrong and the Chinese were right.

Q: How do you feel personally about the dispute?

A: It makes me very angry when I think about it. I don't understand what they are arguing about or why. Instead of arguing they should get together and come to the full support of the liberation effort.

Q: You don't feel the Chinese and the Russians are supporting you and your war sufficiently?

A: No, they are not. They don't care about us. They only care about their arguments. In fact most of what they do for us is because of that argument.

Q: What is it you haven't gotten?

A: Well, for example, coastal anti-ship rockets. The Russians have given them to Nasser and Ben Bella. But not to us.

Q: That's because the Russians don't want to get into a weapons confrontation with the U.S.?

A: It doesn't make any difference. We take risks. So should they.

Q: Still, there is aid, is there not? I mean, there are no arms factories in North Vietnam. All your military hardware comes from the outside, China or the USSR. Isn't that proof of interest and support?

A: No! When I think about this I don't think about what they have done for us. I think about what they have not done for us. That is much more.[7]

Although antipathy for both the USSR and China seemed approximately equal, and although both were judged guilty of insufficiency, different motives were assigned to each by the Vietnamese. (This was in 1969, it should be remembered, when the outcome of the war was uncertain.) The cadres' general sense was that Moscow intended to emerge unscathed from the Vietnam War no matter what the outcome; and that Moscow had aided the DRV in such a way that if the DRV won Moscow could take credit for the victory and if it lost the USSR would not be tarred by the defeat. Further, the cadres felt that Moscow was keeping open options unacceptable to Hanoi, such as a compromise that would leave a neutral South Vietnam and no unification. Moscow was viewed as politely deferential to Hanoi but hypocritically uncaring. By comparison, the Chinese were seen as emotionally committed to the war, so much so that they wanted to dictate procedure. China was viewed as attempting to pressure, even blackmail, Hanoi into using Chinese strategy.

In addition to this visceral sense of things, an intellectualism reinforces the alien nature of the USSR in Vietnamese Communist thinking. It lies in the differences between ideology in Moscow and ideology in Hanoi, and it is a result of the sea change that Marxism-Leninism underwent en route to Vietnam. Although a Vietnamese Communist can hold Marxism-Leninism worthy of dying for—and tens of thousands did exactly that during the war—he does not regard it as something involving intellect. A Vietnamese true believer reveres communism as an icon, not as an intellectual guide. The idea that Marxism is a body of knowledge that, if properly absorbed, can make one infallible in interpreting social phenomena strikes those few Vietnamese who think about it as absurd. No Vietnamese—indeed, no foreigner who lives long in Vietnam and is sensitive to the Buddhist, Confucian, and Taoist influences all about him—can seriously accept the Marxist dogma that nothing is inherently unknowable. The certitude of Marx's historical determinism is utterly smothered by the indeterminism, mysticism, and fatalism of Vietnam.

This disparity confers on the present Soviet-Vietnamese relationship a tenuous quality, delimiting it, hedging it in, and making it appear ephemeral. There never has been the proletarian kinship in Vietnam that was found in Europe. There was and still is an absence of allegiance. The Soviets today remain distant not because they lack sympathy but because of their inherent inability to understand the Vietnamese.

Coupled with these abstractions is the more finite memory in Hanoi of the Kremlin's record of casual indifference to Vietnam's fate and its general unreliability. That this is a familiar experience in the country's long history, illustrated by the Vietnamese proverb about the wolf watching from the mountain as the tigers battle in the valley, makes it no less acceptable.

Understandably, the Vietnamese perception has resulted in something of a backlash in Moscow. Soviet diplomats and academics are not so insensitive as to be unaware of Vietnamese distrust, disdain, and intimations of superiority. Discussing Vietnam privately with Americans, these officials commonly describe the Vietnamese as unappreciative ingrates and double-dealing opportunists. The candid Khrushchev spoke openly, complaining in his memoirs of Vietnamese ingratitude. He was particularly incensed that Ho Chi Minh's last will and testament—more a historical and social document than a legal paper—made no reference to the economic and military aid that the USSR for years had provided Vietnam.[8]

Soviet academic work on Indochina has never been either extensive or intensive. Some demographic and ethnographic work was done in the 1930s along with a few physical geography studies (of North Vietnam) in the 1950s, but less attention was paid to Vietnam than to other countries in Southeast Asia, such as Indonesia and the Philippines. Allan Cameron notes that "prior to 1954 there was little Soviet academic concern with Vietnam and no serious ongoing research." It began, he says, only in the early 1950s and did not start to bear fruit until after 1956. Even later (circa 1970) it remained deficient in many areas.[9] Since the end of the war Soviet academic attention has increased, but it still consists of only a few dozen specialists in the research institutes of Moscow.[10]

Initially this inattention was due to political sensitivity. Theoreticians in Moscow have never been able to fit Vietnam easily into the official doctrinal framework. As Cameron notes, during the early years when there were two Vietnams, Moscow classified both as underdeveloped countries—one as a neocolony linked to imperialism, the other as a fraternal socialist country. Similar conditions and parallel developments were found in both, and Soviet theoreticians were hard-pressed to describe Vietnam in conceptual terms without offending Hanoi. Later it was clear that two separate and competing social systems had emerged, but this fact was denied by Hanoi, which held there was but one Vietnam in differing stages of revolution, Marxist dogma notwithstanding. Soviet theoreticians, as Cameron notes, tended to skirt the matter, lending an air of unreality to much early Soviet doctrinal writing on Vietnam. The problem of trying logically to explain Vietnam was reflected over the years in a general below-the-salt treatment at international party functions, consistently assigning Vietnam a position far down the precedence list.

The more important question here, however, is whether today in Moscow Soviet officials who deal personally with Vietnamese representatives or who make Soviet foreign policy for Vietnam are knowledgeable about this peculiar Vietnamese mindset. Are they trained in Vietnamese language, and are they culturally sensitive? I visited the USSR several times in the 1980s in an effort to determine the state of "Hanoi-watching" there. These trips included attendance at academic conferences and one two-week visit as guest of the Soviet Academy of Sciences for the express purpose of meeting with Indochinese specialists in the Institute of Oriental Studies and in related institutes. With one or two exceptions, work on Indochina is clearly limited and interest in the area is nominal. This is further indicated by the paucity of published literature from Moscow on Indochina. The experience of Soviet academics with little knowledge of and little interest in Indochina was repeated at the ministries, where I met officials from the defense sector, and at the Southeast Asia division of the Foreign Affairs Ministry. Discussions of the broad Asian scene were enjoyable and stimulating. My hosts' comments on topics such as the naval balance of forces in the Pacific or the future of ASEAN, while generously peppered with obligatory ideological references, were generally factual, sophisticated, and urbane. On these matters, the officials were informed and obviously well read, or at least well briefed. But the moment the discussion turned to Indochina, there was a sharp drop in intellectual level. Ignorance of Indochinese affairs on the part of officials who help make Indochina policy was so great as to be embarrassing.

Present-day Soviet-Vietnamese relations, it seemed clear on reflection, have a dangerously unreal quality about them at the Moscow level, because they are rooted in ignorance and based on European assumptions. There is little awareness of what is not known.

The Moscow visit produced a sense of *déjà vu*. Moscow's perception's of Indochina in the 1980s were reminiscent of Washington's perceptions of Indochina in the 1950s. As with Washington then, I found in the Moscow of today simplistic assumptions about and platitudinous explanations of complex issues, a paucity of hard data, a lack of serious sociopolitical analysis (and no perceived need for any), unexamined snap judgments about how history will unroll in Indochina, and a smug certitude about the efficacy of ongoing policies. My demurs and my comments on the meaning for the USSR of events in Indochina were politely brushed aside, just as Washington in the 1950s politely brushed aside suggestions from the French who knew Indochina. I left Moscow convinced that such official Soviet opinions of Vietnam, from which will flow important future decisions, are simple, neat, and wrong—and this history has often shown to be the formula for catastrophe.

STATUS AND POWER

The second dimension of the subliminal level of Soviet-Vietnamese relations involves perceptions of and attitudes toward political/diplomatic authority or, more precisely, toward the components of such authority: power, status, and accomplishment.

The Vietnamese traditionally respect power. Hanoi leaders, especially the old guard such as Pham Van Dong and Pham Hung, still unabashedly admire such figures as Joseph Stalin. There was never any de-Stalinization campaign in North Vietnam, not because of empathy for the Soviet leader but because of regard for the way he exercised power.[11] Vietnamese Communist tributes to the USSR—for instance, in anniversary messages—invariably have used the rhetoric of power. They speak of Soviet iron determination, prowess, the USSR as an irresistable force.[12] In Hanoi's view the USSR is a nation of immense military capability, able to intervene where it sees opportunity to advance progressive causes and revolutionary movements or when necessary to its national interest, as in Afghanistan.[13] Hanoi leaders do not view such ability as an ideological impulse, only as the proper use of one's strength. Their common sense view is that in this hard, merciless world, those who have power use it. The USSR is particularly admired for its toughness in dealing with the United States and China. Soviet leaders also venerate power; hence there is here a harmony of viewpoint.

In projecting its power image, the Kremlin cannot employ orthodox Marxist arguments. Historical determinism falls uncomprehended on Vietnam. Hanoi leaders might like to believe that Marxist thought is infallible and that Soviet communism is the *inevitable* wave of the future. But to arrive at those conclusions they would have to jettison their heritage of traditional, Confucianist, and Buddhist influences. If they believe that the USSR will prevail in the long historical reach, it will be because it has superior material strength and is able to apply force more effectively than its opposition. Mechanistic Western notions such as dialectical reasoning are simply too alien to accept. Almost any other argument, any device—even geomancy—would be more persuasive to the Vietnamese mind.

The opposite side of the coin of power in Vietnamese thinking is *face*, or what a Westerner would call status or prestige. Soviet officials seem to grasp instinctively the importance of status in Vietnam. Their behavior in Vietnam may strike outsiders as somewhat pompous, but it is pomp to engender prestige and it does impress the Vietnamese. However, this status is a double-edged sword because it makes it difficult, even dangerous, for the USSR to accept any sort of defeat or retreat. To do so would reduce prestige, which in turn would undermine the USSR's power. In other words, excessive consciousness of status also diminishes flexibility.

Officials in Hanoi take measure of the Soviets in elemental terms, in a test of success or failure. The only secure hold Moscow can have on Vietnam—dependency is not a long-term hold—comes from demonstrating the continuing ability to apply power successfully. Daily the Vietnamese leaders look around the world, at the various competitions in the international arena, and ask the same question: Who will prevail? In this the USSR must always seem to be successful. To the extent the Vietnamese see Soviet power in the ascendancy, they will adjust their behavior accordingly.

The USSR is locked into an inflexible circle of logic in Vietnam: Its hold is based on power, which rests on prestige, which is rooted in the perceived invincibility of the USSR. In the long run its position there will stand or fall on the fact (or the fable) of its invincible power.

DOC LAP AND MAT NUOC

Vietnam's subliminal relations with the USSR, as with all outsiders, are subject to two stresses that define the degree of intimacy in the association and determine its durability. These two forces are peculiarly

Vietnamese and are the product of Vietnam's tortured history. The first is *doc lap*,[14] commonly translated as independence but connoting a complex ambivalence of assertion of independence and necessary dependency. *Doc lap* does not simply mean freedom from alien yokes, a spirit common to all societies; rather, it refers to a highly complicated amalgam of attitudes toward outsiders, compounded of fear, racial memory, insecurity, ethnic pride, xenophobia, and the need for communion. The term connotes, as with children leaving their parents at maturity, an independence both desired and regretted, one that separates but does not isolate.

Intimately bound up with the *doc lap* concept is a second subliminal force called *mat nuoc* (sometimes *vong quoc*), which literally or superficially means loss of country.[15] However, the term connotes not loss of political sovereignty—colonialism, for instance—but, rather, a condition in which identity becomes so submerged that things Vietnamese cannot easily be distinguished from things non-Vietnamese. Imbedded in *mat nuoc* is the connotation of racial extinction or physical absorption—not the fear of deliberate genocide by the foreigner so much as the fear inadvertent disappearance resulting from foreign intercourse. *Mat nuoc* would reject the American idea of the ethnic melting pot.

In a sense, *doc lap* and *mat nuoc* are opposites or, more accurately, exist in a *yin-yang* relationship. Beyond this, each has within itself the pulls of *yin* and *yang*. *Doc lap* imposes the need for a certain kind of relationship, defined in terms of independence, it is true, but including or implying a connection; in no sense does it mean avoidance of the world, as with monastic Tibet. *Mat nuoc*, while not denying the hunger for deep association, postulates that everything the alien brings, regardless of how beneficent or well intentioned, carries in it the seeds of destruction.[16]

The genesis of this world view unquestionably is the early Vietnamese experience with China. In the beginning, the Vietnamese believe, there lived in what is now south China the Hundred *Yeuh* (Tribes) of which one was the Viets. Then came the Chinese (i.e., the Han), who slowly assimilated the Hundred Yeuh in the process of *han-hua* (Sinoization)—all save one, the Viets, who fled southward from their home along the Yangtze to the delta lands of the Red River. The Chinese pursued them (all of this about the time of Christ), occupying the region for 900 years and pressing their *han-hua* efforts, but without success. The Chinese were forced out, only to return in the thirteenth century and again in the fifteenth century in further wars of attempted conquest. Always the Vietnamese reisisted. In 1945, there was a revival of *han-hua* when the Chinese Nationalists briefly occupied North Vietnam. And there were intimations of it in the 1979 Sino-Vietnamese border war.

The Vietnamese believe, virtually to a person, that in the deep recesses of all Chinese minds remains the undiminished ambition of *han-hua*. China did not simply threaten physical conquest. It also represented the subtle and more insidious danger of *mat nuoc*. Vietnam's identity could be drowned and its culture smothered by the awesome Chinese civilization.

Reinforcing the concept of *doc lap* is the non-Chinese, traditional Vietnamese view of the world, one that contributes to the psychic need for association. Traditional Vietnamese villagers see the world outside their village as a hostile place. The individual himself cannot cope with aliens. Rather, he must establish a network of contractual relations with persons judged to be reliable and successful. This is a necessary protective mechanism meant to fend off the clever and dangerous stranger. The network of relations is not a matter of exploitation. It is a carefully established trade-off of reciprocal responsibilities, all clearly defined although they need not be articulated. The relationship levies on both parties certain imperatives of behavior inasmuch as compliance and satisfaction of demands are part of the arrangement. This is not friendship. It is a power and status arrangement with nonfamily persons. On the broader scene, the arrangement takes on some of the superficial characteristics of early European feudalism, particularly in the way the village deals with the Court at the center or the way the Court deals with other nations (or fiefdoms).

Transferred to the international arena, this traditional view calls for a certain kind of association—namely, the maintenance of minimal relations (but not avoidance of relations) wherever possible, in which one is constantly suspicious of the actions and motives of other nations, anticipates the worst, and establishes one reliable special relationship.

Thus the countries and the peoples who have dealt with the Vietnamese over long periods—particularly the Chinese and the French—have met not simple opposition or xenophobia so much as a people who both wanted and feared their presence. Americans later experienced the same phenomenon. Now it is the Soviets' turn to be told they are both needed and feared. Foreigners are understandably puzzled to find themselves solicited and held at arm's length, treated at one and the same time as savior and threat.

Doc lap, then, carries with it two characteristics—a proudly proclaimed independence and a hunger for intimate supportive relations. During the Chinese *han-hua* efforts and the French colonial experiments, the need for psychic sustenance was met by the external supporter. It may be that this need is now being transferred to the USSR.

The kind of association that results from this condition can best be described as a political umbilical cord. It exists because Vietnamese political movements have regarded it as vital for their survival. The twentieth century has not seen a single important Vietnamese political movement that could be described as independent or self-sufficient. Quite the contrary: Every one of them has had a political umbilical cord to some outside source of support. The nationalist Viet Nam Quoc Dan Dang had ties with China; the Dai Viets, with Japan; the early Catholic and non-Catholic reformist movements, with France; the Buddhists, with Ceylon activists; the South Vietnamese, with the Americans. Vietnamese Communists, both Stalinists and Trotskyites, sought ties with fellow Communists everywhere—Paris, Peking, Moscow. The early history of communism in Vietnam can be written largely in terms of its leaders wandering the earth in search of a foreign connection. All Asian anticolonial movements, of course, had external ties with sympathizers in the metropolitan homeland, but none assumed the life and death importance of those sought by the Vietnamese Communists. The Indian Congress party, for instance, maintained a liaison with support groups in London in the days before it came to power. But it was only a nominal relationship and Congress leaders stayed and worked in India, essentially on their own, knowing they would succeed or fail depending on the efficacy of their party's strategy. The Vietnamese Communists never had this sense of self-reliance. Their leaders and emissaries went abroad not so much to search for specific political and financial support but to find permanent commitment. Revolutionist Ho Chi Minh did not set foot in his homeland from 1912 to 1940. He never got from the Comintern what he needed, in part, perhaps, because Comintern members did not understand the psychic need of the Vietnamese and tended to regard their solicitations as excessive expectations emanating from a not very significant group.

It was long an involuted spectacle. During the Vietnam War, North Vietnam communicated suspicion of betrayal by its two allies. It endlessly proclaimed that its cause depended on no one, that it trusted no one; at the same time it levied extraordinary aid requirements on its allies. At times *doc lap* seemed an irrationally destructive influence. Ho Chi Minh, fully aware of its pernicious effects, filled his speeches with advice to hold its influence in check. His theme was always the same: All moral forces in the world are obliged to support our cause, but we need not depend on them. Ho's handling of this subliminal influence probably was his most important contribution to victory, just as the Saigon leadership's failure to cope with the *doc lap* influence was perhaps the main reason why South Vietnamese lost the war. Ho, from the time of his return to Vietnam during World War II to the time of his death, ceaselessly hammered away at the theme of Vietnamese self-reliance. He and other Hanoi leaders in public statements and interviews through-

out the war asserted, even boasted, that the DRV could fight and win
without any outside assistance. In party indoctrination efforts and *khiem
thao* (self-criticism) sessions the idea was stressed that Hanoi could win
alone and on its own. On the face of it, such a claim was absurd—
Hanoi was totally dependent on outsiders for military hardware—and
many observers at the time put it down as a pitiful effort to save face.
But in fact, as Ho well realized, it was a necessary antidote to *doc lap*
influence, one that had to be administered constantly.

Today the Vietnamese, still aware of the dependent quality of *doc
lap*, struggle constantly to deny it with respect to the USSR. An insightful
example was found in a Hanoi newspaper article entitled "New Hap-
piness,"[17] in which a Vietnamese cadre described a visit to Moscow
during which he came to realize that his view of the Soviet-Vietnamese
relationship was parochial and outdated. He said that he now knows
the relationship "has gone beyond its former seeking aid stage" and
has entered a new "one, big family" stage, marked by parity. In this
new stage, he wrote, "we no longer seek aid. We participate in the
process of international division of labor in which every [country] has
its own tasks, but in our common cause." Vietnam as merely a recipient
of socialist world assistance is "now a proven backward thought." Of
course, he added, this does impose certain conditions on Vietnam. No
longer can Moscow money "be spent by Vietnam in its own way and
choosing." Now it has to be used in accordance with the principles of
international division of labor. There is, however, nothing but advantage
in this for Vietnam, he concluded, because "the more backward and
the smaller is a country, the more it needs to merge with the larger
system. Thus it is pulled forward as the whole system moves forward,
like a box car hooked to a train." This revelation—this "expanded field
of vision"—came to the cadre, he said, on his second day in Moscow.
His article is a strong rationalization in *doc lap* terms, particularly his
use of the family as metaphor.

OIL AND WATER

Clearly these subliminal influences are today's heritage in Vietnam,
affecting relations with the Soviets as well as other foreigners. They
manifest themselves as a contradictory if not schizoid fear of emasculation
that requires Vietnam to escape from foreign influence even while
requiring extensive commitment by foreigners. The legacy is manifold
and dichotomous, an enormously ambivalent attitude toward friend and
foe alike. On the one hand is a desperate psychological need for ties
of sustenance born of past failure, gestures of defiance that for all their
magnificence came to nothing and leave as the only hope the outsider

who could put things right. On the other hand, also reinforced by a long bitter history, is the record of betrayal, abandonment, and subjection by foreigners, a record that has all but destroyed faith in or reliance on them.

The effects of the legacy take a specific form. There is an ingrained indecisiveness with regard to associations, the tendency to temporize in alliances. There is great reluctance to assume the leadership of joint ventures to bring about social change. Responsibility is shunted elsewhere; just as in the past it rested in the royal court, in the village council, with French liberals, and among anti-imperialist friends in China or Moscow.

The Vietnamese, burdened by fear of failure, betrayal, and impotency, impose demands on others—often unreasonable demands. Their anxiety seeks an outlet, often manifested by a meanness of spirit and hatred. In Vietnamese it is known as *cam thu, cam hon*, the spirit of hate: Hate the enemy, hate the traitor, hate the exploiter, hate even those who come to help change the hated condition.

These, then, are the subliminal forces from the past. They remain present and operative in Vietnam today. They are difficult to chart or measure. And they are mutations, constantly being translated into new modes, appearing as new responses. Only a foolish bystander would claim to know in what manner the subliminal influence will affect specific Vietnamese behavior in the future. The subliminal force is genuine and powerful, but by its very nature—its dark irrational quality—it is unpredictable.

The USSR, appearing on the Hanoi scene in such a formidable way, has added another factor to the equation. The Soviets have come on forcefully. Although an aggressive USSR may not in itself trouble the Hanoi leadership in that it imposes no apparent fear of intervention, a hard and unrelenting Moscow approach almost certainly will trigger the old reaction. As Donald Zagoria has pointed out there is in the Soviet character a lack of restraint, even when restraint is a self interest.[18] It was this lack that doomed its ventures in Egypt, China, and elsewhere. Nothing could be more self-defeating in Hanoi than the compulsion to dominate, nor more likely to put the USSR and Vietnam on a collision course.

The USSR may be able to escape this danger and hold itself in restraint. The greater question is whether it can escape history. The clear conclusion to be drawn from the effects of these subliminal forces is what might be labeled the paradoxical law of Vietnamese association: that any relationship with Vietnam has the potential for catastrophe. The demonstrable historical fact is that no nation, no group—not China, not the now extinct Cham, not the once vast Khmer empire, not the

Montagnards of a dozen tribes, not the Thai, the Lao, the fifteenth-century Burmese, not the French, the Japanese or Americans—has ever had a successful relationship with the Vietnamese. In each relationship there were moments of amicability and mutual benefit, but always the relationship carried the seeds of its own destruction.

The Soviet Union today is testing this thesis. Already it can be argued that its close association with Vietnam has gotten it into trouble—tarred as it has been by its support of war in Kampuchea and by the racist expulsion of ethnic Chinese as "boat people"—not because of the USSR's actions but simply because of the result of its association. The Kremlin may not sense the trap that history is preparing, or perhaps it believes it can succeed where others have failed. More likely it will become simply one more victim of the law of paradox.

NOTES

1. Vietnamese music, with its half-tone scale, is so vastly different from Western music that its genius cannot be appreciated by a Westerner without years of special training. There is also a formidable barrier in writing because of the Vietnamese language, which virtually defies poetic yet accurate translation. Hence Vietnamese literature, especially poetry, can scarcely be appreciated or understood except in its original or untranslated form.

2. Nguyen Van Kinh, "Fiftieth Founding Anniversary of the USSR," *Vietnam Courier*, No. 12 (December 1972).

3. See "Vietnam's Unknown Advisors," a 1983 unpublished manuscript by Harry H. Kendall, based on interviews with Vietnamese in Thai refugee camps who had had direct contact with Soviet advisers in Vietnam circa late 1970s and early 1980s. The manuscript is on file at the University of California (Berkeley) Indochina Archive.

4. *An Outline History of the Vietnam Workers Party 1930–1970* (Hanoi: Foreign Languages Publishing House, 1970). Originally published in May 1970 by *Nhan Dan*.

5. *Our President, Ho Chi Minh* (Hanoi: Foreign Languages Publishing House, 1970).

6. These texts were classified as "internal," meaning they were neither put on sale in Vietnam nor made available outside of party circles. Copies of both were captured in South Vietnam, however, and can be consulted at the University of California (Berkeley) Indochina Archive.

7. See the notes found at the Indochina Archive, University of California (Berkeley), *File VIII, National Liberation Front of South Vietnam/General*. The research is the work of Douglas Pike conducted in the late 1960s in Vietnam.

8. See Nikita Khrushchev, *Khrushchev Remembers* (Boston: Little, Brown, 1971).

9. Allan Cameron, "The Soviet Union and Vietnam: The Origins of Involvement," in W. Raymond Duncan, ed., *Soviet Policy in Developing Countries* (Waltham, Mass.: Ginn-Blaisdell, 1970), pp. 166–206.

10. The primary institutes are the Institute of Oriental Studies, the Institute of Far East Studies, and the Institute of Socialist Countries' Relations.

11. Stalin's birthday is still observed as a major event in Hanoi.

12. Typical expression of these characteristics is found in SRV Foreign Minister Nguyen Duy Trinh's speech, "Inexhaustible Source of Strength and Inspiration," published in Moscow as a monograph by the Institute of International Affairs (December 1977).

13. From the start, Hanoi has enthusiastically endorsed Soviet intervention in Afghanistan.

14. The phrase *doc lap* virtually defies translation. Its calligraphic roots are *doc* (meaning toxic, poisonous, harmful, injurious) and *lap* (to build, form, or create); thus the phrase means, literally, to construct a defense against injury. It is the term used by the Vietnamese for the English word *independence*. In English this connotes *freedom* (in English, in fact, the two words are often used interchangeably), but this is not the connotation of *doc lap*. Further, *doc lap* implies controls on the behavior of both parties—a relationship not imposed, but controlled by reciprocity and obligation.

15. The phrase *mat nuoc* is derived from the characters for *mat* (meaning lose, die, vanish, be expunged) and *nuoc* (water, tide, the watery part of a country—literally, loss through inundation); in combination, the two terms mean loss of country; Vietnamese emigrés in the United States tend to use the phrase *vong quoc*, meaning to lose one's country.

16. However, it should be understood that the influence of these concepts is not merely negative. The concepts motivated the resistance offered the Chinese and the French, and out of them have come a community of ideals. They left a general sense of idealism, a sense of the glory of the times. Many of the early Confucianist figures were excellent writers who told their stories of *doc lap* in impressive language and left behind a record that inspired the young of subsequent generations. But the cultural influence of *doc lap* also represents a sword over the Soviet-Vietnamese relationship.

17. See the *Vietnam Courier* (November 1982).

18. Donald Zagoria, ed., *Soviet Policy in East Asia* (New Haven, Conn.: Yale University Press, 1982).

Eight

POST–VIETNAM WAR RELATIONS

IN THE YEARS immediately following the end of the Vietnam War, the USSR and the now unified Socialist Republic of Vietnam moved into a far more intimate relationship than had ever existed before. It was, however, one born more of circumstance than of choice, at least as far as the Vietnamese were concerned, and the direct product of the unanticipated traumatic condition that descended on Indochina at war's end.

The relationship that has emerged rests on the twin pillars of Soviet opportunism and Vietnamese dependence. Moscow has seized what it regards as a great political and diplomatic opportunity in a region from which previously it had largely been excluded. Vietnam inadvertently blundered into regional alienation, which threw it into the arms of the USSR and a dependence that economic troubles have steadily deepened. The original postwar association lasted for the remainder of the decade and was replaced in the 1980s by a vastly altered relationship (as discussed in the following chapter).

POSTWAR YEARS

Nature hates a vacuum, above all a political vacuum, so it was inevitable, from the moment of Hanoi's victory in 1975, that the USSR would be drawn on to Vietnam's stage center to play a far more pivotal role than it had ever anticipated. This was not the result of some carefully conceived and nurtured plan by Moscow. U.S. disengagement from Indochina created a whirlpool so strong that the USSR was irresistably sucked into its vortex.

Moscow's postwar moves in Indochina have been intended to serve general strategic objectives.[1] Its rationale seems reasonably clear. The USSR seeks to counter China—militarily containing it and psychologically diminishing its influence in the region by way of formal treaties, if

180

possible. It wants to enhance its strategic position in the South China Sea, the Indian Ocean, and the waters of the Pacific beyond. It means to stake a claim of legitimacy for involvement in regional affairs and be consulted or have a voice in regional decisionmaking. Vietnam contributes to these goals. The SRV-USSR treaty is a military alliance in all but name. The nature and character of the Soviet military presence in Indochina has been vigorously debated by pro- and anti-Hanoi commentators in Southeast Asia and in the United States. Much of this dispute turns on semantics, particularly on the definition of *military base*. Hanoi and Moscow officials insist that the Soviet air and naval installations in Vietnam are *facilities*, not *bases*. In terms of technical military usage, this is correct. The more important point, however, is that the usage to which the USSR is permitted to put these facilities fully meets all of its strategic requirements in the Southeast Asia region.

At first, for Vietnam and Moscow there was only euphoria. Victory had been achieved against incredible odds, and Communist Vietnam stood on the threshold of a glorious future and was about to become "ten times more beautiful" as Ho Chi Minh had promised throughout the long war. Party Secretary Le Duan in the late summer of 1975 led a high-level DRV delegation on a three-month "victory tour" of the USSR and seven other fraternal nations to offer Hanoi's gratitude for wartime assistance and to outline postwar relations. This high-visibility trip was marked by red carpet treatment by hosts and was studded with hyperbolic and self-congratulatory rhetoric by the Vietnamese. The small cloud on the horizon was the overly correct forced enthusiam of official China.

The next few years saw a constant shuttle of officials between Hanoi and Moscow. Le Duan returned for the CPSU's twenty-fifth Party Congress in February 1976. General Vo Nguyen Giap, with military hardware shopping list in hand, led a PAVN delegation to Moscow in mid-March 1977, followed by Premier Pham Van Dong on a state visit in April and June, crossing paths with Deputy Premier Le Thanh Nghi en route to Warsaw and a major economic aid-solicitation mission to CMEA. In August came Truong Chinh, the party theorist, with a National Assembly delegation. Le Duan was back again in October for a month's celebration of the sixtieth anniversary of the Bolshevik Revolution. Lesser Vietnamese figures came and went with regularity.

Hanoi's earlier reticence in acknowledging appreciation of the USSR vanished with victory. The linchpin of Hanoi's postwar foreign policy became determination to act always in close cooperation with the USSR in the international arena. Le Duan, at the Fifth Party Congress, set forth this policy:

The USSR is our most powerful and firmest ally. . . . To
tighten our friendship and broaden our cooperation (with the
USSR) is the primordial problem in serving the foreign policy of
our Party and State. . . .

(We) once again express our full support of the programs
and the unswerving stands of the USSR . . . [and] warmly hail
the good-willed and constructive proposals of the Soviet Union
in relationship with the west. . . . Solidarity and all-round
cooperation is the keystone of foreign policy of State and
Party. . . .

Close links and all-round cooperation with the Soviet
Union are a matter of principle, strategy and revolutionary
sentiment. . . . Our Party is duty bound to educate all
Vietnamese to grasp firmly this principle, this strategy. . . . Our
people are extremely happy about the brilliant development and
militant solidarity and cooperation between our country and the
USSR.[2]

This message was conveyed by Hanoi officials throughout the
region. Pham Nhu Cuong at a 1978 Bangkok academic conference told
Southeast Asian neighbors that the USSR is central to all Vietnamese
strategic thinking:

In foreign relations, Vietnam's policy is to promote full solidarity
and cooperation with the USSR. . . . The fraternal relations and
solidarity and cooperation between the USSR and Vietnam
started in the 1920's and have been tempered and tested through
the various stages of the hard struggle of the Vietnamese people.
USSR solidarity and assistance has been a factor in the victory of
the Vietnamese people both in the struggle against aggression
and in national reconstruction. The peoples of the two countries
are linked by sincere feelings of friendship, mutual affection,
respect and confidence in the struggle for peace, national
independence and socialism. In our greatest hours of trial and
danger, the Soviet people have always been at the Vietnamese
people's side. At a time when the Peking leaders and other
hostile forces tried to isolate Vietnam and stifle it economically,
the signing of the Vietnam-Soviet Treaty of Friendship and
Cooperation was a timely support to Vietnam and has added to
the moral and material strength of the Vietnamese people in the
new historical stage.[3]

How much prescience there was in Hanoi's gravitation toward
Moscow is something that probably can never be documented. In any

case it was fortuitous. Soon the bloom of victory faded and the world closed in on Hanoi. Relations with China, in decline since the late 1960s, took a precipitous downturn. Alienation from the rest of Southeast Asia deepened. Experiments with land collectivization and a new domestic trade system led to internal economic chaos. Social reconstruction of the South, "breaking the machine," drove out hundreds of thousands of economically valuable middle-class and ethnic Chinese. A holocaust descended on Kampuchea. An atmosphere of grim reality settled on members of the Politburo. The lone reed on which they still could lean was the USSR.

A close relationship with Moscow was to be expected; the dependent relationship that developed was unnatural. It is traceable chiefly to early bad or unworkable Hanoi policies, the result of poor Politburo judgment. The Politburo's intention at war's end was to expand foreign relations and diversify economic relations. There were overtures to Southeast Asia. A liberal foreign investment code was promulgated, and foreign economic aid, both private and governmental, was solicited. The SRV joined the International Monetary Fund and the World Bank and sought to work through the Asian Development Bank to attract outside aid. All of this was nullified by policy mistakes in dealing with China, Pol Pot, the United States, and the ASEAN countries. At one point Vietnam found itself fighting a two-front war. Internal policies became self-defeating. The treatment of the southern middle class and the ethnic Chinese savaged the southern domestic trade sector and the country's transportation and distribution systems, and left nothing in their place. Harsh, overly centralized economic controls stifled agricultural growth and industrial production.

The result, certainly never the intention, was to throw Vietnam into extraordinary dependence on the USSR, one so great it carried implied or potential power of blackmail. Vietnam needed the USSR for 10 to 15 percent of its staple food, without which there would be rice riots. It relied on the USSR for all of its petroleum, chemical fertilizer, and such raw materials as its limited industrial plant could use. Because there are no arms factories in the SRV, it came to be dependent on the USSR for all the armaments, military supplies, and air transportation needed to fight its war in Kampuchea and defend itself against China.

Dependency was such that virtually anything Moscow would have demanded of it, Hanoi would have been obliged to grant. If there was restraint to be shown, it would have been on the part of Moscow, aware that for a sound future the relationship must rest on uncoerced mutual interest cooperation.

THE TREATY

Hanoi's enunciated foreign policy, after the end of the Vietnam War, was one of "independence"—meaning it intended to identify itself chiefly with the Third World. Within the socialist world, it would maintain a position of equidistance. Soon, however, its outward-turning efforts slackened, and its tilt toward Moscow had by 1977 become a distinct lurch. The summer of 1978 was the turning point. The Politburo in Hanoi was drawn or pushed to end its long-standing and previously profitable posture with respect to the Sino-Soviet dispute and come down unequivocally on the side of the USSR.

Two separate acts were involved in this decision: a formal linkup with the Moscow-based economic system known as Comecon, or CMEA, and establishment of a strategic security arrangement within the network of treaties of friendship and cooperation that Moscow had built throughout the world. The context of the Hanoi Politburo decision that summer, it should be remembered, was sharp Chinese brinkmanship against Vietnam, such as reduction and then cutoff of economic and military assistance, apparently intended by the Chinese to shock the Vietnamese back to a more balanced posture. Although Sino-Vietnamese relations were moving toward rupture in mid-1978, the deterioration at this point could have been reversed.

Exactly why the Politburo felt it necessary to forego further exploration of ways to settle differences with China and suddenly and decisively to ally itself with the USSR still is not clear. One interpretation is that Moscow insisted on it. According to this thesis, the USSR was determined not to repeat earlier mistakes in Egypt and elsewhere. It wanted to ensure the value received from its assistance. It wanted to avail itself of Vietnam's strategic position with respect to China, but only if there were guarantees the arrangement would prove durable. An alternate explanation is that the initiative for alliance came from Hanoi, which was frightened by China's saber rattling and sought security assurances from the USSR.

The USSR-SRV Treaty of Friendship and Cooperation was signed on November 2, 1978, in Moscow. It was the first such treaty between the two countries.[4] It was negotiated by Party Secretary Le Duan and Premier Pham Van Dong for Vietnam and President Leonid Brezhnev and Premier Alexi Kosygin for the USSR. Signing came after a last-minute delay of several additional days of hard bargaining that involved Vietnam's top military line commander, General Van Tien Dung.

Signed at the same time were at least five other agreements: a ten-year economic assistance agreement that foreshadowed a new economic relationship, a defense assistance agreement, and three protocols dealing with science, technology, and cultural exchange.

Hanoi's public explanation for entering into the treaty was the China threat. The Soviet explanation was broader:

> At present, the relations between the Soviet Union and Vietnam are based on the Treaty of Friendship and Cooperation signed by the two countries on 2 November 1978. The Treaty defines the main longterm direction in the relations of the two socialist states, and in their political, economic, cultural, and other cooperation.
>
> The Treaty reaffirms the basic direction of Soviet and Vietnamese foreign policy—that of struggle for peace and for just and equal international relations. It contains a special article saying, among other things, that the Soviet Union and Vietnam are firmly determined to promote a more solid peace in Asia and the rest of the world, and that they will support the aspirations of the Southeast Asian peoples to peace, independence, and mutual cooperation.[5]

The treaty commits both parties to "Socialist solidarity" and "consolidation of the world Socialist system." Both affirm support for the "struggle waged by the non-aligned countries and the peoples of Asia, Africa and Latin America against imperialism, colonialism and neo-colonialism," but at the same time also promise to seek the "easing of tension in international relations" through the "principles of peaceful coexistence."

The most important part of the treaty concerns Vietnamese security. It is not clear from an examination of the text what exactly the USSR promises with respect to the defense of Vietnam. The operative clause, Article 6, reads:

> In case either party is attacked or threatened with attack the two parties signatory to the treaty shall immediately consult each other with a view to eliminating the threat, and shall take appropriate and effective measures to safeguard the peace and security of the two countries.

Ambiguity here appears deliberate on the part of the USSR. The treaty varies from what might be called the standard Moscow treaty with other Communist nations: It is not titled a "mutual assistance" treaty, nor does it pledge the USSR "to immediate military aid" as do the others. What the USSR agrees to is "to consult" and to "take appropriate and effective measures." In the case of the Chinese border war, this consultation did not amount to much. The Soviet treaty with Vietnam resembles the USSR treaty with India more than it does treaties with other Communist states.

Moscow spokesmen at the time and since have insisted that the treaty threatens no one and is akin to those signed with ten non-Communist nations such as Finland, Iraq, and Ethiopia. These treaties, however, are not carbon copies. For instance, the Iraq, Angola, and Mozambique treaties commit the signatories to "strengthen the defense capacity" of each, which the Vietnam treaty does not do. Initially, observers interpreted this to mean there would be no Soviet military bases in Vietnam. The Vietnam treaty, like the treaty with India, carefully delimits *threat*. Treaties with other Asian Communist nations are more binding. An attack on North Korea or Mongolia would bring "immediate military aid," a phrase that may have been contained in a secret Vietnam-USSR protocol signed along with the treaty, thus making it equivalent to similar treaties with North Korea and Mongolia. Reports to that effect circulated in Moscow at the time. Some sort of protocol apparently was required, and signed secretly, to permit Soviet use of Vietnamese naval and military installations. Moscow press references link warship calls to the treaty. Moreover, there appears to have been a second secret protocol signed after the Vietnam-China border war in early 1978.[6]

Most other Soviet friendship treaties call for mutual response to threats to regional peace, which the Vietnam treaty does not do. Originally observers believed this omission had to do with Kampuchea, meaning that the USSR was not required by the treaty to join Vietnam in meeting the Kampuchea "threat" and, by extension, that the USSR would not make military assistance available to Hanoi for use there.[7] As with the interpretation on Soviet bases in Vietnam, however, this belief proved to be a forlorn hope.

The treaty specifies that there will no interference in internal affairs by either party (a matter on which other treaties are silent)—apparently a gesture of deference to the Vietnamese *doc lap* spirit. However, the author was told by a former SRV official who had defected that a secret protocol to the treaty was signed in Moscow in November 1978 under which the USSR is automatically authorized to intervene militarily in Vietnam in the event the current government is replaced by non-Communists or is toppled in a coup d'état by a pro-Chinese faction. The existence of such a protocol is highly questionable.

The treaty signing drew a sharp reaction in the region. For China, it represented a direct threat. Beijing reported that Vietnam had become a tool to serve Moscow's hegemonistic dreams in Southeast Asia and that it had become hegemonistic in its own right, to serve its goal of a federation in Indochina and, more ambitiously, in its aim to be the new Cuba of the East. Japan saw the treaty as a move by the USSR to increase its influence in Southeast Asia at Japan's expense and as a blow to the Japanese hope for a nonaligned region.[8] Initial ASEAN reaction was guarded but became more openly critical later, especially in Thailand, Singapore, and Indonesia. East European countries, particularly Romania, Poland, and Czechoslovakia, were also cool to the treaty, regarding it as an unnecessary and dangerous entanglement for Moscow that could increase the risk of war with China.

In the years since the signing, Hanoi has afforded the treaty a prominent place in its conduct of foreign affairs. A Le Duan speech described the treaty as the foundation stone of the country's foreign policies, the single most important element in the conduct of its diplomacy, and the basis of all Vietnamese geopolitical planning.[9] However, Hanoi has also tended to demonstrate a certain ambivalence about the treaty with respect to Vietnamese security. When National Assembly official Tran Quynh reviewed the treaty on its third anniversary, he found it had "made Vietnamese-Soviet friendship increasingly firm and wholesome and the relations between the two countries even richer and more effective,"[10] but he did not say anything about it making Vietnam more secure. *Nhan Dan*'s editorials are laudatory but vague. For instance, one such editorial spoke of the treaty as "an historical event . . . an historical landmark . . . possessing the weight of the Truong Son or Ural Mountains . . . a great contribution to the socialist world's struggle to bring about peace and stability in the world especially in the sensitive (Indochina) region. . . ."[11] This reference to peace and stability is the closest such commentary came to the subject of security. *Nhan Dan* did say that the treaty contributed to the "all sided" development of relations and cooperation in the fields of economics, culture, science, and technology— a statement that can possibly be interpreted as an allusion to security matters. A speech by Truong Chinh to the National Assembly in December 1981 seemed designed to suggest that there were limits to the USSR's ability to defend Vietnam, thus implying a desire on Hanoi's part to trust the USSR but an inability to bring itself to do so.

As far as Vietnam's general public is concerned, however, the treaty is now integral to Vietnam's condition. The fifth anniversary of its signing in 1983 was the occasion for a major emulation-motivation campaign in its name. Following a special training seminar in Hanoi, teams of Party agit-prop cadres fanned out to all districts and most schools in the country to lecture on "the great significance of the Treaty and to popularize its spirit."[12]

ECONOMIC TUTELAGE

The USSR in 1975 moved nimbly to insinuate itself into Vietnam's economic institutions by responding generously to Hanoi's call at war's end for extensive assistance.

The first postwar year in Vietnam saw quick economic improvement, chiefly because southern battlefields had again become rice fields and distribution networks were reopened. With the first two postwar crops (in the tenth month of 1975 and the fifth month of 1976) the South became momentarily self-sufficient, and rice production for the entire country reached a new high. Then southern collectivization was ordered and rice production began to decline, continuing to do so throughout the decade. Remedial measures on the farm and in the distribution sector were ordered, but these did not work and the economy further stagnated. In August 1979 the Sixth Plenum (Fourth Congress) approved a plan to lift some of the controls on agricultural production and domestic trade. This yielded some improvements, although the plan was sabotaged by the ideologues. In December 1983 the Fourth Plenum (Fifth Congress) made a renewed effort to establish a more liberal and pragmatic policy to encourage food production and consumer goods manufacture. It was a program with considerable promise. Rice production increased almost at once, and by 1985 Vietnam for the first time was back to its 1975-1976 rice production level. In June 1985 it made still another effort to get the economic machine moving with the adoption of Plenum Resolution Eight. Throughout this period the USSR faithfully stood by Hanoi, doing what it could under circumstances that admittedly were chaotic.

Soviet economic planners, since 1975, have set for themselves the task of determining what Vietnam's grand strategy for economic development should be, ostensibly so as to fix what will be required of the USSR. Soviet intentions appear to be threefold.

The USSR's first intention is to persuade Vietnam to adopt the Soviet economic model along with the basic components of the Soviet economic system. Specifically, these components include a nationalized means of production in industry and in supportive sectors (e.g., the transportation sector); state planning with outputs and inputs centrally determined; enterprises managed by individuals whose incentive is reward on meeting output targets and minimizing inputs; a government budget supported both by taxes and profits from state enterprises, with expenditures allocated by the center; prices and wages fixed and determined by the state; domestic trade and transport in the hands of state enterprises for the most part; and collectivization of agriculture, with production incentives based on a work point system and with limited acreage assigned as private plots.[13]

At the upper reaches of the Vietnamese leadership, such ideas tend to be regarded more as ideological than technological matters. At root, of course, is the question of the proper role of dogma—Marxism-Leninism, Maoism, or some variant of socialism—in the process of economic development. In Hanoi this question has always been regarded as essentially philosophical, having to do with the nature of human incentives. The result is that an ideological impulse did and still does impinge deeply on all postwar Politiburo economic thinking. The savage, almost mindless attack by Hanoi cadres on southern businesses in March 1978 that destroyed the domestic trade sector as a structured institution and pauperized the middle class was the product of ideological motive. In the process, the domestic trade sector was treated as an expendable function; otherwise, it would have made no sense at all to replace something with nothing. The same influence was behind the gutting of Vietnam's technological base—that is, the driving out of key Vietnamese and Chinese technicians and technocrats simply because they did not fit into the new order.

Doctrine has intruded into other aspects of economic development as well. There is the argument between export-oriented industry and import substitution. Should Vietnam work toward self-sufficiency, producing for itself its industrial necessities (such as trucks, tractors, chemical fertilizer, electric equipment)? Or should it develop enterprises linked to external trade, either those involving agriculture (industrial crops, lumber, fish, and seafood) or labor-intensive assembly operations (television sets, microcomputers) so as to generate hard currency and be able to buy what it needs abroad? Another issue involves the economic development of North versus South—specifically, whether industry should be confined to the North and the South should be turned into a "pastureland." Another has to do with technological labor, the Vietnam brain drain, whether technologists and other experts should be allowed to leave or whether concessions should be made and their skills put to work.

Stated in nonideological terms, the central economic problem for the Vietnamese and their Soviet advisers is to define modernity for Vietnam. Hence the questions to be addressed are these: How far from the present agrarian-based society should Vietnam move? What kind of industrialization should it have? How much industrialization is required for economic development? Is it possible to become modern and still remain agrarian? The Politburo has been wrestling with these questions since 1956. Generally the leadership agrees that industrialization per se is a good thing and a proper goal. But there is some argument over the extent of *heavy* industrialization—for instance, whether Vietnam should be self-sufficient in steel production. It is generally agreed that "industrializing agriculture" is necessary, and that this will require the radical alteration of the country's agricultural sector, that is, conversion of the thousand-year-old farm-village system into district-sized agro-production units or giant farm factories. Increasingly, however, influential party leaders question the feasibility of the agrofactory concept, contending it is unnecessary and probably unworkable.

The industry versus agriculture debate has never been simply a matter of abstract dogma. Advocates of industrialization have always argued on the grounds that there is no alternative, that the economy can never become viable without it. This is the fundamental position of the Soviet theoreticians.

The dispute is commonly portrayed by outside observers, and sometimes even within official Hanoi circles, as an industry *versus* agriculture argument. And among economic cadres and operational planners, there is a persistent tendency to think in terms of either industrial development or agricultural development, despite the fact that there are official strictures against this. Still, in any specific instance concerning the allocation of resources, a choice invariably must be made. Construction of another steel mill, even with massive USSR participation, would draw heavily on the country's scarce supply of technicians and skilled construction workers who might otherwise be employed on, say, a new water-conservancy project. Factory construction, even if financed by free foreign aid, comes at the expense of efforts to mechanize state farms or build up the herds of breeder cattle. Thus there has been and remains a kind of competitive tension between "industrialists" and "agriculturalists" that manifests itself in party-state bureaucratic infighting.

Soviet advisers in Vietnam are thus caught in the middle of both factional political battle and ideological debate.[14] To some extent the USSR itself has an ideological stake in the issue, that is, to wean Vietnam away from Chinese economic thinking and inculcate its own. When the first postwar Five-Year Plan (1976–1980) was being drawn in Hanoi (1974–1975), Chinese advisers on the scene advocated primary emphasis on agriculture, secondary emphasis on light industry, and a distant third priority to heavy industry. The Chinese also impugned the Soviets' motives in their offers to support only "show pieces" in the plan, such as the construction of the Ho Chi Minh mausoleum, leaving the Chinese with mundane projects such as road and bridge construction.

Moscow's second intention with respect to the Vietnamese economy is to integrate it into the socialist/CMEA economic system (as discussed in Chapter 6). As far as can be determined there are no important reservations in Hanoi about the long-term meaning of this integration.

The third intention is entirely pragmatic. It is to help make the economy perform more effectively so as to reduce the economic costs to the USSR. Soviet advisers are thus working to help solve Vietnam's more pressing production problems, find more exportable goods in Vietnam to redress the horrendous trade imbalance, and generally to improve Vietnamese economic efficiency.

It is difficult to judge how influential Soviet economic advisers are in Hanoi today. Some of their advice can be enforced through economic aid mechanisms, although there are sharp limits here. The Vietnamese for ten years have experimented with Soviet suggestions, and most have been found to be neither helpful nor meaningful.

Although it is difficult to document, there appears to be a growing belief in Hanoi among Vietnamese economic planners that no outside economic model—not the USSR, not China, not East European "capitalism"—is appropriate for Vietnam. The reason for this, of course, is the singular set of problems faced by the country and the peculiar cultural and historic burdens it must carry. Therefore, according to this reasoning, Vietnam must devise its own unique strategy for economic problem solving and, beyond that, nation building. If such is the case, the USSR's contribution will by necessity be confined to material support.

MILITARY ALLIANCE

In the decade after the end of the Vietnam War the USSR and Vietnam moved steadily closer together in "fraternal military association," which by the mid-1980s had become a military alliance in all but name. For Moscow the developing relationship represents strategic opportunity, the full dimensions of which it has yet to determine. For Hanoi it means a reasonably reliable source of military hardware and at least limited security guarantees.

Viewed from Moscow the Indochina peninsula offers at least four major strategic uses. First, it can contribute to the USSR's determined augmentation of its surrogate military force and its ability to project that force globally. For most of our lifetime the men of the Kremlin have pressed on unceasingly in arms building at home and enhancement of military prowess abroad. PAVN, the third largest army on earth, can be regarded as a major addition to this potential.

The second use of the peninsula is as a Soviet forward-deployment air and naval base. Vietnam offers a facility midway between Vladivostok (2,220 miles—or 10 days by steamer—from Cam Ranh) and the Indian Ocean. Vietnam also represents an excellent staging area of the sort required to make full use of the technology of modern warfare. And it provides a fixed installation for Soviet military "surge" capability, if required. This utility would be high for limited or regional wars (for instance against China) or for Soviet intervention in Southeast Asia but less so for a war against the United States. In the Soviet presence there is implied protection for Vietnam against China and assurance of reliable sea delivery of armaments and other essential commodities. USSR naval forces are deployed out of three installations—Cam Ranh Bay, Da Nang, and Haiphong—directed chiefly at China. The four major air bases— Da Nang, Cam Ranh, Bien Hoa, and Tan Son Nhut—pose a potential omnidirectional threat to the region.

Augmentation began in the last days of the Vietnam War. Soviet military specialists traveled southward on the heels of the advancing PAVN even as the last battle was being fought. A team from Moscow was inspecting radar installations at Nha Trang before Saigon fell. Chief interest focused on Cam Ranh Bay, the magnificent harbor in Central Vietnam in which the United States had invested nearly $250 million as a commercial port.[15] Emigrés fleeing Cam Ranh reported that within hours of its capture in April 1975 by North Vietnamese troops, Soviet naval officers arrived for inspection.[16] Within days Soviet technicians had restored the radar equipment to operational condition at Cam Ranh and at other installations along the central coast.

This moment, the end of the Vietnam War, coincided with major changes in the USSR's force posture in northeast Asia and the Pacific. New Soviet cruisers, destroyers, and other vessels were added to the Pacific fleet; ground and air forces there were modernized and increased; a high command for the Far East theater of operations was established; and new strategic weapons such as the SS-20 Intermediate-Range Nuclear Missile and the Backfire long-range strike aircraft were being deployed. These were more relevant for Japan, China, and the United States in the Pacific than for Indochina, although obviously there is a strategic meaning for Southeast Asia in the deployment of such weapons.

By the end of 1976 more Soviet than U.S. naval vessels plied the Pacific waters. In the South China seas adjacent to Vietnam were a dozen Soviet naval vessels, a third of them combat-ready. Their calls at Cam Ranh became steadily more frequent and increasingly involved larger capital ships. Soviet usage moved gradually from anchorage to bases. Reportedly in 1981 a Soviet naval command was established aboard a flagship anchored in Cam Ranh Bay. By then there were on average in any one day more Soviet than Vietnamese vessels in Cam Ranh harbor.

It is argued by some observers that the USSR's takeover of Cam Ranh was made possible by China. According to this view, the USSR had long coveted the bases but had been rebuffed by Hanoi on the grounds of Chinese objections and possible dire consequences, an argument lost when China itself breached relations.

Soviet naval presence at Cam Ranh was augmented by Soviet-supplied air defenses: SAM-3 batteries, advanced radar, and fighter-interceptor planes. In 1983 an advanced electronic intelligence complex became operational at Cam Ranh; it is believed to monitor U.S. military installations at Clark Field and Subic Bay in the Philippines.[17] As a major staging complex for the Soviet Pacific Ocean Fleet, Cam Ranh now contains missile storage and missile facilities, a self-contained fuel system, barracks, and other support installations. The air base in 1986 supported Bear and Badger strike and reconnaissance aircraft as well as MIG-23 Floggers that provide air defense and strike escort.

In the 1980s the USSR's use of Cam Ranh quickened in pace. Western and Thai intelligence sources at the end of 1984 said that in the previous four years there had been a fourfold increase in the number of ships calling at Cam Ranh, and that there were twenty-six in the harbor on an average day, half of them combat and the other half service ships.[18] By mid-1986 this figure had risen to an average twenty to twenty-five warships in the harbor at any one time, in addition to about the same number of Soviet freighters and other service vessels.

Probably Cam Ranh Bay's greatest utility is as a submarine base; by the mid-1980s, in fact, there were usually at least a half-dozen submarines in the harbor. Press reports indicated that the USSR had offered Vietnam a flotilla of Foxtrot Class attack submarines and had proposed creation of a joint submarine force. Under this purported arrangement the submarines would fly the Vietnamese flag under nominal command of a Vietnamese captain, although effective control would be in the hands of the ten or twelve Soviet naval officers on board each submarine.[19]

Reliable information about activities at Cam Ranh is difficult to come by because it is a restricted military area, and civilians, whole villages even, have been evacuated to clear a heavily guarded security zone. Vietnamese emigré publications claim that in early 1984 the USSR was granted extraterritoriality status at Cam Ranh port and environs. The reports come from refugees who formerly lived in Ma Ca village on Cam Ranh peninsula but who were moved to a new economic zone in Phu Khanh province as part of the creation of a Vietnamese-free security belt around Soviet installations.[20] Thai intelligence services support the extraterritoriality claim.

Soviet spokesmen contend that the USSR has no military bases in Vietnam, only "access" to certain military installations—a claim echoed by Vietnamese spokesmen. In official terminology, Cam Ranh is not a Soviet naval base but a "fraternal facility." This may be technically correct, in that there are no Soviet flags flying from any building at Cam Ranh nor even from ships in the harbor; nor is use of Cam Ranh reserved exclusively for the USSR. SRV Foreign Minister Nguyen Co Thach, when questioned closely by Malaysian newsmen in mid-1983, acknowledged that the USSR had been granted base use at Cam Ranh, as necessary, he said, "to guard our independence." He assured his questioners that Hanoi would "never allow itself to be exploited by the USSR against any country in Southeast Asia." Pressed by dubious newsmen for details, Thach snapped, "Neither will we allow anyone to inquire into what facilities we have provided the USSR."[21]

Whether Cam Ranh is a Soviet "base," or whether the USSR has extraterritoriality there, is largely immaterial. The Soviet navy and air force and Moscow war planners have in Vietnam what they think they need; that is, Soviet military requirements are being fully met.

The USSR has also shown interest in base use in Kampuchea, particularly the major port of Kompong Som (once known as Sihanoukville) and the smaller port of Ream some ten miles to the south. The first port call at Kompong Som by a Soviet naval vessel was made by the frigate *Petya*, in February 1980. Soviet war vessels now make periodic visits. Soviet technicians in the late 1970s assisted in rebuilding the port's cargo-handling facilities and in channel-dredging work. Kompong Som could act as a back-up port, and Soviet presence in Kampuchea does serve political and diplomatic interests, but it is difficult to believe that Moscow could come to regard Kompong Som as strategically important.[22] Ream appears to be used chiefly as a port storage facility.

Part of the USSR's effort to develop Vietnam as a forward deployment base involves building up the Vietnamese Navy and Vietnamese air defense capability in coordination with Soviet strategic planning. Reportedly there are forty-eight missile battalions stationed at major installations in Vietnam equipped with SAM 2s and 3s and possibly SAM 4s.[23]

The third strategic use of Vietnam by the USSR is as an intelligence-collecting center. At least thirty long-range Soviet spy planes—the famed Bears and Badgers—fly regular missions out of Cam Ranh and Da Nang. Their route is along the China coast to Vladivostok; or they loop out of Cam Ranh past Hainan Island, south of Taiwan, down along the Philippine archipelago[24] and back to Cam Ranh, spying as they can on China, Japan, the Philippines, Indonesia, and Thailand, and on U.S. submarines at sea. Land-based electronic installations in Vietnam eavesdrop on everyone's communications in the region. A string of radar and monitoring stations was built along the China border soon after the war ended. Another network of six electronic monitoring stations operate along the coast (Da Nang, Phu Bai, Cam Ranh, Tuy Hoa, Nha

Trang, and Vung Tao). According to persistent rumors in the Vietnamese emigré community, a vast new electronic intelligence-collating facility is under construction north of Hanoi, similar to the highly sophisticated installation operated by the USSR in Cuba.

The fourth strategic use is Vietnam as a transit facility. The USSR has sheltered-afloat bases at Aden and South Yemen, and at Dehalek Island in the Red Sea, and the first uses of Cam Ranh, Danang, and Haiphong involved similar vessels (i.e., oilers, repair ships, stores ships, and submarine tenders anchored in the harbors to service visiting warships). Late in the 1970s, the USSR began to use the existing shore facilities and in 1981 started constructing new installations at all three ports. The center of this activity is Cam Ranh, where work has begun on a petroleum storage facility, a new road system, and new buildings. In addition, six floating docks (including a 320-foot dry dock), a ship transporter (for repair work), and giant fixed cranes have been installed. A Don Class cargo tanker is usually in the harbor to service nuclear-powered submarines, and a floating dock for repairing Soviet warships has been installed in the Saigon River.

Vessels out of Vladivostok assigned to the Indian Ocean can undergo repairs and obtain supplies in Vietnam, cutting their steaming time in half. In 1985 the USSR had some 20 war ships assigned to the Indian Ocean, and at any one time about 5 of these were either anchored in a Vietnam harbor or sailing to or from Vietnam. These included missile cruisers, destroyers, submarines, and submarine tenders. The Soviet naval vessel presence in the mid-1980s averaged 25–30 ships and submarines on any given day. At the same time, the number of Soviet war ships cruising the waters off Vietnam was rising, from an average of 6 in 1979 to 10 in 1980 to 22 in 1986. Some of these were on patrol and some were transiting the region.

The major port for transit activity is Cam Ranh. Danang harbor is shallow and cannot accommodate large vessels. Vung Tau, to the south, serves chiefly as a rest and recreation center and as a base for oil-exploration vessels. A Soviet flotilla, consisting of a cruiser and two destroyers, called at Cam Ranh Bay in September 1980 for the first time. A second Soviet flotilla—the guided missile cruiser *Varyag* and the guided missile frigate *Razyashiy*—commanded by the Pacific Fleet Deputy Commander Vice-Admiral Nikolay Yasakov, called with enormous fanfare at Danang in mid-October 1981 (as discussed below).

Although Vietnam has considerable strategic value for the USSR, there is no "strategic reciprocity" for Vietnam. Hanoi's geopolitical interests are land based (directed to Kampuchea and Laos), defensive (with respect to China), and as much psychological as military. The chief military value of the USSR to Vietnam is logistical, inasmuch as

Hanoi has no arms factories. It can make explosives, small arms, ammunition, and hand grenades, but the sophisticated weaponry and equipment mandatory for modern war must come from the outside. Without such weaponry Vietnam would be unable to defend itself against China or press the war in Kampuchea.

Whereas economic aid to Vietnam is spread to some extent among Communist nations, military aid is almost exclusively Soviet. At the end of the Vietnam War the USSR was supplying about 75 percent of North Vietnam's military hardware (China about 15 percent and East Europe about 10 percent). By the 1980s these totals were estimated as 97 percent Soviet, 2 percent East German, and the remaining 1 percent from Poland and Czechoslovakia.

Soviet arms shipments to Vietnam (i.e., new aid, not older allocations) in the first two years after the end of the Vietnam War were relatively modest; then they began to increase. Within three weeks of the signing of the 1978 treaty, 20 MIG-24 swept-wing fighter planes were en route to Hanoi—perhaps as a symbolic gesture. A Soviet military mission was established in late 1978, and Soviet military advisers began to appear in numbers in Vietnam. The tonnage of delivered military aid doubled each year from 1977 through 1980 and then leveled off— a reflection of Vietnam's invasion of Kampuchea (December 1978) and the Chinese retaliatory action (February 1979). Soviet military personnel in 1979 began direct support work in Kampuchea, delivering military hardware, ferrying PAVN troops around the country, and operating an air traffic control system. Soviet military assistance since the end of the Vietnam War thus reflected unfolding events. In the last years of the war, aid was running at about $170 million. In the last full year of the war (1974), it was about $168.7 million and for the first months of 1975, about $123.3 million. In the postwar years it is reliably estimated as follows:[25]

1976	$44.7 million
1977	$80 million
1978	$700 million
1979	$890 million
1980	$790 million
1981	$450 million
1982	$900 million
1983	$1.2 billion
1984	$1.3 billion
1985	$1.7 billion
1986	$1.5 billion (est.)

The character of Soviet military aid provided Vietnam in the postwar years has passed through several distinct stages. In the first year or so it was aid of the palace-guard type—that is, routine resupply of PAVN military inventories. With the Vietnamese invasion of Kampuchea, it became counterinsurgency or guerrilla-bashing aid, such as helicopters. With the rise of the threat from China, military hardware for conventional limited warfare was required. Soviet military assistance became increasingly costly.

By the mid-1980s conventional warfare aid comprised the bulk of Soviet assistance to Vietnam. Priority was assigned to air defenses, which including the stationing of MIG-23 swing-wing interceptors in Vietnam and augmentation of the missile defenses of these major cities and installations. Equal priority was assigned to making PAVN more mobile by supplying it with newer and better vehicles, and to enlarging the PAVN Navy. An analysis of this set of priorities indicates that Moscow's primary purpose is to protect Soviet air and naval capabilities based in Vietnam. The USSR has now installed second-generation air defense systems to protect its major air fields at Hanoi and the naval installation at Cam Ranh Bay. Advanced missile systems reportedly have been installed at Haiphong, Huong Khe, Vinh, Da Nang, Nha Trang, and Bien Hoa. The presence of weapons systems such as the SAM-3s is now quite open; they even appear at the national day parades. There are perhaps 70 SAM sites in Indochina (i.e, both Vietnam and Laos). Most of these are SAM-2 (medium-range) weapons, but at least 15 are SAM-3 batteries (five missiles per battery), and possibly some are the advanced SAM-4s. The USSR is also believed to have supplied Vietnam with 200-mile-range surface coastal defense missiles capable of carrying nuclear warheads, although it is assumed that such warheads are not in Vietnam because it is Soviet policy to station nuclear weapons only on Warsaw Pact soil. Reportedly the USSR plans to install ICBMs in remote northern parts of Vietnam and Laos, targeted on China and under complete Soviet control.

Ground-force military aid from the USSR to Vietnam in the three years after the brief two-front war (Kampuchea and China) totaled at least $2 billion. It included 1,800 armored vehicles, mostly medium tanks (T-34/54/55/62) and PT 76 light tanks; about 500 artillery pieces; some 1,500 trucks; and large quantities of individual infantry weapons.

The PAVN Navy, which during the Vietnam War never amounted to much, has been vastly strengthened with the gift of at least 23 combat vessels and a large number of small-sized naval support ships. Moscow has supplied the PAVN Navy with at least 13 missile attack patrol boats, 10 of which are the most modern type in the Soviet Navy—namely, the OSA Class II (240 tons, 40 meters in length, carrying four SSN-2

STYX surface-to-surface missiles). The other three are the older Komar missile attack boats. Additional vessels supplied to the PAVN Navy include: (1) 2 light frigates of the Petya I class (1,140 tons, 82 meters), used for coastal defense and antisubmarine patrol and carrying rocket launchers, torpedo mounts, and 76mm guns; (2) 3 or more Polish-built amphibious assault landing ships (LSMs) of the Polnocny class (1,000 tons, 80 meters); (3) at least 2 Foxtrot-class diesel-powered attack submarines (2,000 tons, 91 meters); (4) 2 SO-1 coastal patrol boats (25mm guns, rocket launchers); (5) several Shershen-class torpedo boats (30mm anti-aircraft guns and 4 torpedo tubes); (6) 1 Poti corvette sub-chaser; (7) one T-58 corvette minesweeper.[26]

Some of these Vietnamese warships are equipped with SSN-3 antiship missiles (21-mile range), SSN-2 STYX missiles (30-mile range), and SS-21 and SS-23 missiles, the latter two being tactical nuclear weapons. Thus the USSR has given the Vietnamese Navy nuclear capability; moreover, although the general belief is that Vietnam is not supplied with nuclear warheads, obviously that option is always open to the Soviets.

PAVN Air Force buildup by the USSR began late in the Vietnam War, then tapered off in the mid-1970s and resumed after the 1979 Chinese incursion. The Vietnamese now have at least 200 tactical aircraft, mostly MIG-21s. Visitors have seen MIG-23s at Hanoi's Noi Bai airfield and elsewhere, but it is not known whether these are Vietnamese or visiting Soviet planes. There are two MIG-21 squadrons (12 planes each), one at Hanoi and one at Ho Chi Minh City, as well as a MIG-21 squadron at Xieng Khouang airfield in central Laos, which now has an all-weather runway. Vietnamese pilots trained in the USSR now can fly TU-16 Badger bombers, used for antiship reconnaissance, and electronic warfare and SU-17 Fitter Swing bombers, used for ground support. In all, Vietnam has received at least 60 Soviet fighter bombers, mostly SU 7/20s. The USSR's largest naval aircraft, the TU-95 Bear D, used for antisubmarine warfare, fly out of Da Nang and Cam Ranh bases, but these are believed to be piloted by Soviets. Some 50 AN-26 Transports service PAVN in Vietnam. An AN-12-Cub squadron of 12 planes is located at Bien Hoa for transport use in the war in Kampuchea. The USSR has also supplied Vietnam with at least 110 helicopters. These include the MI-24 Hind attack helicopter, intended for antitank use but also having counterinsurgency utility; the MI-8 HIP, the world's most heavily armed helicopter gunship (also for use in Kampuchea); the MI-14 Haze and the KA-25 Hormone helicopters for antisubmarine patroling; and the MI-4 Hokum, used for search and rescue missions.

Analysis of the kinds of weapons the USSR supplies Vietnam suggests a dual purpose—to increase Vietnam's defensive capability against China and to increase the USSR's offensive capability against China. Soviet generals, seemingly determined to pass on to the Vietnamese some of the burden of containing China, have assigned them specific missions and given them the military hardware required to perform such missions.

While the Soviet-Vietnamese alliance was being enriched materially it was also being cemented with political and psychological glues, as evidenced by periodic official expressions of enduring support and various goodwill gestures. Typical was the assertion by Soviet Embassy Air-Naval Attaché Colonel Davydov that "the Soviet Union and its armed forces have provided and will provide fraternal SRV with all the necessary assistance for consolidating the SRV's defense capability."[27] A typical goodwill gesture was the arrival in Da Nang of the largest Soviet warship afloat, the *Minsk*,[28] marked by an orgy of parades, girls with flower garlands, banquets, Soviet-Vietnamese friendship society meetings, shipboard receptions, wreath layings, press conferences, and Soviet song and dance ensembles entertaining the people of Da Nang.

General Van Tien Dung headed a PAVN observer team to the West-81 military exercise staged by the Warsaw Pact nations in Eastern Europe in September 1981, and PAVN officers have taken part in other Warsaw Pact war games. In April 1984 a battalion of Soviet naval-infantry (the equivalent of the U.S. Marines) staged amphibious landing maneuvers along the central Vietnam coast about 100 miles south of Haiphong. Nine Soviet warships—including the *Minsk*—took part in the exercise. After the manuevers the 400 troops reportedly returned to Cam Ranh, where they are permanently stationed.

In what probably should be put down as a public relations gesture—although it eventually may have military meaning—the USSR assists the fledgling Vietnamese nuclear industry. A team of Soviet nuclear specialists and technicians restored the nuclear reactor in Dalat to operational capability. The reactor was built by the United States in 1963 to manufacture radioactive isotopes for medical therapy and for agricultural research. The Americans removed its core shortly before Vietnam fell. In 1976 Hanoi asked India for help in renovating the plant; an Indian inspection team visited the site but nothing came of the request, and the matter was put to the USSR, which obliged.

The Hanoi press now reports periodically on "nuclear cooperation" with the USSR. The VNA (March 24, 1986) reported that about 100 Vietnamese nuclear physicists, scientists, and technicians from the SRV Atomic Energy Institute were working at the Joint Institute for Nuclear Research at Dubna, in the USSR. Conferences are staged occasionally in Hanoi by what is called the Program to Use Atomic Energy in the National Economy, at which Soviet nuclear specialists are in attendance.

Little is known about the status of nuclear energy in Vietnam. Although the USSR has clearly assisted in its development, a nuclear war capability on the part of Vietnam seems unlikely to be in Moscow's interests.

Probably the most important quasi-military postwar gesture was the Soyuz 37 space flight by Lieutenant-Colonel Phan Tuan in July 1981. Supposedly the idea of a Vietnamese in space came from Leonid Brezhnev and was proposed to Le Duan in late 1978 at the signing of the Vietnam-USSR Friendship Treaty.[29] Colonel Tuan[30] was the first Asian and the sixth bloc pilot to take part in a Soviet space flight. The launch, from the Baykonur City Cosmodome on July 23, 1981, was attended by Le Duan, General Vo Nguyen Giap, Xuan Thuy, and Tran Dai Nghia, director of the Vietnam Space Research Commission. The space trip received enormous attention in the Hanoi press. For the SRV, it was revenge against Romania (whose candidate was to have been the next space traveler) for its opposition to Vietnamese entry into CMEA, and it also represented one-upmanship against China, which did not allow the matter to go without comment:

> At a time when the Vietnamese people are miserable with
> hunger, the Vietnamese authorities dance with joy over the fact
> that a Vietnamese joined a Soviet cosmonaut on a space flight.
> The Vietnamese who flew into space, Pham Tuan, gleefully said
> this will be the first flight into space by a Vietnamese and also
> by any Asian or citizen of a developing non-aligned country. . . .
> But why the big noise? According to those versed in space plans,
> Pham Tuan was nothing but a passenger. . . . The Hanoi
> authorities (seek) to force the Vietnamese people who are living
> in misery to forget all their sorrows and greet this
> pseudoscientific achievement with smiles.[31]

As of mid-1986 the USSR and Vietnam had twenty-two projects under way in what is called a space research program; as described, however, the program appears to be chiefly an application of space technology for use on earth.[32]

Soviet quasi-military services to Vietnam extend even beyond the call of normal duty. Thai police in May 1983 trapped Lieutenant Colonel Victor Barychev (ostensibly a Soviet embassy trade official in Bangkok but actually, police said, a GRU Soviet military intelligence agent) buying classified Thai Army documents containing information on Thai installations and troop deployment along the Thai-Kampuchean border. Quite probably this was a Soviet intelligence operation run for the benefit of Hanoi, inasmuch as the information would have been of little use to Moscow and hardly worth the risk.

THE SINO-VIETNAMESE WAR

An interesting case history of Soviet-Vietnamese military relations, one that both fixes limits and illustrates dynamics, is the seventeen-day Chinese military incursion into Vietnam in February and March 1979.

To appreciate the USSR's behavior during this short war, it is necessary to review post–Vietnam War Sino-Vietnamese relations. As we have seen, the relationship, once "lip and teeth," had long been on the decline. According to the Chinese, the deterioration began in 1969 with the death of Ho Chi Minh and the loss of his skill in maintaining good relations with both Moscow and Peking. After Ho, say the Chinese, Hanoi began to discriminate against ethnic Chinese members of the Vietnamese Communist party, refusing them higher-echelon jobs and generally treating them like "bees up one's sleeve." China interpreted the quick postwar unification of North and South Vietnam as designed to shut the Chinese presence out of Southern Vietnam. Other grievances concerned the confiscation of ethnic Chinese property in South Vietnam; the fact that ethnic Chinese were made the scapegoat for Vietnam's various economic ills; provocative official Hanoi acts involving flags, maps, and other symbols so important in Asia; and constant hostile or snide references to China in the Hanoi press.

Most important for the ever-suspicious Chinese was Hanoi's behavior toward the USSR. Beijing became increasingly aroused as postwar Vietnam drew economically closer to the Soviets, for this meant it could be held in thrall. Growing Vietnamese-Soviet military collaboration was the least tolerable prospect of all.

Following Hanoi's growing intimacy with the USSR there soon developed a second Chinese grievance—excessive Vietnamese intrusiveness into Kampuchean affairs. Here also the Chinese saw the Soviet hand:

> After 1975 and the end of the Vietnam War, the Soviet Union altered its expansionist policies in Southeast Asia. . . . The Soviet Union's ultimate objective is to create another Cuba in Southeast Asia.
> The Soviet Union is attempting to help Vietnam sell its "Indochina Federation" to the world. . . . The Soviet Union also supported Vietnam in 1977 when it forced Laos to sign "friendship and cooperation" and "border" treaties. The following year Vietnam unleashed its war against Democratic Kampuchea and installed a puppet regime in Phnom Penh.[33]

The last formal Sino-Vietnamese economic and military aid agreement between the two was signed in September 1975, but Chinese aid, for the first time, was no longer *gratis,* a clear signal of worsening relations. Unfriendly gestures came from both sides. Small studied insults grew to large ones. Muted criticism escalated into shrill recrimination. Then came a series of actions by Hanoi and Beijing that set the two on the road to war.

The point of no return probably came in late November 1977 with the visit to Beijing by a large Vietnamese delegation headed by Le Duan. Both sides apparently were spoiling for an argument, and the private sessions were reported to have been marked by blunt exchanges. Even the toasts at the several formal banquest were antagonistic—a matter of lectures on hegemonism or proper socialist behavior rather than of protocol. The Vietnamese departure was frosty.

The chain of events that followed is briefly this: The Vietnamese in December 1977 decided to settle the "Pol Pot problem" once and for all and began a campaign of action: massive border sweeps were made, a Khmer insurgency was organized, and (to hear Pol Pot tell it) Pol Pot's bodyguards were bribed to assassinate him. To dissuade the Vietnamese in this campaign the irritated Chinese cut back on economic aid and canceled some programs. Vietnam responded by applying for Comecon membership, thereby expressly linking the move to China by asking CMEA to pick up the aid projects abandoned by Beijing. China halted *all* aid to Vietnam in July 1978. Vietnam signed the treaty with the USSR in November and on Christmas Day of 1978 sent its tanks across the border in a full-scale invasion of Kampuchea. PAVN quickly captured Phnom Penh and installed a new government. A month later China invaded Vietnam. This triggered what the Chinese considered a racist reaction by Hanoi, the forced expulsion of tens of thousands of ethnic Chinese, many of whose families had lived in Vietnam for generations. PAVN troops or security cadres in the middle of the night would appear at their doorsteps, order them into trucks, take them to a nearby port, put them into small vessels, and push them out to sea.

The problem for China, in policy terms, had been clear enough: how to find a way to reverse the trend of growing Soviet-Vietnamese psychological intimacy, economic integration, and military alliance, preferably by nonmilitary means. What finally pushed China into military action was Vietnam's invasion of Kampuchea, seen by Beijing as the start of a drive to put all of Indochina under Hanoi's control and considered doubly dangerous because it was Soviet instigated. China stepped up its brinkmanship against Vietnam after the invasion—issuing a series of "stern warnings." Border clashes in January 1979 came daily and grew in size. Border forces were reinforced on both sides. The situation grew tense, then taut; then it exploded. At dawn on the morning of February 17, 1979, the People's Liberation Army of China marched into Vietnam.[34]

It was a fairly bloody war for one so short. Reliable estimates made afterward placed the total dead at 60,000 to 70,000, with a ratio of 2:1 against Vietnam. China used a Korean War style of attack with massed infantry[35] and extensive use of armor and artillery. Neither side employed air power during the incursion. Premier Pham Van Dong told an Indonesian visitor in May 1980 that the USSR had offered to send Soviet pilots if Vietnam wished to use air power but that he had refused.

Within a day the PLA had advanced about five miles into the mountainous border region of Vietnam along a broad front. Then the advance slowed and nearly stalled because of heavy resistance by the Vietnamese and because of Chinese supply and logistical problems. On February 21, the advance resumed against Cao Bang in the far north, toward the all-important city of Lang Son, and toward the lesser targets of Dong Dang, Soc Giang, and Nam Cuong. Cao Bang was entered on February 27 and was under complete Chinese control by March 2. Lang Son and Lao Cai were captured two days later. On March 5, the Chinese, asserting that Vietnam had been sufficiently chastised, announced that the incursion was over and PLA forces were withdrawing. It was a slow and Carthaginian withdrawal, however, with the PLA destroying as it went. The last PLA soldier left Vietnamese soil on March 16.

The war viewed from Moscow was, of course, seen against a broader Asian canvas and largely in terms of the Sino-Soviet dispute.[36] The USSR sought to enhance its position in Vietnam, but without altering its general position in the region.

The USSR's behavior during the seventeen days of war was consistently conservative in terms of risk-taking. It took minimal action and carefully labeled each move so as to prevent misunderstanding by China. Pronouncements during the first week of the war were so restrained they could only be interpreted as assuring China that no USSR action against it was being contemplated. A March 5 callup of Soviet reserve forces for border maneuvers was explicitly labeled by Moscow as an annual affair of the same a magnitude of years past—which was correct. There was no reinforcement of the Sino-Soviet border, nor any other hostile strategic gesture toward China. Throughout the USSR clearly sought not to raise the Chinese anxiety level.

Moscow generated a crash delivery program of military assistance to Vietnam. A special air lift brought in needed light cargo, such as medicine, and some heavy cargo in small amounts, chiefly for show purposes. The war was over before sea-dispatched armaments could arrive. There was a good deal of staged demonstration of USSR commitment. Soviet naval air reconnaissance was increased. The USSR mounted a major propaganda campaign charging U.S.-Sino collusion in the attack.[37] And it dispatched a fourteen-vessel naval task force that steamed the South China Seas in circles during the incursion and returned to Vladivostok when the Chinese withdrew. China claimed later that the Soviets also used the war to test some of their new experimental weapons, such as a laser-beam artillery control system.

The Chinese incursion presented the USSR with a choice between boldness and caution—and caution won. Apparently Moscow calculated that China's attack would be as brief as the Chinese had promised, and that Vietnam would be able to contain it. This proved accurate. Hence the Soviets' purpose was inconclusive just as the outcome of the war itself was inconclusive.

Hanoi's official post-incursion view of the Soviet role was that it had been proper and correct: "Loyal to its lofty international duty the Soviet Union through its firm statement, practical actions, and broad mass movement, stood beside us from the very first minutes and was the mightiest support in the struggle."[38]

The Vietnamese maintained that the USSR did everything asked of it. Hanoi did not need troops, so it did not ask for them. What it had needed—certain military supplies—the USSR had delivered promptly. Later, Hanoi officials came to take an almost sanguine view of the incursion. A spokesman explained that China had acted because Vietnam had "liberated" Kampuchea—a move that China regarded as an insult and so felt the need to react. The attack was easily contained, the spokesman continued, and there never had been any doubt in Hanoi about this. Thus, it was implied, Soviet participation would have detracted from the victory achieved by Vietnam. Further, the spokesman said, it was known that the Chinese people opposed the war, and had the Soviet Union become involved it would have rallied the Chinese behind their leaders.[39]

Because of this ambiguity it is difficult to determine exactly what the Hanoi leaders did conclude about Soviet dependability. Their pre-incursion calculation that the 1978 treaty would deter China proved wrong. The treaty probably lost some credibility in Hanoi, even though it is still regarded as a shield against China. Probably the men of the Kremlin drew general satisfaction about their handling of the Chinese. The USSR scored in the international public opinion market by exhibiting "mature restraint," as a West German official phrased it. It managed to provide Vietnam with the logistic and moral support that the latter had needed without seriously jeopardizing Soviet interests in the region. It was fortunate that events never reached the point where the USSR would have been embarrassed by not doing more. On balance it would seem that the 1978 border war with China neither damaged nor improved Soviet-Vietnamese military relations.

Nor did the war solve the Chinese problem that was responsible for precipitating the war in the first place—namely, the danger represented by the Soviet-Vietnamese alliance. This is the heritage of the war for China. It is also a policy problem for Vietnam and the USSR. The Chinese see that a fourfold threat remains:

1. the threat represented by the fact that the 1978 SRV-USSR Treaty of Friendship and Cooperation "explicitly provides for military cooperation and can be considered a military alliance in that it (enables) Vietnam to escalate its aggression and expansion."
2. the threat posed against China because Vietnam's aggressive behavior is underwritten by the USSR; that is, "Vietnam, powerfully backed by the USSR, can step up its acts of aggression along the Sino-Vietnamese border . . . which helps meet the strategic needs of the USSR. . . . (Thus) Vietnam becomes a knife that the USSR holds to China's throat."
3. the threat represented by Vietnamese designs on Laos and Kampuchea, "the 'special relationship' which Vietnam pretends to have with the other Indochinese countries that seeks to speed the plan to establish a Federation of Indochina."
4. the general threat represented by "Soviet military presence in Southeast Asia. Military aid for the invasion of Kampuchea was only the opener. The USSR had been granted use of Cam Ranh Bay, Da Nang and other military bases in Vietnam which effectively moves its Asian and Pacific outposts south by 2,000 miles and completes its naval web . . . menacing international sea lanes, especially the Strait of Malacca linking the Indian and Pacific Oceans."[40]

THE KAMPUCHEAN WAR

A second postwar test of Soviet-Vietnamese military relations, though not as dramatic as the Chinese incursion, has been Vietnam's war in Kampuchea.

The Vietnam-Kampuchea War is many things. It is a flare-up of ancient rivalries deeply rooted in historical fears and ethnic antipathies. It began in 1975 as a land-grabbing effort by both sides that had grown out of decades-long disputes over poorly fixed boundary lines and, until 1978, was mostly a cold war marked by provocation and retaliation on both sides. For awhile it was a quarrel between two brands of communism, one orthodox and one heterodox or, as Hanoi officials put it, "one proper and one radical." Increasingly it became a proxy war between the USSR and China, each deep in the adviser/supplier role, each investing national ego, each determined to frustrate the ambitions of the other.

There was bad blood between the Vietnamese and the Pol Pot Communists prior to the end of the Vietnam War. Following the Communist victory in Indochina in 1975, Pol Pot's hostility toward Vietnam surfaced as total and implacable. Systematically he expunged the Vietnamese influence from the Khmer Communist movement, purging those thought to be sympathetic to Hanoi and institutionalizing anti-Vietnamese policies. For Hanoi, Pol Pot meant a reversal of history, moving Indochina away from federation, the emergence of a generation of Khmer brainwashed to hate all things Vietnamese. The Vietnamese Communists had long considered a federation of Vietnam, Laos, and Kampuchea as the proper and inevitable political configuration for the Indochinese peninsula. Such had been the party's stated goal in the very early years—in the 1930 Indochinese Communist party manifesto, for instance. In 1951, this was replaced by the vague goal of a "special relationship" to be established after victory over colonialism, meaning governments and societies in Cambodia and Laos willing to work toward federation. There was no need for haste toward this end from Hanoi's viewpoint; the important thing was the trend in historical events. Pol Pot clearly was reversing the trend in Kampuchea, moving it away from federation. This was Hanoi's "Pol Pot problem," which it sought to solve by replacing Pol Pot with a more amenable leadership faction in the Khmer Communist party. Possibly this could have been accomplished by assassinating Pol Pot; by psychological warfare and a punitive military "judo chop," to induce a coup d'état in Phnom Penh; by organizing an orthodox war of liberation in Kampuchea; or by conventional military conquest. Vietnam tried them all.[41]

The psychological warfare "judo chop" consisted of a series of shallow military incursions in 1977 and early 1978 designed to cause the Kampuchea political scene to unravel into authentic civil war. In mid-1978 the Vietnamese launched a revolutionary guerrilla war by creating a mass organization united front, carving out a liberated area in Kampuchea, mobilizing a liberation army, and forming a provisional Khmer government. The effort appeared to be progressing but apparently too slowly to satisfy Hanoi. In December 1978 the Vietnamese took their final option—conventional, Soviet-style war. Some 100,000 PAVN troops blitzkrieged Kampuchea. Tank-led infantry plunged across the border and fanned out, and within days it occupied all of Kampuchea. Pol Pot and his followers fled to the Cardamom Mountains to continue the war with assurances of support from China. The newly recruited

Heng Samrin and 300 cadres of the new Khmer Communist party were installed in Phnom Penh as the new government of the People's Republic of Kampuchea.

It is a matter of some debate among Indochina specialists as to exactly what was the USSR role in Vietnam's invasion of Kampuchea. Such hard evidence as exists tends to suggest that the invasion was planned jointly after the signing of the SRV-USSR Treaty of Friendship and Cooperation and that Soviet advisers accompanied the invasion giving tactical advice. This thesis is supported by an examination of the tactics employed. The PAVN attack was of a kind never before seen on the Indochina battlefield—that is, tanks across the border in blitzkreig style, fanning out and occupying the entire country within a few days— in short, classic Soviet warfare. However, a dissenting case can be made that the secretive Vietnamese did not consult their Soviet advisers in advance and in fact only notified them of the invasion a few hours before it was launched.

Third World diplomats stationed in Hanoi during the December 1978 invasion were told by Vietnamese that the campaign would take six months at most, at the end of which guerrilla war resistance would have ended with Heng Samrin in firm control.

Probably this assessment, that a "quick fix" was possible and likely, was also held by Kremlin generals, just as it was by most outside observers. But the quick fix was not to be, and eight years later the war, now a protracted conflict, had no apparent end in sight. Whether the USSR played an important role in conceiving and executing the Kampuchean invasion is not merely a matter of historical interest, it involves Soviet and Vietnamese estimates of one another and a decision as to where to place the blame for the bogdown in Kampuchea.

PAVN's commander in Kampuchea, Colonel General Le Duc Anh, in an article in a PAVN military journal, set forth the PAVN High Command's thinking about the war in Kampuchea after six years of struggle. His major point was that the security of Kampuchea is directly linked to the security of Vietnam: "Indochina is a single battlefield and the militant strategic alliance among the three Indochinese countries involves the law of survival and development for each as well as the three collectively."

General Anh's formula for victory was the more or less standard *dau tranh* (struggle) strategy: The burden of combat must be carried by the Khmer, with the fraternal PAVN and Lao armies performing their "internationalist duties" only to the extent absolutely required. His discussion of prospects for building a "revolutionary proletarian army" in Phnom Penh was sober and anything but optimistic.[42]

In retrospect, the Vietnamese invasion of Kampuchea appears to have been based on the assumption that a quick successful takeover would force the Chinese to accept a changed status, and on the strategic estimate that Pol Pot had neither political depth nor military staying power—and hence that a dispersal of his forces would cause the Khmer people overwhelmingly to rally to the new government. The assumption proved wrong and the strategy didn't work. The invasion did not solve the Pol Pot problem; instead, it bogged Vietnam down in a costly protracted war, tarnishing Hanoi's image abroad and ruining a relationship with China that might have been salvaged. It also drained Hanoi's coffers and unleashed a host of tangential problems.

The Kampuchean brush tarred the USSR as well. Moscow's funding of the invasion hurt its image in Southeast Asia, although the USSR has managed to dampen some criticism by dissembling. For instance, in July 1980 the Soviet ambassador to Thailand, Yuriy Kuznetsov, assured Thai Deputy Foreign Minister Arun Phanuphong that the USSR had halted all arms shipments to Kampuchea. From time to time the USSR attempts to straddle the line between Vietnam and Southeast Asia on the Kampuchean issue. In December 1979, following the Carter-Brezhnev meeting in Vienna, there was an exchange of letters in which Brezhnev said that Vietnam forces would not cross the border into Thailand. This assurance was ignored by the Vietnamese press. The USSR has also attempted to maintain an independent position on the question of a negotiated settlement in Kampuchea, which Hanoi generally opposes on the grounds that the Kampuchean situation is "irreversible." For several years USSR spokesmen employed the word *irreversible* to describe Kampuchea, but in the mid-1980s it substituted *respect the reality of the situation*, which implies a willingness to negotiate. Such usage is stonily ignored by Hanoi.

With the arrival of Mikhail Gorbachev as top leader in Moscow came new Soviet overtures on Kampuchea. In a series of early 1986 pronouncements the USSR restated its general position: (1) that the Kampuchean problem is due almost entirely to pernicious external forces—that is, China, the United States, and ASEAN; (2) that the issue can and should be settled through negotiations; (3) that in a settlement the franchise can be used as the mechanism to allocate political power among the contending Khmer factions (and that elections need not be staged under the present People's Republic of Kampuchea (PRK) constitution but can be staged under other arrangements; (4) that PAVN forces can and should be withdrawn within one year of a settlement; and (5) that the USSR is willing to act in some sort of good offices/guarantor role in a Kampuchean accord. The Gorbachev administration at the time seemed to be anxious to get some kind of talks going quickly.

In July 1986, when Gorbachev unveiled his new policy approach for Asia in his speech at Vladivostok, he seemed resigned to the war, specifically excluding discussion of Kampuchea even though the address was otherwise a comprehensive examination of all of Asia's problems and conditions.[43] However, the USSR's treatment of the Kampuchean War has always been fully supportive of Vietnam. Moscow "summit" conferences, involving Le Duan and Kampuchean officials, periodically map out Kampuchean battlefield strategy and joint positions on a negotiated settlement. Possibly there is a sense of kinship between Moscow and Hanoi because of the perceived similarities between the USSR in Afghanistan and the Vietnamese in Kampuchea.

Soviet public support of Kampuchea generally has stressed two themes—humanitarianism and anti-Chinese sentiment:

> The Soviet Union welcomed the victory of the Kampuchean people in January 1979 [i.e., Vietnamese invasion and installation of the Heng Samrin regime in Phnom Penh] because that victory deposed a man-hating anti-people's regime, because it saved the Kampuchean nation from suffering and extermination, bringing it back from medieval barbarity to the 20th century, and because it created good conditions for the country's advance along the road of democracy and social progress. . . .
>
> The Soviet Union supports humanitarian international aid to the Kampuchean people. Along with Vietnam and other socialist countries, it is giving the People's Republic of Kampuchea considerable assistance on a bilateral basis in rehabilitating its economy and normalizing life as rapidly as possible. In 1979, the Soviet Union granted Kampuchea free aid amounting to 85 million dollars' worth of commodities. Under the 1980 programme, free deliveries of goods will total nearly 134 million dollars, including 164,000 tons of food (of which more than 100,000 tons have already been delivered), 130,000 tons of oil products, 8 million metres of fabric, 420 automobiles, and various consumer goods. In addition, the Soviet Union is helping the PRK to restore a number of factories, medical institutions, and educational establishments. Funds earmarked for these purposes add up to more than 68 million dollars. . . .
>
> The Soviet Union considers the People's Revolutionary Council of Kampuchea the country's sole lawful government that is dealing with all its internal and international problems. It therefore supports PRK efforts to assume its lawful seat in the United Nations and other international organizations. The changes in Kampuchea are irreversible. Any maneuvers interfering in its internal affairs, including attempts to use the UN for these purposes, can only complicate the situation. Highly

regrettable, too, are the attempts to use the territory of other
Southeast Asian countries to deliver military and other help to
forces engaged in subversive activity against the PRK.[44]

The chief Soviet role in Kampuchea is that of quartermaster. Soviet
tanks and Soviet weapons led the initial assault. Sufficient war materiel
was on hand for a six-month campaign, which was considered sufficient.
When the campaign bogged down, a pipeline from the USSR was opened.
In the first three years of the war, the USSR supplied PAVN in Kampuchea
with some 300 T-54 and T-55 tanks and armored personnel carriers,
some 4,000 military trucks, 300 heavy artillery weapons, thousands of
infantry weapons with ammunition, and the helicopter and close combat
support aircraft noted earlier. Military machine shops, fully equipped,
were installed by USSR technicians outside Ho Chi Minh City to repair
war-damaged trucks, tanks, and other vehicles. From 1980 to 1984
military shipments from the USSR to Kampuchea increased 500 percent.
By 1986 it was estimated that the war in Kampuchea was costing Vietnam
about $12 million a day, about 80 percent of which came directly or
indirectly from the USSR.

"Air Russia," as it is unofficially dubbed, was established in 1979
to provide PAVN with air transport within Kampuchea. It consists of
a fleet of AN-12 (four-pod turbo-prop) cargo planes and IL-62 transport
planes flown by Soviet pilots, together with the necessary Soviet air
traffic controllers and cargo-handling specialists on the ground—a total
of perhaps 500 personnel. In the early 1980s Air Russia averaged about
30 flights a day and suffered losses from hostile fire as well as casualties
on the ground.[45]

The USSR may have used the Kampuchean War (and the Vietnamese
struggle against the resistance in Laos) as an opportunity to field-test
new forms of chemical warfare. Reports of "gas warfare" in Kampuchea
and Laos are so extensive and come from so many diverse sources that
there simply must be a basis in fact that someone was engaged in
chemical warfare. Certainly mycotoxin agents were used, although the
side responsible cannot be identified with certainty. Most of these
substances are incapacitating but not highly lethal, as might be expected
with new sophisticated chemical warfare agents that required field testing.
They are also virtually undetectable. Most observers have concluded
that the "yellow rain" of Kampuchea and Laos can plausibly be explained
in terms of the research and development work done by Soviet scientists—
that is, the field-testing of a new generation of chemical warfare agents.[46]

Moscow also attempted to use the Kampuchean War as a means
of establishing more direct bilateral relations with the PRK government
in Phnom Penh. This effort began in mid-1980, when the number of

Soviet advisers in Kampuchea had risen to about 500. Apparently Moscow had gained sufficient confidence to engineer a leadership change in the PRK that would bring about a more suitable figure than Heng Samrin.[47] In the Phnom Penh struggle for power, Heng Samrin was opposed by Pen Sovan, a major party figure. With Soviet backing Pen Sovan eased out Heng Samrin. This did not go down well with Hanoi, which for a few weeks bided its time. Then in December 1981 came the brief announcement that Heng Samrin had returned to power as prime minister and chairman of the Council of Ministers, followed shortly by a second announcement that Pen Sovan had left for Moscow "for reasons of health." The meaning of this affair can be interpreted on several levels, one of them being that Hanoi administered an object lesson to the USSR—that Kampuchea is Hanoi's ballpark and the game there is not played by Moscow rules. Not an important incident perhaps, but illustrative.[48]

During the 1980s, despite the war, the USSR has pressed on with its economic aid program for the PRK, which runs at an estimated annual rate of about $250 million. Soviet specialists have established a Russian Language Polytechnic School in Phnom Penh; have reestablished and reorganized along socialist lines the PRK State Bank; have built a state farm outside Battambang and restored to good operating condition the port facilities at Kompong Son; and have delivered some 3,500 badly needed trucks and buses for civilian use. A five-year (1986–1990) trade agreement signed by the PRK and the USSR in January 1986 called for doubling trade volume above the level of the past five years (then averaging $60 million p/a)—chiefly Khmer timber, rubber, and agricultural products for Soviet petroleum, motor vehicles, and tractors.

THE DIPLOMATIC FRONT

In addition to military and economic assistance, the USSR, by the 1980s, was providing the SRV with psychic support in the form of diplomatic and political backing, some of it also designed to contribute to other Soviet purposes such as legitimizing its regional presence or neutralizing China. Soviet diplomats defended Vietnam's invasion of Kampuchea at the United Nations and other international gatherings. The USSR vetoed a UN Security Council resolution, sponsored by the ASEAN nations, calling for withdrawal of foreign troops from Indochinese countries. It delivered frequent *demarches* to the ASEAN countries supporting the Hanoi position on the Kampuchean problem.

Despite the stigma attached, the USSR supported the SRV policy of expelling middle-class Vietnamese and ethnic Chinese from Vietnam. The Moscow position on these "boat people" echoes Hanoi's assertion that their exodus is merely a Chinese conspiracy to slander Vietnam and obscure hegemonistic dreams:

> Beijing's propaganda machine and the Western countries' mass media have mounted another anti-Vietnam campaign, with the so-called "Indochina refugee problem" as the pretext. A real problem does exist. Approximately 300,000 people have left . . . (because) of reluctance to bear the burden of a hard working life . . . and many refugees are former employees of the puppet administration and army accustomed to a parasitic way of life and not wishing to work. . . . The SRV government is doing everything in its power to ease the lot of the refugees.[49]

Illustrative of the Soviet attitude is a 1980 incident involving fleeing refugees and a Norwegian aid project. Norway donated a sophisticated fishing trawler to Vietnam and sent along a Norwegian crew to demonstrate its use. At sea, the trawler encountered some refugees in a small open boat. An SRV security squad aboard the trawler opened fire with machine guns, killing all the refugees. The horrified Norwegian fishermen immediately returned the trawler to port and boarded the first available plane for Oslo, refusing official gifts offered them at the Hanoi airport. The Norwegian government backed their action by rejecting a Hanoi "complaint," whereupon the USSR volunteered to send a crew to replace the Norwegians.[50]

The Soviet Union's treatment of the refugee problem reduced a cruel human condition to simplistic sloganeering and generated some of the baldest examples in recent history of the big-lie technique at work in international propaganda: "An objective analysis of the refugee situation proves that the governments of Vietnam, Laos, and Kampuchea have nothing to do with the problem of refugees. The problem was invented in Washington and Beijing to promote their own political designs."[51]

The Indochinese exodus is one of the great migrations in modern history involving more than 1 million persons. Yet throughout, Moscow has treated it as a nonproblem, as a mere question of the fate of a few scum of society—drug addicts, criminals, and subversives. Soviet officials, when pressed by outsiders in private sessions, tend to fall back on the argument that the refugee question is an internal matter that cannot concern the USSR.

Moscow has paid a considerable price for this uncritical support, in terms of lost influence and lowered prestige in Southeast Asia. Many in the region believe that Vietnam sends out the "boat people" to destabilize the countries of the southeast where they land, and that this is done with Moscow's encouragement. This probably is not true, but it is widely believed.

The USSR's unreserved backing for Vietnam's refugee policies and for its pursuit of war in Kampuchea undoubtedly stems in part from Moscow's conclusion that it cannot dissuade the Vietnamese in any case. Moscow may also believe that a politically isolated Vietnam, the inevitable result of such policies, increased SRV dependence on the USSR. Certainly it has become a lonesome association. No non-Communist country in the region supports Vietnam's policies, and even in the socialist world— with the exception of the USSR and Cuba—support is *pro forma* and minimal.

Hanoi has reciprocated Soviet support gestures by enthusiastically backing the USSR on virtually every important international question with across-the-board endorsements of all Soviet foreign policies. It has also dutifully welcomed Moscow's disarmament proposals. Truong Chinh has called them an "important contribution to the consolidation of international security to the easing of the danger of global nuclear conflict and to detente."[52] For Truong Chinh—who believes in neither coexistence nor disarmament—to say, as he did, that SALT-2 "represented important progress in our struggle for disarmament and peaceful co-existence" is little short of black humor.

The problem of Afghanistan has been afforded special treatment by Hanoi. The SRV Foreign Ministry in July 1981 issued a statement supporting the "correct stand of the USSR in Afghanistan and . . . the noble internationalist assistance being provided there." Ha Van Lau, SRV Ambassador to the United Nations, during a debate on the subject on November 17, 1983, declared: "The main cause of tension about Afghanistan obviously is the policy of interference and aggression of the U.S., in collusion with China. The correct way to solve the present situation in Afghanistan is to stop the undeclared war against the country and end all forms of aggression and interference in its internal affairs."[53]

'The festering "solidarity" challenge in Poland seems to have touched a special nerve in Hanoi, as if for Vietnam it is the Ghost of Christmas Future. As Hanoi has asserted: "All patriotic Poles consider Poland's friendship with the USSR to be the most vital interest of the nation. . . . The danger threatening Poland is caused by a counterattack by reactionary forces against Socialism . . . not by the nature of socialism nor from shortcomings and mistakes in economic management."[54]

Soviet-Vietnamese relations in the 1980s were marked by periodic "summit" conferences. The one in Moscow in mid-July 1980 was attended by four of Vietnam's top leaders, although they also were in Moscow for other reasons: Le Duan, to receive the Lenin Peace Prize and for medical treatment; Premier Pham Van Dong, to attend the annual meeting of the Council for Mutual Economic Assistance; General Vo Nguyen Giap, to witness the joint Soviet-Vietnamese space launch; and chief economic planner Nguyen Lam, to negotiate a petroleum exploration and exploitation agreement. This was the first gathering of the top leadership since the 1978 treaty signing. A similar "summit" conference, held the following year (June 1981), was attended by Le Duan and To Huu from Vietnam and the Kampuchean Premier Pen Sovan, shortly before his fall from power. Le Duan addressed the CPSU twenty-sixth Congress, while To Huu discussed economic aid and Pen Sovan undoubtedly discussed the Kampuchean War. Le Duan made periodic visits to Moscow, including one in June and July 1985, when he reportedly had long and systematic discussions with the USSR's newly installed General Secretary Mikhail Gorbachev on virtually all of Vietnam's major internal and external problems.

There were other gestures as well. The *Sao Vang* (Order of the Golden Star), Vietnam's highest decoration, was presented in June 1980 to Leonid Brezhnev, the first foreigner to receive the honor. The decoration reflects what probably is a consensus in the Hanoi Politburo: that Brezhnev was held in higher regard than any other Soviet leader, past or present, because he better understood Vietnam. The *Sao Vang* was presented to CPSU Central Committee Secretary Mikhail Suslov, the USSR's chief theoretician, shortly before his death; and later to Soviet Council of Ministers Chairman Alexi Kosygin. In January 1982 the CPSU reciprocated by awarding the Order of Lenin of the Supreme Soviet to Le Duan and Truong Chinh.

THE AMBIENCE TODAY

By the mid-1980s the Soviet-Vietnamese relationship had evolved into a new form—even an affectionate one, if official Hanoi description is to be believed. This deepening of relations has gone on largely unnoticed abroad. Only in Thailand and, of course, China (given the closely watching, ever-critical Chinese) has the "russianization" of Vietnam become a matter of concern.

A decade after the end of the war, the Soviet presence in Vietnam was ubiquitous. Aeroflot flights from Moscow landed in Hanoi to disgorge a seemingly endless variety of visitors: Leningrad editors, Uzbek painters, Latvian ballet dancers, satellite specialists, generals, tennis teams, admirals, psychologists, Russian Buddhists, Estonian Catholics, linguists, trade representatives, vocational rehabilitation therapists, nuclear physicists, typography experts, and Russian language teachers. The typical visitor first makes the obligatory courtesy call on his respective counterpart in the yellow sandstone Vietnamese Communist Party Headquarters building on Ba Dinh Square and the obligatory visit to Ho Chi Minh's home, office, and mausoleum to sign the obligatory guest book; he or she then departs on a tour of the country. Some visitors go to the mountain resort town of Dalat and eat strawberries or sunbathe on the beaches of Nha Trang or Vung Tau. Others explore the emperors' tombs outside Hue, poke through the antique stores in the Da Cao section of Ho Chi Minh City, or dance away the night beneath the stars of a rootfop nightclub in Da Nang. Still others in comfortable limousines tour the battlefields of Kampuchea.

In Ho Chi Minh City, Soviet visitors are sequestered at the city's hotels according to their status. The most important hotel is the Doc Lap (formerly the Caravelle), which also houses the Soviet brass stationed in the city and their families, guarded by a fifty-man security team. Lesser guests stay at the Huu Nghi (Palace Hotel), the Ben Thanh (Rex BOQ), and the Cuu Long (Majestic); the latter also houses a large contingent of Cubans. The Thanh Loi (Victory) is reserved for Soviet military officials. The Duc Hotel, more heavily guarded than even the Caravelle, apparently is reserved for Soviets in sensitive occupations such as intelligence and missile installation. In Vung Tau, Soviet oil engineers have taken over the best villas. In Da Nang, Soviet sailors are housed in the former U.S. Marine Corps barracks and at what once was called the China Beach enclave.

In major Vietnamese cities special Friendship Stores have been established, open only to Soviets or East European visitors with special connections. The Friendship Stores are resented because the Vietnamese government, which runs them, is obliged to purchase goods, such as liquor and cigarettes, in hard currency from Singapore and then sell to Soviet patrons for rubles. Such goods are rationed, but refugees say most patrons blackmarket their rations if they do not consume them.

Soviet housing in Vietnam is generally located in compounds set geographically apart from the Vietnamese. The largest of these, called Camp Russia, is outside Haiphong and houses some 2,000 people. It is surrounded by barbed wire, and along the road leading to its main gate is a sign reading "Restricted Area For Foreign Experts Only." Reportedly there is a red light district at Ha Long beach near Haiphong that also serves only foreign experts. The swimming pool at what once was Saigon's Cercle Sportif is reserved on Saturday mornings for Soviet citizens.

Many Vietnamese regard the Soviet presence with a malicious disdain, referring to them as "our latest barbarians." Soviet behavior in the street and public places is often crude, and the xenophobic Vietnamese react adversely to it. The term *Lien-Xo* (Russian) has become an ephithet among many adult Vietnamese. Said one antique dealer to a visiting foreign journalist: "They come in to my shop, pick up an 18th century work of art and offer to barter it for a Soviet airline flag, a bottle of fingernail polish or a nylon shirt."[55] The Chinese, with their sense of the psychological jugular, picture the Soviet presence thus:

> In Vietnam, Mr. Soviet Union has now replaced Mr. United States. From the Soviets in Vietnam you see the shadow of the Americans and smell the neocolonialism. On the highways near Hanoi you can see Soviet made command cars, trucks and tanks. The port of Haiphong is crowded with Soviet vessels. Soviet fighters are flying over Vietnamese skies. . . .
>
> These facts show that the relationship between the Soviet Union and Vietnam is one between a large hegemonist and a small hegemonist, between a master and a lackey, and that such a relationship is founded on mutual collusion and utilization.[56]

Soviet culture, whether influential in Vietnam or not, is ubiquitous. Book stalls in the cities are filled with Russian language works that are inexpensive because they are heavily subsidized. Friendship Society chapters are found in every city and district town. Statues of Lenin have been erected in Chi Lang Garden in Hanoi, and in Haiphong. And there is a Lenin Park in Ho Chi Minh City. Soviet films are common fare at movie theaters throughout the country, and Soviet science and education films are used widely in the schools. Television has perhaps the greatest impact in introducing the Vietnamese to the USSR. Half the items on an average two-hour news/feature program on Hanoi Television are Soviet programs. Given television's insatiable appetite for broadcast material and Vietnam's limited television production capacity (about a dozen feature films a year), it is inevitable that much of the air time is filled with Moscow-supplied materials.

The Vietnamese-Soviet ambience of the 1980s has a darker side as well. At least forty Soviet citizens have been killed in Vietnam in recent years. Their deaths in many instances have been committed by unknown parties, either criminals or the Vietnamese resistance. Snipers shot into a beach café in Da Nang from a passing boat one night in January 1980. A hand grenade was thrown into a Soviet tourist bus at Vung Tau in February 1980, killing four and injuring ten. A Soviet colonel was shot in the back while walking along the Saigon River in August 1981. Two other Soviet citizens were wounded by pistol fire from two young men on a motorcycle in Cholon in December 1984. Soviet officials hush up these incidents if possible, and the details never appear in the Vietnam press. When night-time attacks increase markedly (as they did in 1983), Soviet officials order a curfew on their citizens.

Vung Tau and the Cholon section of Ho Chi Minh City appear to be the two most dangerous places in the country for Soviet citizens.

Unfortunately for non-Russians in Vietnam, the Vietnamese are often unable to distinguish among foreign visitors. Some blond European students at the Da Nang train station in 1981 found themselves surrounded by a threatening mob; one of the students spoke enough Vietnamese to convince the crowd they were Swedes.[57] East German sailors in late 1981 were roughed up and one of their group was knifed in a Haiphong bar; they were told later that their assailants had mistaken them for Russians. A similar case of harassment was reported by the French counsel general and his wife, who had been strolling in Dalat.[58] When a Belgian Postal Union official was killed in Da Nang in 1979, his widow subsequently received a formal letter of apology from the SRV, which said that the killer had been captured and had told the police he thought the victim was a Russian. Swedish technicians at the Bai Bang Paper Plant, when in Hanoi, wear T-shirts emblazoned *Khong Lien Xo* (Not a Russian). A refugee in a Thai camp described an incident at the main Saigon market in Ho Chi Minh City in 1980. A young thief had slipped a watch from the wrist of a Soviet tourist. He ran through the market with the tourist in pursuit. Near the entrance a Vietnamese security agent tripped the thief, drew a pistol, put a bullet into the thief's brain, then calmly handed the watch back to the horrified Soviet tourist.

Official Soviet presence in Vietnam has grown steadily since the end of the war. By mid-1977 the Soviet mission headquartered in Hanoi was estimated to number about 100 members, all of whom were working in some military capacity. By 1986 this total had reached nearly 10,000, of whom 60 percent were military.

The Soviet Embassy in Hanoi was presided over by Ambassador Boris Nikolaevitch Tchaplin (known privately among the more sophisticated Vietnamese as "Charlie Chaplin") from 1985 until his departure in 1986. In the embassy are some fifty foreign service officers, thirty-two with diplomatic rank. In 1985 the military attaché office, which was a staff function, was headed by Colonel Vladimir Alexsandrovich Davydov and dealt with the PAVN High Command. A second Soviet technical military advisory mission was headed by General Petrov Nikolai Alexandrovitch and coordinated military assistance activities such as training Vietnamese pilots, dredging river and harbor channels, air traffic control work, and stevedoring on the Haiphong docks. A third office handles delivery of military hardware and supplies. The one Soviet official who is clearly the czar of Soviet economic assistance is A. P. Sukunof, on loan from the USSR General Department of Technology and carrying the title "plenipotentiary representative." In Ho Chi Minh

City is the fifteen-person Soviet consulate general headed by Oleg Alexandrovich Volkov, who lives in the former U.S. ambassador's residence at No. 12 Mac Dinh Chi Street. The consulates in Da Nang and Vung Tau have ten and eight officers, respectively.

The chief mechanism for nongovernmental and nonparty relations between the two countries is the Vietnam-USSR Friendship Association, founded on May 23, 1950.[59] The current president (since 1983) is Nguyen Vinh, director of the Marx-Lenin Institute in Hanoi and a member of the Central Committee. He is assisted by fourteen vice presidents and a sixty-person standing committee. The Association has branches in all major cities and provincial towns throughout Vietnam. These groups stage Soviet plays, sponsor lectures and film showings, and mount exhibits. They also handle goodwill tours and exchange visits not classified as party- or government-related. The Association supplies interpreters, runs Russian language schools in which interpreters are trained, and arranges for the translation and publishing of current event materials from the USSR. The publication of Soviet writings has become big business in Vietnam. The Su That Publishing House in Hanoi by mid-1980 had published 333 editions of Lenin's works for a total press run of 2,177,696 copies. Earlier it had published 50,000 copies of the fifteen-volume set *The Collected Works of Lenin*.[60] The Association in 1981 was instrumental in changing the name of Thong Nhut (Unification) Park in Hanoi to Lenin Park, thus effacing a once-sacred term; it also supervises the observance of Lenin's birthday, now a national holiday in Vietnam.

This "friendship" activity is reciprocated by a corresponding organization in the USSR, the USSR-Vietnam Friendship Association headed by one A. P. Shitikov. It receives Vietnam visitors, stages friendship festivals and Vietnam day observances (mostly in the provinces), and generally tries to rectify the woeful ignorance of Soviet history and culture displayed by most Vietnamese. Vietnamese ambassadors to the USSR are also active in this work.

NOTES

1. USSR military interest in Vietnam, of course, flows from broader strategic considerations. By way of providing context it should be borne in mind that (as of mid-1986), of the 184 divisions of Soviet ground force (about 1,950,000 men), 52 (or one-fourth) were deployed mainly along the Sino-Soviet border against China and Japan. Of these about 39 divisions (402,000 men) were deployed east of Lake Baikal. Of the Soviet air force totaling about 8,500 planes, some 2,060 (or one-fourth) were deployed in the Far East (about 450 bombers, 1,450 fighters, and 160 patrol craft). Of the Soviet naval force of about 2,620 warships totaling about 5 million tons, about one-third, or 785 warships (1.5

million tons), were deployed to the Soviet Pacific fleet. This fleet included 130 submarines, half of which are atomic powered.

2. Le Duan, *Political Report to the Fifth VCP Congress,* Radio Hanoi (March 27, 1982).

3. Pham Nhu Cong, *Revolution in the Village* (Hanoi: Foreign Language Publishing House, 1976).

4. The VNA published its official English language text of the treaty on November 3, 1978; it was broadcast that day by Radio Hanoi.

5. Genady Chufrin, *Southeast Asia: History and the Present Day,* Oriental Studies in the USSR, No. 6 (Moscow: Social Sciences Today, 1982).

6. For example, see L. Edgar Prina (Copley news service) in the *San Diego Union* (March 22, 1979).

7. Two days after the signing, Peking dispatched a high-level delegation, including military figures, on a mission to Cambodia.

8. Some Japanese critics of the government in Tokyo suggested that the treaty was a reaction by the USSR to the earlier (August) signing of the PRC-Japan treaty.

9. VNA (June 25, 1981).

10. Tran Quynh, "Great Comprehensive and Highly Effective Soviet Assistance," *Nhan Dan* (November 3, 1981).

11. *Nhan Dan* (November 2, 1981).

12. VNA (June 24, 1983).

13. I am indebted to Robert F. Dernberger (University of Michigan) for the criteria used in this section. They were drawn from his working paper entitled "The State Planned, Centralized System," which was presented at the Conference on Economic Development and Models in the Present and Future, Tokyo (September 19–22, 1983).

14. An interesting and authoritative discussion of official Soviet thinking on Vietnamese economic development is found in A. Volodin's "The Effectiveness of Soviet-Vietnamese Cooperation," *Far Eastern Affairs* (Moscow), No. 1 (1984), which interprets Lenin's words to mean that "with the aid of the proletariat of the advanced countries, backward countries can go over to the Soviet system and through certain stages of development to communism without having to pass through the capitalist stage." The author adds that "the entire history of Soviet-Vietnamese relations confirms the brillance of Lenin's foresight."

15. Cam Ranh Bay figures in Czarist Russia's history, at least as a footnote. In May 1905 the Russian Baltic fleet, under the command of Admiral Rozhdestvenski, dropped anchor there for a month-long stopover, en route to its rendezvous with the Japanese and its destiny in the Tsushima straits. It was a "fantastic presence," wrote a French colonial official at the time; some 52 vessels dotted the immense bay.

16. George McArthur, *Los Angeles Times* (September 14, 1976).

17. *New York Times* (March 13, 1983).

18. See *Sankei Shimbun* (Tokyo) (March 1, 1985). See also John McBeth, "Buildup on the Bay," *Far Eastern Economic Review* (December 29, 1983).

19. Le Anh Tuan, "Vietnam No Longer Sovereign over Cam Ranh," *Tin Viet Nam* (Beijing), No. 38, (April 1984). Thai intelligence also claims that Cam Ranh is under complete Soviet control.

20. *London Daily Telegraph* (July 10, 1979).

21. *Bernama* (Kuala Lumpur) (August 10, 1983).

22. Radio Democratic Kampuchea (April 3, 1980) reported on Soviet activity in Kampuchea, some details of which has been confirmed by Thai intelligence sources. See the *Far Eastern Economic Review* (March 10, 1985) for reporting on the USSR base at Ream.

23. See Kyodo News Service (Tokyo) (July 4, 1978), quoting a defecting SRV diplomat. See also Thai Quang Trung's "The Moscow-Hanoi Axis and Soviet Military Build-up in Southeast Asia" (unpublished manuscript, circa mid-1986).

24. The Philippine air force frequently scrambles its fighter planes (i.e., sends them up) when the Soviet reconnaissance planes intrude into Philippine air space.

25. In terms of tonnage, military aid rose from about 40,000 tons in 1976 to about 100,000 tons in 1980; since then the tonnage has leveled off at around 300,000 tons p/a.

26. See *Yomiuri Shimbun* (Tokyo) (October 10, 1979), quoting Japan Defense Agency officials. See also *Lak Thai* (Bangkok) (July 25, 1985).

27. Radio Hanoi (February 22, 1981).

28. The *Minsk* is the most famous Soviet warship in Vietnamese waters, constantly tracked by the Vietnamese resistance, the Japanese Self-Defence Force, and the intelligence services of a dozen nations. It is one of two of its class, the other being the *Kiev*, in the Northern Fleet. (Reportedly two more of this type are under construction.) Its formal designation is Guided Missile Vertical Short-Takeoff and Landing (V/STOL) Air Craft Carrier (37,000 tons). Technically not an aircraft carrier, it has the capability of deploying 35 fixed-wing and 25 rotary-wing aircraft, primarily on anti-submarine missions. Its repeated presence in Vietnamese waters seems intended largely for psychological purposes.

29. *Vietnam Courier,* No. 8 (August 1980) and No. 9 (September 1985). The latter is an article by Dao Vong Duc, vice-chairman of the Vietnam Space Research Committee.

30. Colonel Tuan was born in Thai Binh province in 1947. He joined the PAVN air force at the age of 18, was sent to the USSR in 1967 for two years training as a fighter pilot, and then returned to Vietnam and the war (and, according to Soviet press reports, shot down several U.S. fighter planes and a B-52 bomber). In 1978 he returned to the USSR for space flight training.

31. "Look to the Sky to Ease Hunger," Radio Beijing (July 30, 1980).

32. See the Dao Vong Duc interview in VNA (July 24, 1986). The Soyuz-37 landing module is now at the Giang Exhibition Center in Hanoi.

33. See *Beijing Review*, No. 39 (March 1, 1982).

34. The war is commonly referred to in the Chinese press and elsewhere as the Seventeen-Day War. The Chinese attack began on the morning of February 17. At noon on March 5 (Beijing time), China announced it was withdrawing

its forces from Vietnam. This is the 17-day period. However, fighting continued during the withdrawal, completed March 16—a total of 28 days.

35. China had some 250,000 troops in the immediate battle area (not all were committed to combat), as compared to the 100,000 Vietnamese defenders.

36. For an interesting if somewhat purple account of the Chinese attack through the eyes of a Soviet observer, see V. Skvortsov's "Thirty Days of War," *Kommunist* (Moscow), No. 6 (April 1979).

37. Moscow offered as evidence of U.S.-Chinese collusion the Teng visit to the United States just prior to the start of the war and his statements (in Washington and again in Tokyo) on the necessity of "teaching Vietnam a lesson"; U.S. Treasury Secretary Michael Blumenthal's trip to China during the war; the United States' redeployment of naval vessels into the South China Sea (also the deployment by China of its naval vessels from the Taiwan straits to the waters off Vietnam); and, finally, the internal logic of the situation—namely, that the United States was forging a military alliance with China.

38. *Nhan Dan* (February 15, 1980).

39. Ibid.

40. Tang Shan, "Source of Southeast Asia Tension," *Beijing Review*, No. 46 (November 1983).

41. For a detailed account of Hanoi–Pol Pot relations in the years immediately following the Vietnam War, see Nayan Chanda, *Brother Enemy: The War After the War* (New York: Harcourt Brace Jovanovich, 1986). See also Elizabeth Becker's *When the War Was Over: The Voices of Cambodia's Revolution and Its People* (New York: Simon and Schuster, 1986).

42. Colonel General LeDuc Anh, "PAVN and Its Noble International Mission in Friendly Cambodia," *Tap Chi Quan Doi Nhan Dan* (December 1984).

43. See FBIS *Daily Report* for the USSR (January 8 and 28, 1986), and *Far Eastern Economic Review* (January 16, 1986). For Gorbachev's Vladivostok speech, see FBIS *Daily Report* for the USSR (July 29, 1986).

44. G. I. Chufrin (Institute of Oriental Studies, Moscow), "Problems of Peace and Security in Southeast Asia," in Khien Theeravit and MacAlister Brown, eds., *Indochina and Problems of Security and Stability in Southeast Asia* (Bangkok: Chulalongkorn University Press, 1983).

45. Both Radio DK (Democratic Kampuchea) and Radio Beijing over the years have reported Soviet casualties in Kampuchea. Refugees in Thai camps also say that Pol Pot's troops have captured and executed Soviet advisers. These reports could never be verified, but given the nature of the Kampuchea War, some Soviet casualties seem likely. One report that was confirmed by Western intelligence sources concerned a rocket attack on a Soviet barracks in Kompong Som on January 13, 1986, in which two Soviets were killed and four were wounded.

46. See U.S. Department of State, "Chemical Warfare in Southeast Asia and Afghanistan," Special Report No. 98 (1983). See also Sterling Seagrave, *Yellow Rain* (New York: Evans and Co., 1981).

47. The Vietnamese had recruited Heng Samrin out of a refugee camp in Vietnam and installed him as PRK president. He is a man of no perceptible

governing talents—the Chinese describe him as a "failed horse thief"—but he is acceptable to the Vietnamese because of his tractableness.

48. See Nayan Chanda, "The Indochina Linchpin," *Far Eastern Economic Review* (January 1, 1982).

49. *Novoye Vremya* (Moscow), No. 27 (July 1, 1979).

50. *Aftenposten* (Oslo) (March 27, 1980).

51. Radio Moscow (June 27, 1980).

52. VNA (June 25 and 28, 1979).

53. *Nhan Dan* (August 19, 1983).

54. VNA (June 18, 1981).

55. *Newsweek* (April 17, 1981).

56. Radio Beijing (March 21, 1980).

57. Keyes Beech, "Why Russian is a Dirty Word in Vietnam," *San Francisco Chronicle* (February 12, 1982).

58. Ibid.

59. Through the years, many Vietnamese were identified with the association and regarded as pro-Soviet: Vice-Minister of Education Vo Thuan Nho, Duong Bach Mai, the intellectual Nguyen Khanh Toan, Nguyen Xien, Nguyen Thi Thap, Vu Quoc Uy, and early USSR ambassador to the DRV, Suren Tovmasyan. I. S. Shcherbakov in Moscow heads the counterpart organization.

60. The SRV-USSR Politio-Socio Book Publishing Agreement was signed on June 9, 1983, between Truth (Su That) in Hanoi and Progress Publishers in Moscow to facilitate translation and distribution of printed Soviet materials. The first project was publication of the works of Leonid Brezhnev, in seven volumes.

Nine

THE EVOLVING RELATIONSHIP

SOMETIME IN EARLY January 1981, a delegation of senior Soviet military and economic aid officials sat down at a conference table in Hanoi across from an assemblage of their Vietnamese counterparts. They had come to fix the agenda for trips to the USSR later in the year by Vietnam's top leaders, including two visits by Le Duan.[1] The meeting continued for several days, during which it broadened into a discussion of what the Soviet-Vietnamese association had become in the six years after the war. There is good reason to believe (although probably it will never be documented) that these sessions turned into a brutally frank exchange in which grievances and complaints were traded and each side set forth in detail what it considered to be the inadequacies, shortcomings, and misbehavior of the other. This exchange of recriminations proved to be a therapeutic clearing of the air, however. Out of it came the consensus that the relationship needed readjustment if it was to stand the test of time. An outline of what later was to be termed the "new all-around relationship" went to the principals for their consideration at the meetings later in the year in Moscow, where it received a stamp of approval. It ended what might be called the post–Vietnam War era of Soviet-Vietnamese relations and launched the association on a journey into the uncharted, more complicated, and more uncertain 1980s.

Even before the January meeting in Hanoi, it was clear that the basic relationship formed in the chaotic days of 1975 was undergoing subtle but profound change. The first few postwar years, in retrospect, constituted a kind of shakedown cruise for a longer voyage. Certain characteristics of the association disappeared and new ones developed even while the original pillars of the relationship, Soviet strategic opportunism and Vietnamese dependence, continued to stand. The passage of time, the rush of events, and the chemistry of leaders' personalities combined to transform a relationship that had served its

223

original purpose. By 1980 it had proved to be, for Hanoi, an association without firm policies, and for the USSR, a policy without much focus. It was a time for change.

As the final chapter of this book is being written, signs of significant change are appearing in the corridors of power in Hanoi. Le Duan has died, some Politburo-level figures are clearly in the political ascendency, some are losing power. The long-anticipated generational transfer of power appears to be under way. At the same time there is a new order in Moscow. Mikhail Gorbachev gives every sign of seeking certain fundamental alterations in the Soviet system and at least some degree of change in the USSR's geopolitical stance in Asia. These leadership developments provide further impetus to the change in Soviet-Vietnamese relations, and they also make its future more problematical.

This last chapter is divided into three parts. The first is a description of the "new all-around relationship" that is emerging as a result of the concerted effort by both parties to restructure and institutionalize their association, to rationalize it and make it more cost-effective, and to share more equally the burden that the relationship represents. The second deals with the two overriding issues that dominate thinking in both capitals with respect to the association: (1) the nature, meaning, and value to each party of continuing close and integrated military and economic relations; and (2) the regional struggle for power that both joins and divides Vietnam and the USSR, involving the ASEAN states and, more important, China. Virtually all present or future USSR-Vietnamese differences—or contradictions as the two parties would say—can be traced to these two issues. The third section contains some concluding thoughts, a few cautious projections, and a comment on the implications for future U.S. policy.

THE "ALL-AROUND" RELATIONSHIP

What might be called the post-postwar Vietnam-USSR relationship began in the early 1980s. At first, the changes were barely perceptible; then they became slow and evolutionary. Some were minor, some transitory, some probably have yet to surface, but the general outlines are now clear. Specifically, these changes reflect the trend toward institutionalization, the search for increased rationality, and the determination to achieve greater equity in burden sharing.[2]

The first characteristic of the evolving relationship is the determination to create a more institutionalized, more formal association, to make joint decisionmaking more systematic and less *ad hoc*, and generally to add structure to the association. New mechanisms have been created to conduct day-to-day activity, particularly in the economic and military sectors. Economic intercourse is now formally coordinated at the national level by a rather formidable CMEA-related bureaucratic process called the annual state plan coordination system. Military relations, particularly those activities concerned with contingency planning for war with China, are increasingly integrated in terms of missions. PAVN forces are equipped and deployed in such a way as to complement—not duplicate—the Soviet military. There is combined military planning, weapons standardization, and war gaming.

The Vietnamese describe this new arrangement as an "all-around relationship," by which they mean a mutual interaction at all levels and in all sectors. A typical expression of the concept came from Hanoi theoretician Nguyen Khac Vien, who used a railroad train as a metaphor:

> The USSR is the locomotive, Vietnam one of the boxcars, the entire train a single unit. No longer does the SRV solicit aid from the USSR. Now each side performs its respective share of duty in the international division of socialist labor. Vietnam now is a member of the socialist community and we should now integrate ourselves with it.[3]

Although, as Nguyen Khac Vien has noted, the economic burden may fall disproportionately on one partner in any one case—consider the vast new Soviet-built electric power system in Vietnam, for instance—the balance will soon be redressed elsewhere, perhaps with increased Vietnamese rubber exports to the USSR. Vien raises to the international level the Marxist notion of "from each according to his ability, to each according to his need."

The substitution of the idea of integration for dependency, of course, can be a face-saving device for the Vietnamese. Nonetheless, such a device is important to Hanoi, for it heightens Vietnam's sense of security by making Moscow seem a more reliable partner. For the USSR, the institutional association increases both the kind and degree of influence that can be wielded, facilitates planning, and generally steadies the relationship. For both parties, an increase in structure may lock them into a more common destiny than either realizes.

All of this presumes Soviet skill in working closely with the Vietnamese. Soviet representatives commonly seek to dominate others; should this practice become widespread in Vietnam, it would cause serious difficulties, as would any Soviet move interpreted by the Vietnamese as seeking to imprison them in an alliance. There can be no doubt, because of the enormous subliminal pressure generated by *doc lap*, that Hanoi leaders have difficulty dealing with a more intimate embrace. The Chinese, with their usual mix of insight and obtuseness, sense well the dilemma posed:

> The Vietnamese press for some time has highlighted the so-called all-around Vietnamese-Soviet cooperation. The Le Duan clique and the Vietnamese propaganda machine have hailed this cooperation as a panacea that is helping the Vietnamese people to successfully overcome difficulties, increase their overall strength and advance directly from small-scale to large-scale socialist production. It is, they claim, proof of the inevitability of objective historic laws. They have even gone so far as to claim that the Vietnamese-Soviet cooperation is a prerequisite for the Vietnamese people's nation building and national defense.
>
> All that fuss has prompted this question: The Le Duan clique previously boasted about carrying out a policy of independence and sovereignty. Why is it making much publicity about the so-called all-around cooperation with the Soviet socialist imperialists? In fact, this is further proof of the Le Duan clique's complete dependence on the Soviets and of its selling out Vietnam's sovereignty and independence in the hope of extricating itself from domestic and international predicaments. . . .
>
> To hold on to power, the Le Duan clique looks to the Soviet hegemonists for support and assistance, ignoring the fact that it is moving further along a reactionary path, because to get Soviet support and assistance, it must sell cheaply Vietnam's national sovereignty, making Vietnam a Soviet satellite. The so-called "all-around Vietnamese-Soviet cooperation" is just a euphemism; "selling out one's country" is the right term.
>
> To get rubles from the Soviets, the Le Duan clique has acted against the dictates of its conscience, despite its claim to the contrary. It calls for opposition to China, controls Laos, invades Kampuchea, has intruded into Thailand and threatens the other Southeast Asian countries. It has become a pawn for the Soviets' expansionist scheme. . . .
>
> Comrade Hoang Van Hoan has correctly said: Vietnam is no longer independent. The much touted "all-around Vietnamese-Soviet cooperation" panacea is in fact a poison killing Vietnam's independence.[4]

The integration process still is only in its incipient stage and could unravel even given continued dependency by the Vietnamese, so strong is the ever-present undercurrent of xenophobia in Hanoi. A reversal or at least a halt could come when Vietnam is able to feed itself and Kampuchea is settled, or if a new Hanoi leadership decides to make peace with China. It is not likely as a deliberate decision by the present Politburo, and therefore it may be assumed that the trend will continue as long as the current leadership remains.

The second characteristic of the evolving relationship is the joint effort to make the association more rational and more serviceable. This effort is under way chiefly in the economic sector. It involves a search for ways to solve Vietnam's more pressing economic problems, to reduce economic drain on the USSR, and to redress the trade imbalance. Privately it is described in party circles as an effort to end the Vietnamese "supermarket mentality" in which the Vietnamese turn to Moscow for every economic need. The initiative here clearly was on Moscow's part. After a few years of luxuriating in its diplomatic victory over China, it began to examine its Vietnam investment portfolio with a view to measuring Vietnam as strategic opportunity against Vietnam as economic liability.

By the mid-1980s the annual cost of Vietnam to the USSR was estimated at between $4 and $6 billion. It is difficult to determine how great an economic bite this represents in Moscow. In comparative terms it is one-fourth the cost of Afghanistan. Some observers, particularly the Chinese, believe the two adventures, plus East European economic demands, represent an enormous financial drain. Others argue that, while significant, the costs are not such as to affect Kremlin strategy.

During several Moscow visits in the 1980s, I attempted to explore the subject of Vietnam as a financial burden with my Soviet hosts. The general sense of their comments was that, while significant economic cost is involved with respect to the resources allocated, it is not so great as to cause the USSR to abandon such support. This view was put forth unenthusiastically, however, as aid for Vietnam is the necessary fulfillment of a socialist duty.

Whatever degree of burden Vietnam represents, the USSR actively seeks ways to offset or reduce it. Soviet trade officials constantly scour Vietnam in search of exportable goods and seem determined to remit every ruble they can so as to equalize the horrendous Soviet-Vietnamese trade imbalance. Unfortunately, poverty-stricken Vietnam has little to offer beyond handicraft and limited amounts of agricultural products. Moscow does not take certain valuable exports such as coal because they would cut into Hanoi's scarce hard-currency earnings and in the end redound fiscally on the USSR.

The economic rationalization trend manifests itself in the Soviet demand for greater managerial authority over certain Vietnamese economic activities—a delicate matter. Initially the USSR sought more controls over the economic aid flow within Vietnam, including checks on final utilization. Soon this control was extended to the planning process. Inasmuch as it is the Soviets' opinion that many of Vietnam's economic ills are due to factors outside the economic sector, some demands reach into such delicate matters as state maladministration and party personnel shortcomings. Soviet advisers argue that unless Vietnam's fundamental causes of economic stagnation are removed, Soviet economic aid is simply a bottomless rathole. Haiphong port in 1979 reportedly was the scene of an early showdown of Soviet determination. Losses there due to pilferage and mishandling of cargo had reached staggering proportions. The Soviet ambassador in Hanoi formally requested that management of the port be turned over to PAVN, and subsequently PAVN was given administrative control.

At various "summit" conferences between Vietnamese and USSR officials, Soviet officials have tabled suggestions in the form of "firm policy recommendations." Among these have been recommendations that the SRV cabinet be reorganized along USSR lines, with some new personnel assignments (with Moscow supplying a list of "suggested" appointments); that the PAVN militia be reduced from 1.9 million to 1 million and the excess personnel converted as units to agricultural production teams and construction brigades; that the PAVN standing army be reorganized with a view to making it more modern and more cost-effective; that Soviet economic monitors be assigned to various levels of the Vietnamese economy, from national to the factory/commune level; that there be forced retirements of some Central Committee members and a purge of incompetent and corrupt cadres; that Hanoi announce a timetable for withdrawal of its forces from Kampuchea; that decisionmaking authority be centralized in the Vietnamese internal security *apparat*; and that there be a major campaign mounted to reduce corruption, pilferage, inefficiency, and red tape in the administration of Soviet economic aid. Some of these suggestions have been accepted, but most have not. Soviet advisers seem particularly unrelenting in their efforts to improve the party and state cadre structure in the economic sector. After considerable effort they persuaded Hanoi officials in 1982 to establish a major Soviet-run crash training course for economic cadres.

The advisers have also attempted, without much success, to end the sinecure practice of filling economic and educational posts with retired PAVN personnel, sometimes at the expense of those trained for the positions. They also have suggested a refined system of aid monitoring, by two-man teams (one Soviet and one Vietnamese who is Soviet trained), which currently is being tested.

To emphasize its seriousness, or perhaps to get Hanoi's attention, Moscow from time to time makes aid reduction gestures. In 1981 its canceled plans for the second enlargement of the Bim Son Cement Plant, Vietnam's largest, where earlier expansion work had gone so badly (later the program was resumed). In the 1980s it has sharply boosted the price charged to Vietnam for Soviet petroleum products. Occasionally it stages slowdowns in delivery of commodity aid shipments. Japanese sources report that in 1981, unknown Vietnamese deliberately set several warehouses in Haiphong afire the night before the arrival of a high-level Moscow inspection team, apparently to hide missing inventories—a cover-up the Soviets considered so blatant as to be insulting.

It is possible to sympathize with Moscow in its attempts to ensure better use of its aid and in its campaign to extract a better return on its Vietnam investment. But it is a dangerous game, one that at any time could trigger a Vietnamese response that is self-defeating for the USSR.

Moscow believes that the great hope for rationalizing the Vietnamese economic scene, as is clear from an analysis of its aid programs, lies in the massive application of science and technology. On this point there appears to be complete Vietnamese agreement. Indeed, Vietnamese ideology has long depicted science and technology as the panacea for Vietnam's internal ills. Soviet technicians and advisers, often with missionary zeal, seek to impart the benefits of Soviet expertise and scientific knowledge. At least 6,000 of them are on duty in Vietnam at any one time,[5] and thousands of Vietnamese are in advanced training at some thirty-five institutions of higher learning in the USSR.[6]

Le Qui An, a top official in Soviet-Vietnamese scientific cooperation, has expressed the Hanoi leadership's attitude as follows:

> Scientific-technological cooperation between Vietnam and the Soviet Union has developed in an unprecedentedly vigorous manner. The two countries have defined long-term scientific projects involving joint research efforts for 5–6 years . . . aimed at solving the current problems facing 23 major sectors of the national economy. . . . Every year hundreds of specialists are exchanged by the two countries to carry out these projects under contracts and agreements signed between the two sides. The Soviet Union has designed and manufactured modern machinery for various joint Vietnam-USSR research facilities in Vietnam to facilitate the work of Vietnamese and Soviet scientists. . . . With the generous and disinterested assistance of the Soviet Union scientific and technological potential nearly 20,000 university cadres have been trained in the Soviet Union and more than 50 percent of our doctors and candidate doctors have graduated from Soviet universities and institutes. Apart from training our cadres, the Soviet Union has helped Vietnam build and equip many

important scientific establishments, such as the Vietnam institutes
of science and the Hanoi polytechnic colleges.[7]

The USSR has reported that, largely due to its efforts, Vietnam
today has 165 scientific organizations, more than 80 educational institutions, and 300,000 scientists engaged in 300 major research projects.[8]
These statistics may be technically correct. However, they imply a depth
of knowledge and a scientific research capability in Vietnam that simply
does not exist.

The USSR has helped establish or develop a network of some 125
research institutes in Vietnam parallel to the system used in the USSR—
that is, a system under which research is done not in the universities
or colleges but in a separate institutional matrix. Of the 125 about 84
are administratively part of the SRV State Commission of Science and
Technology and are devoted chiefly to applied science with some basic
science work being done. Of the 84, 73 are integral parts of individual
state ministries and commissions, while 11 form the prestigious Scientific
Planning Research Center.[9] In addition to the hard-science research
facilities there are 21 economic planning institutes that do technical and
scientific planning for their respective ministries and commissions and
about 20 social science research institutes also attached to ministries.
Almost all of these research institutes are believed to be supported in
part or entirely by the USSR. Many have Soviet technicians and advisers
on their staffs. Most major ongoing research, at least 160 of the 300
current research projects, are joint efforts in which Vietnamese and
Soviet scientists and technicians work side by side.[10] Three Vietnamese
scientists are foreign members of the USSR Academy of Science. Institute
libraries are largely supported by the USSR. The SRV Scientific Research
Center has about 300,000 books, half of them in Russian; about 6,000
Russian language books are being added yearly to its collection.[11]

The third characteristic of the emerging "new type all-around"
Soviet-Vietnamese relationship is a move to redress the burdens each
thinks it unfairly carries. Both parties see a need for more balance in
the assumption of responsibility.

To a considerable extent what is involved here is perceptional
change. For the USSR there is the need to end the view of Vietnam
not pulling its own weight with the common problem of China; of
Vietnam being less than serious about improving the trade imbalance;
and of the general Vietnamese attitude of "taking much, demanding
all, giving little," as a Soviet academician in Moscow characterized it
to the author. On the Vietnamese side there is the need to end the
perception of the USSR "exploiting" Vietnam for geopolitical purposes;

of Moscow tokenism in many assistance programs; and of impure Soviet motives in its relations with China.

As far as specific policies are concerned, the chief adjustments required are in the economic sector (the main concern for Hanoi) and in military and security affairs (which are of greater concern to the USSR).

In actuality there is not much Vietnam can do to contribute to greater economic parity. It can marginally increase exports to the USSR and supply more export labor if that is feasible. Probably the USSR would be satisfied with a more serious effort on Vietnam's part to reduce the economic strain of the trade imbalance.

Greater burden sharing in the military relationship is chiefly a concern of the USSR. Moscow appears to want a more integrated military association, but due to the natural secrecy surrounding such matters, exactly what it has in mind is difficult to determine. Based on what is known—about combined military planning, about the design of certain types of military hardware provided Vietnam by the USSR, and about joint military exercises and frequent military conferences—it seems clear that the USSR is attempting to move toward a joint command structure. The formal military planning mechanism established in 1982 has become more than simply a military hardware coordination effort; however, whether the two engage in joint military contingency planning is not known. Changes in PAVN's organization and ordnance inventory appear to have been designed to fit into USSR contingency planning for conventional war against China. PAVN is structured and equipped in such a way as to complement, not duplicate, Soviet military preparedness on the China front. It follows that there must be some overarching defense plan that determines the kinds of war materiel to be delivered and positioned in Vietnam. It seems certain that Kremlin generals increasingly will expect to play a more direct role in future Vietnamese military planning and, if it comes to that, in the conduct of future Vietnamese military operations.

Thus the USSR and Vietnam seek to readjust their initial close postwar relationship. Each has grievances that need addressing; each has its own singular problems with the marriage. In reading about their many problems in the Hanoi press, where complaints often are candidly discussed, an observer could be led to the erroneous conclusion that the marriage is headed for the rocks. Eventually this may happen, but as of the mid-1980s such a judgment is not warranted. The important point to bear in mind with respect to the "new all-around relationship" is that, by all evidence, it is a sincere joint effort to eliminate or make manageable existing differences.

INTERNAL ISSUES: DEPENDENCE VERSUS INFLUENCE

All bilateral relations in international affairs are inherently subject to divisive forces because of competing national objectives and conflicting interests. This divisiveness can be controlled but seldom eliminated entirely.

The Soviet-Vietnamese relationship as it is now emerging is—and by all evidence will continue to be—dominated by two general forces, each composed of a cluster of specific issues. Some of these issues are normal or orthodox; others are singular, even peculiar. Taken collectively, the two forces will largely shape the future Soviet-Vietnamese relationship and, beyond this, will influence the unfolding of history in the Pacific region for the rest of this century. The first of these has to do with the adverse quality of the relationship itself, with its chemistry. It is partly psychological and partly perceptional. It is the product of the Vietnamese sense of acceptable and unacceptable kinds of dependence on the USSR and, for the USSR, the permissible and impermissible ways to influence Vietnam. The first force is explored in this section. The second, having to do with complementary and conflicting Soviet and Vietnamese external national interests, is discussed in the section that follows.

The dependence versus influence force is *yin* and *yang* in nature and should not be regarded as a polarized either-or condition. Nor is it a case of good and bad tradeoff. There is in the Vietnamese dependency on the USSR both benefit and liability for both parties, just as there is both benefit and liability for each side in the heavy Soviet influence on Vietnam.

The major positive factor for Moscow is the opportunism the Kremlin always finds difficult to resist. It can be argued that the present close USSR relation with Vietnam is the direct result of Soviet political and diplomatic failures suffered earlier in Asia. The opportunity presented Moscow by Vietnam's postwar dependent condition was an irresistible lure for Moscow, one it has seized with the determination to develop sustained influence in Vietnam. For its part, Vietnam's dependence stemmed from initial economic failure and from the growing danger posed by its alienation from China, a situation in which the USSR was the only reliable source for arms. The practical meaning for the USSR was access to Vietnam and through Vietnam, to Southeast Asia. Moscow saw great advantage in binding Vietnam in alliance.

Soviet leaders, judging by their pronouncements, regard USSR foreign policy in Indochina as highly successful; and, based on their criteria, this may be so. But there is tarnish on the claim. The USSR is burdened with supporting what at times has been an economic invalid whose economic future is dismal at best. The USSR has paid a price for its Vietnam bargain within the region. Its intimacy in Hanoi has all but frozen its relations with China, and it is difficult to envision how this condition can significantly improve without a major change in the Soviet-Vietnamese relationship. Moscow's association with Vietnam has put sinew in ASEAN and moved it in a direction that the USSR always sought to avoid—toward military alliance. It has also triggered a buildup of U.S. naval strength in the Pacific.

Probably the chief negative factor at work here, and the heart of the case against perpetuating the relationship over a long period of time, centers on impermanence due to its inherently alien quality, the working out of *doc lap* influences and the manifestation of the Soviet personality. These factors make the association unpredictable if not unreliable.

An imponderable here is whether Vietnam in the years ahead will continue to be as strategically important to the USSR as is now the case. Under Mikhail Gorbachev the USSR appears to be making a bid for geopolitical power and influence in Asia by the method it has long used to challenge Western Europe and the United States. If this bid proves successful, Vietnam will retain its strategic value. However, it can be argued that the traditional "command of the sea" concept is falling into geopolitical dispute[12] and that the USSR had invested in a strategic white elephant in Vietnam. Or, it may be that the USSR will find that it does not need Vietnam as a base for power projection, that simply having great influence in Hanoi is sufficient and, in fact, far less expensive.[13]

Another imponderable that also may be a negative factor is ideology. Hanoi's external relations are more subject to ideological influence, are more ideologically oriented, than those of most other socialist countries. At the same time, Gorbachev's policies in Asia seem less ideologically oriented. Strategic thinking is also at work in Hanoi, but it is so mixed with the iron and thunder of ideology as to make the two inseparable. This is not to say that there cannot be compatibility between Moscow and Hanoi. There is considerable congruence in their respective foreign policies. However, the ideological influences at work in Hanoi are so anachronistic that at times they undercut the Soviet interests they hope to facilitate. Further, it is a truism that a shared outlook does not always either equate with mutual national interest or translate into national influence. Finally, as we have seen, this ideological impulse is not something that fits easily in the process of rational governmental decisionmaking; indeed, it can impede policy implementation.

What might well prove to be the most negative factor of all for the USSR (and this is also an imponderable) is the generational transfer of power in Vietnam that is now under way. There is no certain way of knowing what will be the mindset or the state policies of the next generation of rulers in Vietnam. They may move even closer to the USSR or they may put distance between the two countries. Since changes of guard in Communist systems are almost always somewhat volatile, the prospect for the USSR when the change comes is for a period of prolonged uncertainty about its future in Vietnam. The kind of leadership that appears to be emerging in Moscow may prove to be an additional exacerbation in Vietnam. The rulers in Hanoi are not sure of what to make of Mikhail Gorbachev and in fact may be wondering if they might not have another Nikita Khrushchev on their hands—that is, a Soviet leader without much empathy for the Vietnamese "revolution," one who sees Vietnam chiefly in terms of entrapment and who has his own domestic priorities to pursue, if necessary at the expense of Vietnam.[14]

What will remain is the strong emotive Vietnamese sense of the Russian. But this is in no way as intricate or psychologically complex as the attitude toward the Chinese. The Vietnamese see the people of the USSR as alien Europeans with whom they have little in common, and as sharing far less common a heritage than with others (the French, for example). Official figures in Hanoi have long considered (and privately described) their USSR associates as crude, chauvinistic, sometimes racist. In their memory is fixed a record of Kremlin leadership that was often indifferent to Vietnam's fate and frequently untrustworthy in day-to-day dealings. Past feelings among Vietnamese can be exacerbated by the present-day Soviet compulsion to dominate the association. But insofar as the Vietnamese leaders perceive Soviet power and prestige in the ascendancy in the region, which currently seems to be the case, to that extent they will adjust their behavior. This is the psychological influence among Vietnamese that underlies the present Soviet-Vietnamese closeness, augmented and rationalized by economic and military dependency. Their natural propellant, however, is the opposite—away from the USSR, pressed by an ingrained suspiciousness that will largely shape the ultimate or long-range relationship.

The major positive factor for Vietnam in the present integrated relationship with the USSR is economic benefit. The price may be an embarrassing dependency, but the benefits obtained are necessary and obtainable nowhere else. But that is why this is an issue between the two.

Because Hanoi once could play the USSR against China so that Moscow was not able to exert excessive leverage, some observers of the postwar scene have tended to dismiss the idea that somehow Vietnam can fend off excessive Soviet presence or unwanted Soviet demands. This is not the case. Moscow may show restraint, but should it choose to exert influence it would be nearly overwhelming. Even if dependence for daily necessities ends, there will remain the need for Soviet assistance in economic development. Hanoi lags so far behind in nation building that vast amounts of money are required just to make up for lost time. The only source for that kind of financing—tens of billions of dollars— is the USSR.

The major negative factor for the Vietnamese, as made clear earlier, is the affective quality of the relationship, the *doc lap* syndrome. It manifests itself in Vietnamese behavior through bristly assertion of self-reliance and almost desperate expressions of need for psychic sustenance. The Soviets repel and attract the Vietnamese at the same time—such is the influence of *doc lap*. It causes the Vietnamese to act in ways that hurt themselves; their history is full of examples. The Vietnamese almost certainly will never be satisfied with the USSR relationship, no matter what it becomes. The Soviets forever must deal with an associate that is volatile, uncertain, difficult even to understand. Soviet efforts to exert controls on the manner and means by which Vietnam tackles its economic difficulties can themselves become an issue between the two. And there are other negative factors. The USSR lacks moral authority in Vietnam. It is respected for the fire power it can command and is needed for its material resources, but it is not the model of a society to which the Vietnamese can aspire culturally.

Vietnam is now held to Moscow by steel bands of necessity. But there are centrifugal forces at work that are pressing it away from the Soviet center. On balance it would seem that for the short run the positive or binding factors in the relationship outweigh the negative ones. The play, of dependence against influence, serves Soviet-perceived opportunities and Vietnamese economic and security needs. But in the long run, dependence/influence are likely to become issues engendering conflicts of national interest.

EXTERNAL ISSUES: CONFLICT OF INTEREST

The second general force at work in Soviet-Vietnamese relations has to do with the respective national interests of the two, chiefly in the Pacific region. Whereas the cluster of issues involved in the first force are bilateral and largely manageable by the two parties, the second force involves issues beyond their control.

What is involved here is a triangular struggle for power. The first side is ASEAN (in association with Japan, the United States, and the other Pacific nations); the second side is Vietnam (more correctly, perhaps, Indochina) in alliance with the USSR; the third side is China. Imposed on this triangle are separate sets of bilateral relations, of which the overwhelmingly most important one in Hanoi's view is its relationship with China.

External influence raises both positive and negative issues for Vietnam and the USSR, issues that are both burden and asset. The considerable mutuality that now exists for the two is the result of Vietnam's minimal relations with its neighbors and the rest of the world. As the years pass, mutuality is bound to dissipate as regionalism grows and the triangular struggle for power deepens.

China is and will remain central in Soviet-Vietnamese relations. The USSR in dealing with China pursues one set of goals: to increase its status in Asia, extend its military and naval influence, and find new allies for its collective security system, all at the expense of China. Vietnam approaches China with a different set of goals: to resist its hegemonism and, ultimately, to achieve a viable relationship. The USSR must protect the long porous border that it shares with China; it must compete for influence and leadership in the Communist nations and the Third World; it must relate China to its complicated bilateral relationship with the United States. Vietnam must forestall military attack by China, by either improving relations or invoking Soviet protection; must improve relations with the ASEAN countries at the expense of China; and must achieve a preeminent position within Indochina in the face of Chinese opposition. These two sets of interests may coincide but can never be simply Moscow and Hanoi united against Beijing. If that pattern appears so at times, it is only that the conflict of interest is glossed over or buried.

The Sino-Soviet dispute, as we have seen earlier, was the product of the combined ideological and geopolitical competition between the USSR and China, which by the mid-1980s had taken on additional meaning. It still influences the course of Sino-U.S. relations and largely conditions both Chinese and Soviet behavior toward Vietnam.

Future Soviet-Vietnamese relations will be subjected to the constant pull and haul that results from the obvious geopolitical fact that Vietnam cannot deal with China in the same manner and by using the same policies as does the USSR. Moscow may be able to afford a permanent cold war with Beijing, but because of China's proximity and size, Hanoi cannot.

The USSR appears fully aware of the meaning of the fact that it stands between China and Vietnam. Moscow leaders seem tempted at times to play a "China card" in Hanoi but probably realize that this strategy could blow up in their faces. China and the USSR meet periodically at the deputy foreign minister level, always watched carefully by Hanoi. Both Soviet and Chinese leaders and official spokesmen, when asked about the future of the Sino-Soviet dispute, offer the same outlook:

that relations between the two will gradually improve, that this will be a slow and measured process, that neither is prepared to predict how long the dispute will continue or what exactly will be the character of the final association.

Hanoi leaders are (or profess to be) in constant anxiety over the possibility of a Sino-Soviet rapprochement, and they continually demand assurances from Moscow that its interests will not be negotiated away nor Vietnam abandoned. Dutifully, Soviet officials make these assurances after every meeting with the Chinese.[15] Hanoi's assumptions about the Sino-Soviet dispute today appear to be these:

- that it will continue essentially on a straight course, neither seriously worsening (say, to the point of war) nor vastly improving (for instance, to the point of permitting Sino-Soviet collusion against Vietnam).
- that there will be swings within the relationship—with improvements in the form of new economic agreements or cultural exchanges offset by moments of tension and difficulty—but with a slow general trend in the direction of harmony.
- that both the USSR and China will continue to place their respective national interests over those of Vietnam, meaning that in the long run the USSR is no more to be trusted than China.
- that whatever form the dispute takes, frontal militancy or some more peaceful form of competition, it will remain the chief determinant in Vietnamese external relations.

If the dispute holds firm at its present implacable level, it will continue to limit Hanoi's room for maneuver with either party. A lessening of hostility could lead to a new condition, but it would still be in the context of a power struggle. An improved Sino-Soviet relationship might not diminish Moscow's interest in Vietnam, but it probably would alter Moscow's attitudes toward Vietnam.

The starkest sort of development involving China, of course, would be war—either war between Vietnam and China or war between the USSR and China. A war similar to the 1979 Sino-Vietnamese border war would probably give the Soviets few serious problems; arms would be air-lifted in and a barrage of rhetoric launched, and that would be the extent of Soviet involvement. A longer, more determined conflict (or a war that involved a struggle for power in Hanoi) would present the USSR with exceedingly difficult choices. It is unlikely that Moscow would ever send ground troops to fight in Vietnam, although in the event of a long Sino-Vietnamese war it might encourage "volunteers" from other socialist countries. The chief danger to the USSR in a protracted conflict would be a chain of events that gradually and inexorably draws it in, the familiar small steps into the swamp: military assistance, advisers, fighter pilots, "volunteer" ground troops, full commitment.

A Sino-Soviet war independent of Hanoi—that is, one waged over some issue not involving Vietnam—quite possibly might not involve Vietnamese participation. Almost certainly Hanoi's leaders would maintain that the USSR should fight alone, reasoning that when elephants battle, the ant has little to contribute. Hanoi's generals are probably of the opinion that the USSR cannot defeat China militarily; that although the USSR could occupy Chinese territory and deliver devastating blows, China could still frustrate Soviet military goals; and that anyone who had collaborated with Moscow would pay a high price.

The future political configuration of Indochina, one turning on the idea of a federation of Indochina, represents another dimension of the Sino-Vietnamese struggle for power. It also represents a latent divisive force between Vietnam and the USSR. China strongly opposes a Federation of Indochina. Hanoi holds that such a federation is inevitable and desirable. The USSR supports the idea nominally, although it has never actually committed itself. It is a complicated matter for Moscow, for it involves its bilateral relations with Phnom Penh and Vientiane.

Hanoi's attitude toward Kampuchea and Laos is now, and always has been, strongly paternalistic. Early Vietnamese Marxists regarded the Indochina revolutionary movement as a single entity and assumed that the eventual outcome of the struggle against French colonialism would be a French Indochina without the French. Ho Chi Minh and other early Marxists saw the region as a natural economic entity and concluded that single Indochina was the proper ultimate political configuration for the peninsula. During World War II, for tactical reasons and later as a concession to the bourgeoning Lao and Khmer nationalism, the idea of a unified or federated Indochina was replaced by the "special relationship" concept. This term was never precisely defined, probably by way of a deliberate obfuscation, but in general it meant close mutual relations built around a paternalistic Vietnamese preeminence. Other terms now commonly employed are "alliance" and "solidarity zone."

Hanoi's long-range goal clearly seems to be the creation of a federation. To achieve this it must overcome a number of problems, including, of interest to us here, opposition by China (and possibly by the USSR). China's feelings on the matter are evident from its actions in Kampuchea today: It means to prevent federation if it can. The USSR's views are somewhat less clear. As a tactic it may support the idea because it is anathema to China, although, given a choice, Moscow probably would prefer to deal with three Indochinese states rather than one. Soviet officials speaking privately are unenthusiastic about the idea of a Federation of Indochina.

Kampuchea serves both to unite and to divide Vietnam and the USSR—a supreme example of the dualistic nature of external relations impinging on the relationship. In Kampuchea as surrogate war,[16] the triangular nature of the SRV-USSR China competition is most clearly revealed. Both China and Vietnam maintain that the central issue between them is Kampuchea and the excessive influence each is attempting to establish there. Theoretically, at least, this means that an acceptable settlement would be one in which both had less influence. A new governing arrangement in which both Vietnamese and Chinese influences diminish, but in which each is left with a Khmer faction on which to pin future hopes, could end the present suffering. But what of the USSR in this matter? One can raise the question, as the Chinese continually do, whether the USSR wants to see the region return to a stability that would tend to shut it out of the area. The question is this: To what extent does the Leninist vision of a world transformed through conflagration of the hinterland still drive the Kremlin? Will Moscow try to keep its hand in Southeast Asian affairs by perpetuating instability and maintaining local tensions?

It is difficult to build a persuasive and logical case for long-term Hanoi collaboration with the USSR against China. The Hanoi-Beijing faceoff came about not by choice but by error, on the part of both. Vietnamese leaders could have handled the Chinese more carefully and avoided a breach. China's attempt to force distance between the USSR and Vietnam was clumsy and proved to have the opposite effect. What seems clear is that there can be no peace in the region, no reduction in tensions, no rapprochement until there is more balance in the three-way relationship. China is simply too large and too near to permit Vietnam the luxury of treating it as a permanent enemy. That is a psychological fact of a thousand years' standing. A viable Vietnam requires peace with China. However, this does not and cannot mean capitulation to China. Rather, it requires the proper mix of Vietnamese assertiveness and deference to China, which is difficult to achieve because of the premium Asia places on face-saving. Somehow, sooner or later, it will be accomplished.

Just as the USSR and Vietnam have contradictory interests with respect to China and intra-Indochinese relations, so they have them with the ASEAN states and elsewhere in Asia. This is the major inevitable result of the outcome of the Vietnam War—that is, the altered geopolitical condition in Southeast Asia, which has pushed a linked Vietnam and USSR in one direction and the ASEAN states and China in the opposite. Soviet presence in the region has become a growing concern for most of the nations in the Pacific Basin, more so than the Hanoi leaders realize. Japan's anxieties were aroused by Soviet war vessels cruising across the sea lanes traveled by the oil supertankers from the Mideast to Yokohama. ASEAN countries viewed the altered balance of power in the region resulting from the Hanoi-Moscow linkup first with alarm and then with growing self-confidence in their ability to stand up to it. China's reaction has been the attempt to bleed Vietnam in Kampuchea and to move closer to Thailand. U.S. strategists have taken a new hard look at U.S. naval requirements for the Pacific, and the United States is increasing the size of the U.S. fleet there.

To some extent the Hanoi-ASEAN relationship that has emerged since the end of the war was inadvertent. In 1975 Hanoi seemed to have a strong sense of identification with the Third World—even with the capitalist nations of Southeast Asia. It said at the time that it wanted to maintain equidistance both within the socialist world and outside of it. It was forced off this policy by internal difficulties that threw it into dependence on the USSR. It said it wanted flexible external relations with Southeast Asian countries. Confrontation with ASEAN over Kampuchea has resulted in polarization. Presumably Hanoi's long-range intention is to reverse this process, eventually moving back first to flexibility, then to equidistance.

Some observers have argued that for this reason and others, the USSR has a vested interest in perpetuating instability in Southeast Asia. A case can be made here, but it would seem on balance that even the USSR is not served well by the present regional condition and that it would serve its own interests better by contributing to reversing polarization and ending instability.

In the long run, Moscow's close association with Hanoi may prove short-sighted. Possibly, as some in Southeast Asia have suggested, Moscow hopes eventually to parlay its winnings into a bigger payoff: an influential relationship with ASEAN nations by becoming a buffer between them and Vietnam, protecting them and acting as a restraining force on the "Cubans of Asia."

Thus there are both centrifugal and centripetal forces in the Soviet-Vietnamese relationship, each at work in its own matrix of internal and external issues. By all presently available evidence, these forces are not such as to overwhelm the relationship, particularly given the determination of Hanoi and Moscow to delimit or minimize that which divides. The prospect for the foreseeable future, to the end of this decade, is for continued close and reasonably harmonious relations.

However, there is nothing permanent in the association. The USSR has had close relations with other countries that have ended suddenly even when a breach seemed unlikely. China, Egypt, Indonesia, and

Poland (in a different way) are examples. The general subject of the breakup of Moscow's relations with various associated countries is an interesting but largely unexplored one. More data and analysis are required before firm conclusions can be reached. A cursory examination of such ruptures in Asia and Africa suggests that they resulted from three factors working singly or in combination: (1) for reasons of exigency or changed circumstances, such as a newly perceived advantage or a better offer from elsewhere; (2) because of developments within the host country leadership, either change of leadership or an altered leadership perception of Soviet motives and intentions; (3) because of an internal flux or a domestic politics that is reflected in foreign affairs but has little to do with the USSR itself. The potential for each of these factors is present in Vietnam, the most likely being the second, leadership change.

U.S. POLICY IMPLICATIONS

The U.S. policymaker, viewing the Soviet Vietnamese relationship from Washington, faces two almost paradoxical policy questions, one evaluative, the other operational. The assessment question is whether it is in the United States' interest that the present symbiotic Moscow-Hanoi relationship be continued, or whether an effort should be made to force distance between the two, or even to rupture the relationship. The operational question, assuming the implementation of either policy (i.e., force them together or drive a wedge between them), is what measures can be taken that will be effective yet still not destructive to U.S. interests elsewhere in the region?

U.S. policy turns on broader regional considerations. Southeast Asia is vulnerable to Moscow pressure, whether augmented by the Vietnamese or not, and the United States sees its role in the area as helping the ASEAN countries to avoid coercion or intimidation by either Moscow or Hanoi as Soviet surrogate. The United States wants the ASEAN states to be self-reliant and independent, as they themselves would wish, but fending off Moscow is one thing they cannot do for themselves.

In the first few years after the end of the Vietnam War, it was clear that the Hanoi leadership neither cared what the United States thought about its relationship with the USSR nor gave the matter much attention. Its sole concern was possible U.S. intervention (as in Kampuchea). Outsiders speculated that the Hanoi Politburo at times entertained the idea of "trading" the USSR for the United States, but there is no evidence that this was ever seriously entertained. The Hanoi leadership remains highly distrustful of all U.S. leaders and dubious that any gain can be had in Washington. Further, it has long been clear that a factional division exists at the Politburo level over how best to handle the Americans. One faction holds that only the hard-line approach works, arguing that history demonstrates that everything Hanoi has ever gained from the United States has been the result of protracted, unremitting pressure. The other faction holds that what is now appropriate is a more forthcoming approach. Since the leadership in Hanoi is collective, the policy toward the United States swings back and forth, from hard-line, to less hard-line.

U.S. interest in Indochina after the Vietnam War, to the extent there was interest, turned largely on assessment of the benefits and burdens of the Soviet naval and military presence in Indochina. The Soviet presence in Indochina flanked China on the south and, as a threat to China, represented a factor in the emerging U.S.-Chinese relationship. The mere presence of Soviet prowess in the region forced redeployment of U.S. military and naval forces. The new Soviet-Vietnamese relationship injected a certain degree of division into U.S. relations with its allies and friends. The United States' concern turned mostly on the ever-expanding, ever-hardening naval and air installations at Cam Ranh and Da Nang. There is some disagreement among American experts and strategic planners in the Pentagon as to the exact strategic significance of these bases. The general conclusion of Japanese (and probably Chinese) strategists is that the chief Soviet value of the Vietnam facilities is for regional war (including war with China) and, short of war, for intimidative political and psychological purposes. In a war with the United States, most observers believe, the naval installations at Cam Ranh could easily be closed by U.S. action. Hence Moscow war planners can not assume the availability of these installations. This is less true with respect to Vietnamese airfields that put Soviet planes within range of U.S. installations in the Philippines.

Hanoi seems convinced that the United States is excessively concerned about Cam Ranh Bay as a Soviet naval base. Its diplomats frequently tell Third World officials that the only U.S. interest in establishing diplomatic relations with Vietnam is to get the USSR out of Cam Ranh.

Assuming its desirability, then, how can the United States and its friends and associates in Asia force Hanoi to distance itself from Moscow? In Asia, at least, there is little argument that this should be done if possible. Hardly a day passes that some ASEAN official does not warn of danger. Conferences are held on the subject. From Tokyo to Singapore virtually all governments openly or tacitly agree that it would be desirable if Vietnam did not provide bases for Soviet military forces. Opinion on how best to reduce the Soviet military presence in Vietnam falls into two schools of thought. The first holds for the carrot-and-stick approach: Vietnam should be treated with a mix of economic inducement and economic punishment, making it profitable for it to move away from the USSR, painful if it does not. The ASEAN nations and Japan generally belong to this school, although there are differences among them regarding the size of the carrot (i.e., the fear that economically building up Vietnam may eventually make it a major threat in its own right). The second school of thought is endorsed chiefly by China. It holds that far from trying to wean Vietnam away from the USSR, interested parties should drive them even closer together. The calculation here is that the dynamics of the relationship will eventually cause it to self-destruct.

If it is assumed that the Vietnamese would like to end their dependency on the USSR and that they see it in their long-range national interest to distance themselves somewhat from the USSR, and if it is a fact that Vietnam desperately needs outside economic assistance, it would seem logical that great opportunities present themselves to the United States, the ASEAN countries, Japan, and others. All the outsiders need to do, it would appear, is to mount a campaign of economic overture in Hanoi designed to end Vietnamese dependency on the USSR and wean it away from Moscow, ideally to the point where it becomes economically dependent on the non-Communist nations of the region. Such campaigns of economic leverage have worked elsewhere and logically should work in Vietnam.

However, both the experience of outsiders and the internal logic of Hanoi Politburo politics belie such a conclusion. The history of attempts to apply economic leverage in Hanoi is an unbroken record of failure. Neither economic blackmail nor economic inducement has ever worked for anyone. The United States in effect tried to bribe North Vietnam into ending the Vietnam War, but without success. Both Moscow and Beijing tried economic aid to seduce or coerce Vietnam into taking sides in the Sino-Soviet dispute, and both failed. Khrushchev cut aid to Vietnam in a futile attempt to influence Vietnamese behavior. China's 1978 ultimatum on aid was ignored by Hanoi, which then shrugged off China's subsequent total curtailment. Non-Communist nations in 1979 reduced or ended economic aid to Vietnam—a loss running to several hundred millions dollars—in a vain attempt to discourage Hanoi's war making in Kampuchea. The central reason for this intransigence is the ideological influence at work on the singular mindset of the men of the Politburo. It is a potent mixture of dogma and ego that has produced an implacability that knows no compromise. The meaning is abundantly clear: Money does not talk in Hanoi the way it does elsewhere.

Based on the past, then, and on our analysis of Hanoi leadership, it appears that the idea of using economic leverage to rid Vietnam of the Soviet military presence is infeasible and unworkable. However, although the past is usually prologue, it is not always so. What prevents us from rejecting the notion outright is that all things change, this being the one immutable law of history. The present condition in Hanoi will probably obtain so long as the present leadership continues to rule. A new set of leaders might offer the United States and its allies an opportunity to start a process that would markedly affect the Soviet military base arrangement in Vietnam. If a new leadership group takes the helm in Hanoi and it is the United States' estimate that the time is ripe for an economic inducement campaign, even then, the odds against success will be great. A dozen things must go right, and one wrong development could ruin the effort. However, the United States would have much to gain, and nothing to risk, by eliminating Soviet bases; hence the attempt would be worthwhile.

CONCLUSIONS

I end this study of the Vietnamese-USSR relationship with a summary of my findings and a discussion of the conclusions I've drawn.

The first conclusion is that Vietnam and the USSR for the foreseeable future will remain locked into a relationship bound by self-interest, but that there are forces at work that in the longer run will force a distance into the present highly intimate association. A breach of relations, while possible, is unlikely. More probable is a cooling into a more reserved kind of association. The pace at which this takes place will depend in part on the behavior and policies of outsiders, especially China, and it could be accelerated by a generational transfer of political power in Hanoi.

The essence of the present relationship is a material and psychic dependency on the part of Vietnam and a perceived geopolitical opportunity on the part of the USSR. It is more the product of historical accident than premeditated scheming by either party. It will continue at least as long as Vietnam's condition of dependency continues and/or Moscow sees utility in continuing the present relationship.

The second conclusion is that relations are still nominal and formative. There are, between the two, no deeply imbedded national perceptions—neither ingrained fear, ancient grievance, nor memory of common heroic stands. Because Vietnam and the USSR hardly know each other historically, they are still in the process of defining their relationship. The meaning of this, among other things, is that outsiders should avoid dogmatically treating the relations as if they were set in concrete.

The relationship in the early 1980s developed serious problems, which both sides sought to address in a forthright manner. This was no fundamental change but, rather, a case of tinkering with the machinery. Success remains to be determined.

Many Asians fear that Vietnam will eventually become a Soviet satellite. The Vietnamese do not share this view; they are confident that the USSR could never impose the kind of authority and influence it has in East Europe. Nor do the Vietnamese fear Soviet (Afghan-style) intervention, which is prevented, they say, by the spirit of Vietnamese nationalism and by geography. Probably this assessment is correct. Vietnam can be considered a client state of the USSR but not a satellite, and one would find it virtually impossible to imagine Vietnam under the kind of control that Moscow has established in, say, East Germany.

The third conclusion is that the major force influencing the relationship (and also the best indicator of the direction it will take) is the geopolitics of the Sino-Soviet dispute. To the extent that the future of the dispute is uncertain, Soviet-Vietnamese relations will remain contingent and fluid. This triangular relationship among China, Vietnam, and the USSR also has great meaning throughout Southeast Asia.

The ideological competition and geopolitical struggle between China and the USSR largely shaped Hanoi's relationship with Moscow in the early days, and this remains true today. Vietnam is important in the Kremlin's eyes chiefly because of China. Therefore, the underlying impulse of the Soviet Union in dealing with Vietnam has been an ideological one. Moscow's orientation in influencing Vietnamese policy and behavior has consistently been a determination to influence Vietnamese actions in ways that will contribute to reducing Chinese strength and influence throughout Asia.

Aside from China, the factors influencing the USSR's relations with Vietnam include its interests in ASEAN; the Japanese potential to shift the power balance and create a new power center in the Pacific hostile to the USSR; the challenge Moscow faces in East Europe (a challenge that undercuts orthodoxy and challenges Soviet authority); and Soviet internal difficulties, economic troubles, and other deficiencies.

The Soviet-Vietnamese alliance continues to face hostile forces to the north and south of Vietnam. The Vietnamese occupation of Kampuchea has turned into a protracted conflict, but Hanoi seems confident it can eventually prevail and has fixed 1990 as the date for a full pullout of its troops. China's efforts to force Vietnam out of Kampuchea have not succeeded. The two-front war threat has enabled the USSR to consolidate and expand the military presence in Vietnam. Moscow has also helped strengthen PAVN forces along the border of Northern

Vietnam, thus making another Chinese attack more difficult and costly and therefore less likely.

The fourth conclusion is that there is a fundamental incompatibility in Vietnamese-Soviet relations that will sharply delimit the association in ultimate or long-range terms.

The heritage of the relationship—the conviction of Hanoi leaders that in the past the USSR was always prepared to sacrifice Vietnamese interests for marginal Soviet interests—is the absence of a strong sense of Vietnamese obligation. The same leaders believe that Soviet economic assistance, past and present, was given for the wrong reasons (competition with China) and deserves little gratitude.

Vietnamese theoreticians and other influential persons in Hanoi believe that the Soviet leaders neither understand Vietnam nor have much to offer by way of ideological guidance. The USSR is stigmatized as having a barbarian mentality that makes it incapable of grasping the Vietnamese world view—a shortcoming privately labeled Soviet cultural chauvinism. At best, in ideological terms, the USSR serves as a vague inspiration.

Ideological incongruence has conferred on the Vietnamese Communist–Soviet Communist relationship a quality of tenuousness. Without Vietnamese proletarian kinship, there is little sense of allegiance. The Vietnamese consider the men of Moscow to be distant, not because they lack sympathy but because of their innate inability to understand either the Vietnamese cause or the Vietnamese themselves. All of this means that there is not, and can never be, much psychological closeness between the two.

FINAL THOUGHT

The process of change in the affairs of the Asian nations often seems to operate under its own separate laws of political science. Although it may occasionally come with blinding speed, most change in Asia is glacial in pace. Conditions sometimes will stand immutable against what seems to be irresistible forces that defy logic, even common sense; in other instances there will occur truly fundamental change for what seem to be only light or transient reasons. Only a foolish determinist would claim to see the future of the Soviet-Vietnamese relationship.

We have examined the forces that hold together these two unlikely partners as well as the issues that divide them. We have found the two sets of factors to be more or less counterbalanced. We have found a balance of burden and benefits extending in both directions. As far as we can see ahead, a few years at most, the relationship will continue on down the present straight road.

There is one final peculiarly Vietnamese factor at work in the Soviet-Vietnamese relationship, a factor that is perhaps not so much an issue as a transcendental historical fact that must be noted. Vietnam's external relations are and always have been singular, one might say even unique among nations. It is a demonstrable fact of history that no nation, no group, has ever had what could be called a successful relationship with the Vietnamese. Such is the experience of the Chinese for a millenium, the Khmers of once vast empire, the now near-extinct Cham, the Thais, the Burmese of the fifteenth century, the Lao, the Montagnards of a dozen tribes, the French, the Americans. All of these relationships began with or had moments of amicability and mutual benefit, but each carried the seeds of its own destruction. Hence it appears that a paradoxical law is at work in Vietnamese associations: Any success is a potential catastrophe. Such is the historical challenge facing Moscow.

We are thus left with the unanswered question as to whether Moscow and Hanoi have a permanent alliance, as permanent as any alliance can be, or merely a marrige of convenience that is neither close nor durable. It is a question no one—not even the members of the Hanoi Politburo or the men of the Kremlin—can answer with any certainty. A survey of the current scene suggests the former, Vietnamese history suggests the latter. What is past is not always prologue, but it is still one of our best guides; therefore, it would seem that the wisest choice is to go with history.

NOTES

1. Le Duan's first trip, to the twenty-sixth CPSU Congress, lasted from February 20 to March 10, 1981. At this time (March 10) Le Duan met with Brezhnev to discuss future economic relations. The second trip, billed as a party/state visit, came in early September; Le Duan and Brezhnev met on September 7. Other high-level meetings during the year included the SRV State Planning Commission delegation (headed by Nguyen Lam) in early July; a foreign trade mission (headed by Minister of Foreign Trade Le Khac) in late July; and a science and technology cooperation delegation (headed by State Council Vice Chairman Tran Quynh) in September.

2. Source material on this "new relationship" is fragmented and usually found buried in broader policy statements, exchanges of goodwill messages, and so on. For a typical early account, see Nayan Chanda, "As Moscow's Ardour Cools, Hanoi Looks Elsewhere," *Far Eastern Economic Review* (April 16, 1982). A recent Moscow treatment of the problems in the relationship is found in Yevgeniy Kachanov's Radio Moscow commentary for November 2, 1985.

3. *Nhan Dan* (October 21, 1981).

4. "All-Around Cooperation or Thorough Sell-Out?" *Xinhua*, Radio Beijing commentary (September 19, 1980).

5. Radio Moscow (May 15, 1984).

6. Radio Hanoi (January 29, 1985).

7. VNA (March 14, 1984).

8. *Izvestia* (March 6, 1984), and *Pravda* (March 8, 1984).

9. Separate institutes exist for Biology, Chemistry, Cybernetics, Computer Technology, Earth Sciences, Mathematics, Mechanical Engineering, Machine Design, Nuclear Energy, Oceanography, and Physics.

10. *Pravda* (March 8, 1984).

11. VNA (July 14, 1980).

12. Soviet thinking on naval strategy is based on the writings of Soviet Admiral S. G. Gorshkov, who is widely quoted in foreign naval circles.

13. For further discussion of this idea, see Joseph G. Whelan, *The Soviet Union in the Third World, 1980–1982: An Imperial Burden or Political Asset? The Soviet in Asia, an Expanding Presence* (Washington, D.C.: Library of Congress CRS Report 48-56-S, 1984).

14. For further discussion of this matter, see Richard Nations, "A Mild Chill in Moscow," *Far Eastern Economic Review* (July 17, 1985).

15. Typical expression of Hanoi fears is found in Nguyen Co Thach's speech at the United Nations (October 7, 1983). See also the editorial entitled "Andropov's September 28th Address," *Nhan Dan* (October 1, 1983).

16. China has firmly and deliberately injected Kampuchea into the Sino-Soviet dispute, making Vietnamese withdrawal from Kampuchea one of its three requirements for improved Sino-Soviet relations (the other two being Soviet withdrawal from Afghanistan and reduction of Soviet troop strength along the Sino-Soviet border). SRV Foreign Minister Nguyen Co Thach, in a UN speech on October 7, 1984, claimed that the USSR had "categorically rejected Beijing's demand that Kampuchea be on the agenda of Sino-Soviet talks." This may be true, but quite probably the subject was discussed without being on the agenda.

SELECTED BIBLIOGRAPHY

Becker, Elizabeth. *When the War Was Over: The Voices of Cambodia's Revolution and Its People.* New York: Simon and Schuster, 1986.

Borisov, X. "The Monetary System of the Socialist Economic Union." *Tap Chi Cong San,* No. 2, February 1981.

Boudreau, Robert Nelson. *Vietnam and the Soviet Union: Implications for Europe and American Foreign Policy Options.* Ph.D. Thesis, Monterey, Calif.: U.S. Naval Postgraduate School, March 1983.

Budanov, A. G. "Invincible Vietnam." In V. A. Zharov, ed., *Southeast Asia: History, Economy Policy.* Moscow: Progress Publishers, 1972.

Buttinger, Joseph. *The Smaller Dragon: A Political History of Vietnam.* New York: Praeger Publishers, 1958.

———. *Vietnam: A Dragon Embattled* (2 vols.) New York: Praeger Publishers, 1967.

Cameron, Allan. "The Soviet Union and Vietnam: The Origins of Involvement." In W. Raymond Duncan, ed., *Soviet Policy in Developing Countries.* Waltham, Mass.: Ginn-Blaisdell, 1970.

———. *Vietnam Crisis: A Documentary Study, Vol. I.* Ithaca, N.Y.: Cornell University Press, 1971.

Cassen, Robert, ed. *Soviet Interests in the Third World.* Beverly Hills, Calif.: Sage, 1985.

Chanda, Nayan. *Brother Enemy: The War After the War.* New York: Harcourt Brace Jovanovich, 1986.

Chang, Pao-min. "The Sino-Soviet Conflict Over Kampuchea." *Survey,* Vol. 27, Nos. 118, 119, 1983.

Chufrin, Genady. *Southeast Asia: History and the Present Day.* Oriental Studies in the USSR, No. 6. Moscow: Social Sciences Today, 1982.

Cohen, Stephen F. *Rethinking the Soviet Experience: Politics and History Since 1917.* Oxford: Oxford University Press, 1985.

"The Communist International and the Indochinese Communist Party." *Tap Chi Cong San,* No. 2, February 1986.

Communist Parties and the Crisis of Imperialism. Moscow: Pravda Publishing House, 1932.

Crankshaw, Edward. *The New Cold War: Moscow vs. Peking.* New York: Penguin Books, 1963.

Dang Xuan Ky. "Nguyen Ai Quoc: Course of Searching for a National Salvation Path." *Vietnam Social Sciences* (Hanoi), February 1986.

Dau Ngoc Xuan. "Improving Economic Ties." *Ekonomicheskoye Sotrudnichestvo Stranchlenov Sev* (Moscow), JPRS-SEA 84-074, February 9, 1984.

Duiker, William J. "SRV Longer Ranged Relations with the USSR and PRC in an International Context." Paper read at U.S. Department of State conference, April 1977.

Duncanson, Dennis J. *Government and Revolution in Vietnam.* New York: Oxford University Press, 1968.

Eudin, J. *Soviet Russia and the East.* Stanford, Calif.: Stanford University Press, 1957.

"Facts and Figures on Vietnamese-Soviet Economic and Cultural Cooperation." *Tap Chi Cong San,* No. 11, November 1985, JPRS-SEA 86-034.

Fall, Bernard B. *The Two Viet-Nams: A Political and Military Analysis.* New York: Praeger Publishers, 1967.

Fforde, Adam. "Economic Aspects of the Soviet-Vietnamese Relationship: Their Role and Importance," Discussion Paper 156. London: Birbeck College, October 1984.

Fusheng, Dong. "The Soviet Drive into Southeast Asia." *Beijing Review,* No. 9, March 1, 1982.

Gafurov, B. G., ed. *Study of the History and Economy of the Countries of Southeast Asia.* Moscow: Nauka Publishing House, 1968.

Garrett, Banning N., and Glaser, Bonnie S. *War and Peace: The Views from Moscow and Beijing.* Policy Paper in International Affairs No. 20. Berkeley: University of California, Institute of International Studies.

Gelman, Harry. *The Soviet Far East Buildup and Soviet Risk Taking Against China,* Project Air Force report. Santa Monica, Calif.: U.S. Air Force, RAND Corporation, August 1982.

————. *Soviet Expansionism in Asia and the Sino-Soviet-U.S. Triangle.* Marina del Rey, Calif.: Security Conference on Asia and the Pacific (SeCAP), March 1983.

————. *The Brezhnev Politburo and the Decline of Detente.* Ithaca and London: Cornell University Press, 1984.

Girling, J.L.S. *People's War.* New York: Praeger Publishers, 1969.

Gorbachev, Mikhail. Vladivostok Speech, July 28, 1986. Published in Foreign Broadcast Information Service (FBIS) *Daily Report* for the USSR, July 29, 1986.

Government of Japan. *Soren To Betonamu Tono Kyoryokukankei* [Soviet-Vietnamese Cooperation Relations]. Tokyo, February 1984. (In Japanese.)

Griffith, William E. *The Sino-Soviet Rift.* Cambridge, Mass.: MIT Press, 1964.

————. *Soviet Losses in Asia.* Cambridge, Mass.: Center for International Studies, MIT, November 1978.

Gupta, Bhabani Sen. "The Soviet Union and Vietnam." *International Studies* (New Delhi), Vol. 12, No. 4, October–December 1973.

————. *Soviet Asian Relations in the 1970's and Beyond.* New York: Praeger Publishers, 1976.

Gupta, Surenda K. "Moscow and Southeast Asia Policy Towards Recent Developments in Vietnam, Cambodia and Laos." Paper read at the Western

Conference of Association of Asian Studies, San Diego State College, October 30, 1971.

Heinzig, Dieter. *Soviet Interests in Indochina,* Monograph. Cologne: Institute for International Studies, 1980.

———. "Soviet Policy in Asia in the Seventies and Eighties." *Asian Thought and Society,* Vol. 10, No. 29, July 1985.

Hellmann, Donald C. "Future Strategic Alternatives for the U.S. and the Soviet Union in Asia." Unpublished paper, 1977.

Honey, P. J. *Communism in North Vietnam: Its Role in the Sino-Soviet Dispute.* Cambridge, Mass.: Center for International Studies, MIT, July 1963.

Hong Chuong (*Tap Chi Cong San* editor). Interview by Radio Moscow, *Tap Chi Cong San,* No. 10, October 1983, JPRS 84-017.

Hong Tung. "The Great Force of Solidarity." *Pravda,* October 25, 1983; JPRS 85020, December 28.

Horelick, Arnold L. "Soviet Policy Dilemmas in Asia." *Asian Survey,* June 1977.

Horn, Robert C. "Soviet Influence in Sea: Opportunities and Obstacles." *Asian Survey,* August 1975.

———. "Soviet-Vietnam Relations and the Future of the Sea." *Pacific Affairs,* Winter 1978-1979.

Isaacs, Harold. *No Peace for Asia.* Cambridge, Mass.: MIT Press, 1947.

Isayev, M. "Fraternal Unity of the Countries of Indochina." *International Affairs* (Moscow), July 1983.

Jukes, Geoffrey. *The Soviet Union in Asia.* Berkeley: University of California Press, 1973.

Khrushchev, Nikita. *Khrushchev Remembers.* Boston: Little, Brown, 1971.

Kozhevnikov, V. A. "Laos." In V. A. Zharov, ed., *Southeast Asia: History, Economy Policy.* Moscow: Progress Publishers, 1972.

Kudinov, M. (Department Chief of USSR State Committee for Science and Technology). Speech on Soviet educational programs for Vietnamese and other cooperation programs, Radio Moscow, March 7, 1985; FBIS *Daiy Report* for the USSR, March 9, 1985.

Lancaster, Donald. *The Emancipation of French Indochina.* New York: Oxford University Press, 1961.

Le Duc Tho. "Let Us Advance Under the Revolutionary Banner of Lenin." Speech at the 110th anniversary of Lenin's birth. Hanoi: VNA, April 21, 1980.

Leighton, Marian. "Vietnam and the Sino-Soviet Rivalry." *Asian Afairs,* Vol. 6, No. 1, September-October 1978.

Le Khac. "The Soviet-Vietnamese Treaty." *Foreign Trade* (Moscow), No. 4, April 1983.

Le Ngoc. "Why Our Party Was Able to Seize the Right to Lead the Revolution." *Tap Chi Cong San* (Hanoi), No. 2, February 1986.

"Lenin's Image in Ho Chi Minh's Writings." *Vietnam Courier* (Hanoi), No. 4, April 1985.

Luxmoore, Jonathan. *Vietnam: The Dilemmas of Reconstruction,* Conflict Studies Monograph 147. London: Institute for the Study of Conflict, 1983.

MacKintosh, J. M. *Strategy and Tactics of Soviet Foreign Policy.* London: Oxford University Press, 1953.

McBeth, John. "Buildup on the Bay." *Far Eastern Economic Review,* December 29, 1983.

McConnell, James M., and Dismukes, Bradford. "Soviet Diplomacy of Force in the Third World." *Problems of Communism,* January-February 1979.

McLane, Charles B. *Soviet Strategies in Southeast Asia: An Exploration of Eastern Policy under Lenin and Stalin.* Princeton, N.J.: Princeton University Press, 1966.

———. "The Russians and Vietnam: Strategies of Indirection." In the winter 1968-1969 edition of *International Journal* (Toronto), Vol. 24, No. 1. (Also contains a useful chronology of DRV-USSR interrelated events [1955–1968].)

Michael, Franz. "Moscow and Peking." *Asian Affairs,* Vol. 6, No. 4, March-April 1979.

Milestones of Soviet Foreign Policy 1917–1967. Moscow: Progress Publishers, 1967.

"Nguyen Ai Quoc and the International Communist Movement and the Indochinese Revolution: 1930–1940." *Tap Chi Cong San,* No. 2, February 1984, JPRS-SEA 84-070.

Nguyen Chan. (article on Soviet aid to Vietnam coal sector). *Nhan Dan,* October 19, 1983; JPRS 84-008, January 16, 1983.

Nguyen Hoa. "Soviet Cooperation and Assistance to Vietnam's Oil and Natural Gas Sector." *Nhan Dan,* October 28, 1983; JPRS 84-008, January 16, 1983.

Nguyen Ngoc Huy and Young, Stephen B. *Understanding Vietnam.* Bussum, Netherlands: DCP Publishing Co., 1983.

Nguyen Thanh. "The Communist International and the Indochinese Revolution." *Vietnam Courier,* February 1984.

Ojha, Ishwer C. "China and North Vietnam: The Limits of the Alliance." *Current History,* January 1968.

Papp, Daniel S. *Soviet Perceptions of the Developing World in the 1980's: The Ideological Basis.* Lexington, Mass.: Lexington Books, 1985.

Parker, F. Charles. "Vietnam and Soviet Asian Strategy." *Asian Affairs,* November-December, 1976.

Petrov, Vladimir. *New Dimensions of Soviet Foreign Policy,* Reprint Series No. 87. Washington, D.C.: George Washington University, Institute for Sino-Soviet Studies, 1983.

Pfaff, William. "Reflections: The Soviet Myth." *New Yorker Magazine,* November 6, 1978.

Pike, Douglas. "Conceptions of Asian Security: Indochina." Paper read at the International Studies Association Annual Meeting, Toronto, Canada, February 1976.

———. *Vietnam's Future Foreign Policy.* Study prepared for the U.S. Senate Committee on Foreign Relations. Published as Committee Print 33-241, Washington, D.C., 1978.

———. "Vietnam and the USSR." Paper read at the Conference on the Soviet Union in the Third World. Carlisle Barracks, Penn.: U.S. Army War College Strategic Studies Institute, September 1979.

———— . "Soviet Response to an Intra-Communist Crisis: Indochina, 1979." Paper read at the 18th Annual Conference on Slavic Studies, Loyola University, New Orleans, Louisiana, October 1979.

———— . "The USSR and Vietnam." In Robert H. Donaldson, ed., *The Soviet Union in the Third World*. Boulder, Colo.: Westview Press, 1981.

———— . "Impact of the Sino-Soviet Dispute on Southeast Asia." In Herbert J. Ellison, ed., *The Sino-Soviet Conflict: A Global Perspective*. Seattle: University of Washington Press, 1982.

———— . "Vietnam's Military Assistance." In John F. Cooper and Daniel S. Papp, eds., *Communist Nations' Military Assistance*. Boulder, Colo.: Westview Press, 1983.

———— . *PAVN: People's Army of Vietnam*. Novato, Calif.: Presidio Press, 1986.

Polmar, Norman. *Guide to the Soviet Navy*, 3rd ed. Annapolis, Md.: Naval Institute Press, 1983.

Quested, R. "Further Light on the Expansion of Russia in East Asia 1857–60." Paper no. 86, read at the International Conference on Asian History, Kuala Lumpur, August 1968.

Randle, Robert F. *Geneva 1954: The Settlement of the Indochinese War*. Princeton N.J.: Princeton University Press, 1969.

Rosenberger, Leif. "The Soviet-Vietnamese Alliance and Kampuchea." *Survey* (London), Vol. 227, No. 118/119, Autumn-Winter 1983.

Sakharov, Nikolay. "Soviet-Vietnamese Cooperation in the Coal Sector." Interview of *Quan Doi Nhan Dan*, November 9, 1983; JPRS 84-001, January 3, 1984.

Scalapino, Robert. "The Political Influence of the USSR in Asia." In Donald S. Zagoria, ed., *Soviet Policy in East Asia*. New Haven, Conn.: Yale University Press, 1982.

Scalapino, Robert, ed. *The Communist Revolution in Asia: Tactics, Goals and Achievements*. Englewood Cliffs, N.J.: Prentice-Hall, 1965.

Scalapino, Robert A.; Seizaburo, Sato; and Wanandi, Jusuf, eds. *Asian Economic Development—Present and Future*, Research Papers and Policy Studies (RPPS) No. 14. Berkeley: University of California, Institute of East Asian Studies (IEAS), 1986.

———— . "Legitimacy and Institutionalization in Asian Socialist Societies." In Robert Scalapino et al., eds., *Asian Political Institutionalization*. Berkeley: University of California Institute of East Asia Studies, 1986, pp. 59–64.

———— . *Asian Political Institutionalization*. RPPS No. 15. Berkeley: University of California, IEAS, 1986.

———— . *Internal and External Security Issues in Asia*. RPPS No. 16. Berkeley: University of California, IEAS, 1986.

Seah, Chee-Meow. "Asian Vulnerabilities to Soviet Influence and Manipulation: A View from Singapore." *Asian Perspective* (Seoul), Vol. 9, No. 1, Spring-Summer, 1985.

Simon, Sheldon. "The Soviet Union and Southeast Asia: Interests, Goals and Constraints." *Orbis*, Vol. 25, No. 1, Spring 1981.

Sochevko, G. G. "Cambodia." In V. A. Zharov, ed., *Southeast Asia: History, Economy Policy*. Moscow: Progress Publishers, 1972.

Southeast Asia Research Council (Tokyo). "Cooperative Relations Between the USSR and Vietnam 1975–83." Tokyo, February 1984.

Soviet-Vietnamese Cooperation Relations [Soren To Betonamu Tono Kyoryoku-kankei]. Tokyo, February 20, 1984. (In Japanese.) Translated by JPRS-SEA 85-048, March 19, 1985.

Spragens, John, Jr. "Vietnam and the Soviets: A Tighter Alliance." *Indochina Issues*, No. 51, November 1984.

Thai Quang Trung. "The Moscow-Hanoi Axis and Soviet Military Build-up in Southeast Asia." Unpublished manuscript, circa mid-1986.

The Tap. "Nguyen Ai Quoc and the International Communist Movement and the Indochinese Revolution: 1930–1940." *Tap Chi Cong San*, No. 2, February 1984.

Thomas, John R. "The Soviet Union." In Gene T. Hsiao, *The Role of External Powers in the Indochina Crisis*. Edwardsville: Southern Illinois University, 1973.

Thornton, Richard C. "Soviet Union and the Future of Southeast Asia." Prepared for the 25th annual meeting of Association for Asian Studies (AAS), Chicago, March 30, 1973.

————. "Soviet Strategy and the Vietnam War." *Asian Affairs*, March-April 1974.

————. "Soviet Strategy in Asia Since WWII," No. 67. Washington, D.C.: George Washington University, Institute for Sino-Soviet Studies, Spring 1977.

Thrombley, Woodworth G. *The U.S., the USSR and China in Southeast Asia: Issues and Alternatives*. Published by Indiana University, Bureau of Public Discussion, 1969.

To Huu. "Close Friendship and Cooperation Between Vietnam and the Soviet Union." *Nhan Dan*, July 18, 1980.

Tran Quynh. (Article on Vietnamese participation in CEMA). *Tap Chi Cong San*, No. 11, November 1983; JPRS 84-028, February 21.

Trigubenko, M. "On the Participation of the Soviet Union's Far Eastern Areas in the USSR's Trade and Economic Cooperation with Vietnam." *Far Eastern Affairs*, No. 4, 1983.

Trinh Ngoc Thai. "The Leninist Foreign Policy of the Soviet Union." *Tap Chi Cong San*, No. 4, April 1980.

"The Truth About Sino-Vietnamese Relations During the Last Thirty Years." *Nhan Dan*, October 6, 1979.

"Twenty Five Years of Vietnam-Soviet Union Trade Relations." *Nhan Dan*, July 21, 1980.

Ulyanovsky, R. A. *The Comintern and the East: The Struggle for the Leninist Strategy and Tactics in National Liberation Movements*. Moscow: Progress Publishers, 1979.

United States Government, Department of Defense. *Soviet Military Power: 1985*. Washington, D.C.: GPO, 1985.

United States Government, Department of the Navy. *Understanding Soviet Naval Developments*. Washington, D.C.: U.S. Navy, 1981.

United States Government, Department of State. "Report to the Congress on Forced Labor in the USSR." Washington, D.C.: GPO, February 1983.

United States Senate, 86th Congress, Committee on the Judiciary. *Soviet Peace Agreements and Results.* Washington, D.C.: GPO, 1959.

Van Dyke, Jon M. *North Vietnam's Strategy for Survival.* Palo Alto, Calif.: Pacific Books, 1972.

Viet Nam-Lien Xo: Xa Ma Gan [Vietnam and the USSR: Far But Near]. Foreign Languages Publishing House (Hanoi) and Novatni Publishing House (Moscow), 1983.

"Vietnam-USSR: 25 Years of Economic Cooperation." *Vietnam Courier* (Hanoi), No. 8, 1980.

"V.I. Lenin on Vietnam and Indochina." *Vietnam Courier* (Hanoi), No. 8, August 1985.

Viner, Kimberly Douglas. *Implications of the Soviet Military Presence in Southeast Asia.* M.A. thesis, U.S. Naval Postgraduate School, Monterey, Calif., December 1984.

Volodin, Anatoly. "The Party Tempered in Struggle." *Asia and Africa Today,* No. 4, 1985.

Wall, Irwin M. *French Communism in the Era of Stalin.* Westport, Conn.: Greenwood Press, 1983.

Wolfe, Thomas W. "Union and Non-Intervention: Evolution of Soviet Military Policy." RAND Corporation monograph, February 1968.

Yermovlayev, A. "Soviet-Vietnamese Scientific and Technical Cooperation." *Far Eastern Affairs* (Moscow), No. 1, 1985.

Zagoria, Donald. "Into the Breach: New Soviet Alliances in the Third World." *Foreign Affairs,* Spring 1979.

_____. "Soviet Policy and Prospects in East Asia." *International Security,* Fall 1980.

_____. *Soviet Policy in East Asia.* New Haven, Conn.: Yale University Press, 1982.

Zharov, V. A., and V. A. Tyurin, eds. *Southeast Asia: History, Economy, Policy.* Moscow: Progress Publishers, 1972.

INDEX